Lucky
Loser

Lucky Loser

Adventures in Tennis & Comedy

MICHAEL KOSTA

HARPER
INFLUENCE

HarperCollins books may be purchased for educational, business, or sales promotional use. For information, please email the Special Markets Department at SPsales@harpercollins.com.

Unless otherwise noted, all photos are courtesy of the author.

FIRST EDITION

Designed by Bonni Leon-Berman

Part title art by Milan Bozic

Library of Congress Cataloging-in-Publication Data has been applied for.

ISBN 978-0-06-341806-6

24 25 26 27 28 LBC 5 4 3 2 1

To Dad, we miss you.

Lucky Loser:

A tennis term: A player who loses in the deciding qualifying round, but then still gains entrance into the Main Draw tournament when a main draw player withdraws unexpectedly—that is, a player who wins an opportunity even though they lost.

A life term: A loser, who gets lucky.

Contents

Contents

Part IV: Comedy, Seriously . . .

Author's Note

I have fact-checked this book as much as possible. Trying to find information about minute events that happened before the internet is hard. Many results and locations for my tennis matches seem to be gone. I relied on my memory and my friends' memories plus what tiny information I can find online. So, if you find out later that I lost 6–4 6–1 not 6–2 6–1, you are probably right and good job to you. Thanks for reading my book.

Happy

BEST
GIFT
EVER

KOSTA FAMILY TENNIS

JUNIOR
TENNIS

PART 1
Growing Up
1984–1998

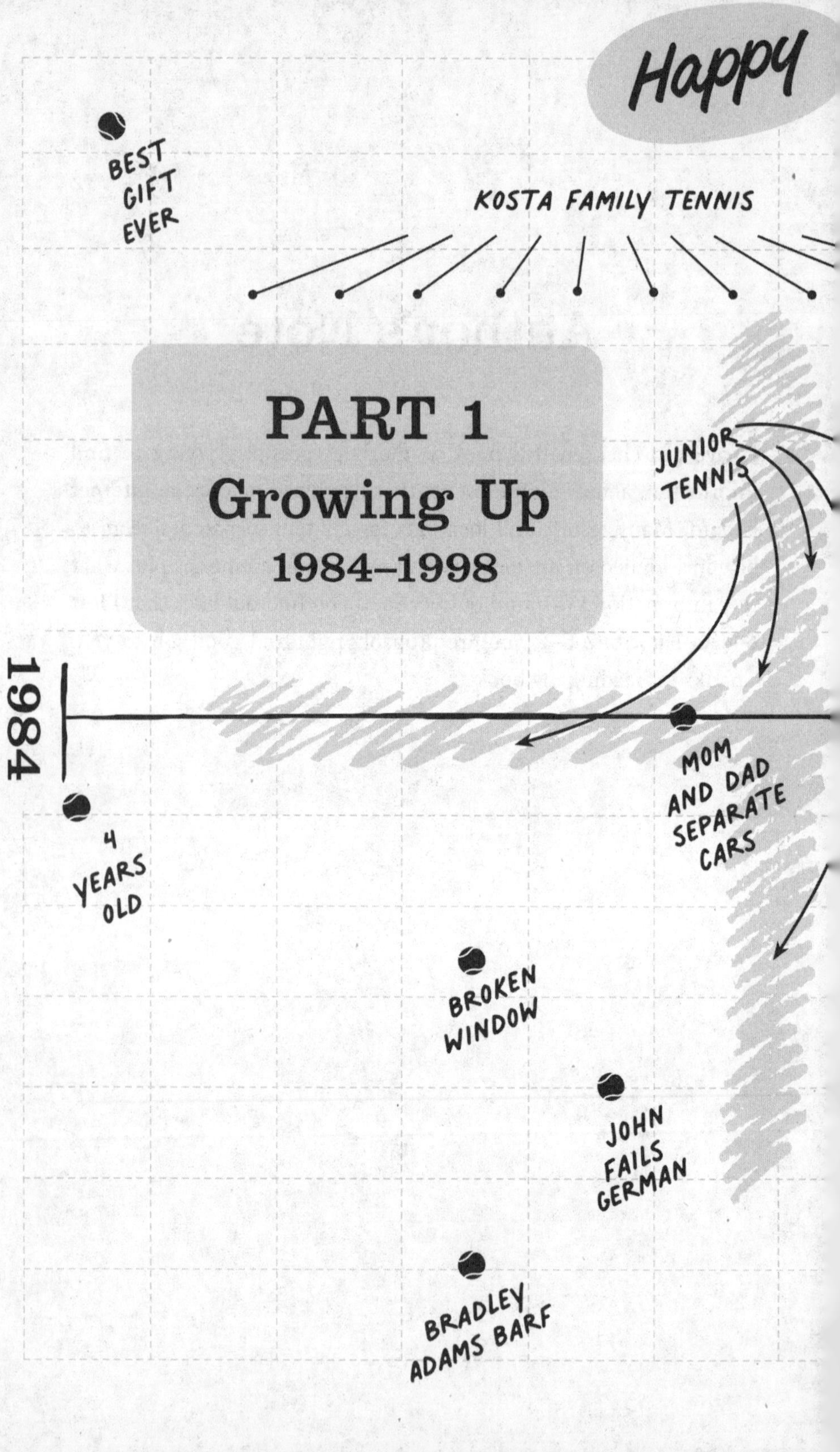

1984

4
YEARS
OLD

MOM
AND DAD
SEPARATE
CARS

BROKEN
WINDOW

JOHN
FAILS
GERMAN

BRADLEY
ADAMS BARF

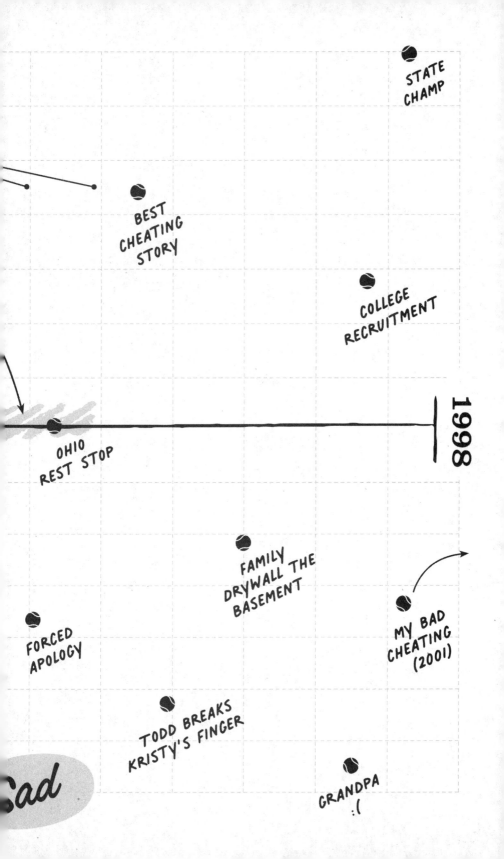

STATE
CHAMP

BEST
CHEATING
STORY

COLLEGE
RECRUITMENT

1998

OHIO
REST STOP

FAMILY
DRYWALL THE
BASEMENT

FORCED
APOLOGY

MY BAD
CHEATING
(2001)

TODD BREAKS
KRISTY'S FINGER

GRANDPA
:(

ad

Chapter 1

Roddy Racket

THIS ALL STARTED when I was four years old. It's a vague memory but it's significant that it is a memory. I listen to NPR a lot so I'm pretty smart and I learned, listening to an interview, that we remember things when emotions are present. Emotions signal to our mind that something is important, and we remember important things. It's a survival tactic. That's why you remember where you were when 9/11 happened or when Obama got elected or when Sally told you she wasn't going to marry you—a lot of emotions were present and your brain said, "Hey, let's hold on to this, to protect ourselves in the future." That's also why you don't remember folding laundry last Wednesday or your neighbor's name, because you don't care and emotions aren't involved. That's also why it hurts so much when someone you love forgets your birthday or anniversary or graduation, because what that really means is they don't attach emotions to you and your significance. How's my tennis book so far?

What I'm trying to say is that when I was four, in 1984, I got a Christmas gift that changed my life forever. And I remember that. I remember getting the gift. I remember how I felt. I remember that my older brother John gave it to me. I remember feeling immediately happy and warm and excited. Even as I type this thirty-six years later in an Atlantic City hotel (show tonight eight p.m., tickets still available) I feel the excitement that I felt that early Christmas morning on Huntington Drive in Ann Arbor, Michigan. We were sitting in the living room opening gifts, as we always did, the six of us. I don't remember anything else about that day, or even that year. I think my next memory starts when I was nine and, trying to find my golf ball, I got stung by twenty-one hornets (my other older brother, Todd, still says I maybe got stung by one bee). That's how important it must have been to me, to receive that gift: a Roddy tennis racket. Silver (aluminum?) with a black grip, nylon strings (15 gauge?), and a giant "R" stenciled on the strings. It was beautiful. There was a red ribbon attached to the center of the racket head, exactly where you would want to strike each ball, the sweet spot. Looking back, that was a nice subtle touch by my mom to remind me to watch the ball at its contact point. A tennis racket is a beautiful thing. Truly an outstanding tool, and by far one of the most ridiculous pieces of sports equipment out there. It's basically one third baseball bat, one third lacrosse stick, and one third trampoline, made out of metal (those days, at least). The strings make it elite in my opinion; it's like a violin but for athletes. If it didn't have strings it would just be a club, a bat, a stick, something Neanderthals use to hit objects (ever meet a baseball player?). A tennis racket is fascinating to look at. To this day, if there is a tennis racket in any room, I have to look at it. I have to hold it and spin it in my hand. If you threw a party and there was a dog and a tennis racket nearby, I could easily not speak to a single human all night.

Part of the significance of this gift was who gave it to me: my oldest brother, John. He was my favorite sibling. Todd and Kristy were great older siblings, too, but when I was four, they were more obstacles and nuisances. While Todd was just brute force and Kristy was a girl, John was thirteen and he was cool. He was old enough to protect me and help me but still not act like a parent. He had a skateboard and a Walkman and he was really nice to me. He still is. One hundred percent I would have loved getting a tennis racket for Christmas that year from anyone, but the fact that it came from John made it really special. And it changed the course of my life.

One thing I really hate about people from the South is that as children, they got to play with their Christmas gifts the same day they received them. Because the sun was out. The driveway was clean. It wasn't -12 degrees. Getting a racket that year was amazing but it was kind of like getting a savings bond: "You hold on to this, someday this will be worth something." As a kid growing up in Michigan I had to wait and wait and wait to get to play with my gifts. Unless you got a snowmobile or a shovel for Christmas, there was a lot of patience involved. When I received the tennis racket, I remember being really excited, but then also really bummed. I was four. Waiting five months to use my gift was roughly fifteen percent of my life.

Years later, as I entered competitive tennis, it was for a similar reason that I kept hating people from the South. They had good weather. They got to practice more. They didn't have to save up money to buy one hour of indoor court time in January. Kids from the South were always better at tennis. Us Northerners would look at the draw before a tournament and assess how good our opponent would be by which state he was from.

"Who you playing?" someone would ask.

"I don't know but he's from Florida."

"Shit, good luck."

I don't think the players from Georgia had the same worry when they saw my name in the draw with "Ann Arbor, Michigan" under it. If anything, they probably knew they would have to book a practice court after the match, because beating me wouldn't be enough of a challenge. But that's not the point right now.

What you're about to read all started because of this gift from John. I realize now it's very likely John didn't actually buy this gift for me. It's very likely that my mom, who knew John was my favorite, bought the racket for me and said it was from him. I could ask John that now, but part of me doesn't want to know the answer. When you're the youngest in your family, there is a lot you don't know. There was a whole family before you even showed up. I remember coming to that realization one day as a kid and feeling sad for weeks. As the youngest, there's also a constant struggle for your parents' attention. Yes, it is true that life is usually easier for the youngest in big families: typically the family has more money, rules are more relaxed because the parents are worn down, but Mom and Dad are also over it. They're over you, a little bit. My mom made a scrapbook for my brother John the size of six bricks with journal entries describing his first words, first haircut picture, an actual piece of hair, picture of his outfits, birthday cards, ribbons from his crib, etc. I asked my mom one time where my baby scrapbook was, and she left the room and didn't come back until I had left for soccer practice. I say it in interviews all the time: I think I became a stand-up comic because I'm still just trying to get my parents' attention. YOU HEAR THAT, MOM AND DAD! (No way they have read this far.)

But credit goes to them, because they most certainly paid for the Roddy racket, and it remains by far the greatest gift I ever got. I love tennis and I've always loved tennis and that racket was like someone buying me a lifetime ticket into a world that I wasn't invited to previously. Do you remember a moment like that in your life? Maybe it was the time you first strummed a guitar or hammered a nail or stepped into a foreign city that you love. (I guess it could work negatively, also: the first time you tried a double cheeseburger, or meth.) Thirty-five years later I still have no clue what brand "Roddy" is. I've never seen another racket like it; even Google struggles when I search for it. It doesn't matter. For the next six years of my life, it was the racket that I used to learn to play tennis, and as you will read, tennis sent me on many adventures. Thank you to John for the gift, thank you to Mom and Dad for buying it for him to give to me, and thank you to everyone else along the way who helped me become a somewhat decent tennis player.

Chapter 2

The Tennis Ball Game

MY FAMILY DID everything together. That was just how it was. I didn't have a vote on what we were doing—and as the youngest (and sadly the least important), I certainly couldn't ask why we were doing it. I have many memories of sitting in the car in the driveway with my seat belt on, waiting for us to leave while my parents packed the car. *Where were we going? Why were we going there?* But it didn't matter. "We're going on a family adventure," my dad would announce. An adventure it most certainly was.

Dinner was at six p.m. every day. We ate *together*. The phone was taken off the hook to keep outsiders from intruding (imagine that now, what's "the hook"?). Ironically, for the first two minutes, the phone would make a noise reminding you that it wasn't connected. So we would sit and listen to the phone-is-off-the-hook noise that represented a quiet and uninterrupted dinner experience. And we didn't just eat, we talked. We answered questions and were expected to ask questions in return.

"Kristy, how do you feel you did on your math test today?"

Then it was Kristy's turn to ask a question: "Todd, did you score any goals in your soccer game?"

I'm serious. This is how it went, around and around. Looking back now, it was tremendous social training.

This was all fine, but sometimes we were all just tired from school and basketball and teenage anxieties, and then family dinner became another lesson in our day, when we really just wanted to eat and not talk to anyone, least of all our parents.

This all came from Jan, my tremendous mother, who loves and cares for us deeply and also created wonderful ways to trick us into becoming prepared and well-rounded adults. If my mom was everyone's mom, we wouldn't have war or hunger or social anxiety or loneliness. We might all behave the same, but a lot of problems would be solved. (Shout out to all the moms out there creating and developing real human beings. It helps; it makes the world better.) I observe so many different types of people throughout my travels, and I often interact with someone at a hotel or comedy club or airport and think, "That person had a great mom."

Unfortunately, I can also tell when someone didn't.

One of the tricks my mom used to help us learn how to converse was called the Tennis Ball Game. She would sit us down, one-on-one, and ask us a question. "Michael, I see you're wearing a jacket, is it cold outside today?"

She would then toss me a tennis ball. The goal of the game was to pass the ball back to the person who handed it to you, but you could only pass it back if you asked a question in return. So, if I just said, "Yes, it's cold," I couldn't pass the ball. Instead I would say, "Yes, it's cold. Do you like the cold weather, or do you like warm weather?" Then I could toss the ball back to her.

"I like warm weather, thank you for asking, because I like gardening outside. Do you like gardening?" my mom would say. Back and forth we'd go. Like a tennis match, get it? This could presumably go on forever. And anyone that has ever sat with my mother knows that it sometimes did. That was, and still is, okay with her.

As an adult, when I tell people this story it's interesting to hear their reactions. Some people say, "Oh my god, that's amazing." Other people, like my wife, look perplexed and confused: "She trained you to ask questions, like you were circus animals?"

"Yes," I say. "Do you like the circus?"

Say what you want about the training, I think it's great. I tend to like people that ask me questions, and people tend to like that I ask them questions, too. When I first started interviewing people on TV, the segment producers would always give me so many questions to ask each subject before the interview. Like fifteen questions on a card, for a four-minute interview. Then we would do the interview and the producers would say, "You're so good at that, it seems like you've been doing that for years."

Ah yeah, I have, since I was four, it's called the Tennis Ball Game.

• • •

For the first half of my life, I was surrounded by athletes. In general, athletes are very well-trained members of society. They show up on time, put the right clothes on, know how to shake hands, converse clearly, thank people, win and lose with class, go to bed on time, and wake up early. Sure, a couple of exceptions usually make the news, but you can't really be a successful athlete if you can't follow rules and sit through awards banquets or coaches' meetings.

Most athletes know how to play the Tennis Ball Game, often because they had a coach or parent in their life like my mom. So when I switched over to comedy, I was absolutely baffled at how poorly trained comics were. Comics are some of the most socially awkward, difficult to be around, unpleasant individuals you will ever spend time with. They talk either a hundred percent of the time or zero percent of the time. They show up really late or really early. They stand too close to you or too far away. Their clothes are, somehow, always dirty. I have example after example of socializing with comics where really basic standard rules of social interaction were violated and violated very badly. I really love comedy and I really love comics, and there is a freedom and creativity that comes with the craft (it takes a crazy individual with at least a small delusion to get up on stage each night, so I guess it is understandable that many stand-up comics don't comply with these societal norms), but damn, sometimes when I stand outside the Comedy Store in LA and talk to a few comics I find myself thinking, "I really need to bring a tennis ball out here next time, this guy hasn't asked me a question in twenty-five minutes."

It's not like I was always good at this stuff. And I'm sure the comics that I'm complaining about didn't have the same upbringing as I did. How could they? I had Super Mom over here teaching me the subtleties of conversation. I remember sharing the Tennis Ball Game with a fellow comic while golfing one day and he looked at me like I was a hippopotamus.

"What was your mom like?" I asked.

"I used to come home from school and my mom would be cutting lines of cocaine on the only clean plate in the house," he replied.

"OK . . . well, huh, you laying three or four?"

Back to the Kosta family's six p.m. dinners. I remember at one point my mom told me that she and my dad were worried about my brother John. He was supposedly failing German and my parents were worried that he was a druggie or something. That's how it worked in my house: if John was getting a C in German, it was most definitely because he was on drugs, not because John hated German and hated his German teacher, Frau Stolt.

Before dinner one night, my mom said to me, "Michael, you have a tendency to interrupt at the dinner table and your father and I want to talk to John as much as possible tonight. So tonight, let us talk to him without trying to turn the conversation to you."

Okay, Mom, whatever you say. Well, that didn't work. Apparently, every time my parents tried to talk to John that night, I would butt in and ruin the German class intervention. Remember that part about me wanting my parents' attention? It was even worse back then. (I always chose the seat at the dinner table that was directly across from the sliding glass door, because as the sun would go down, the glare would turn it into a mirror, and I would just sit at the table and stare at myself and make faces and perform for an audience of one [myself]. My parents eventually switched my seat.)

By the next night, my parents still had not figured out why John was failing the hardest language class his school offered, so they tried a new tactic. Before dinner, my mom pulled me aside again and said, "Michael, tonight when we start talking to John about German, if you interrupt, I'm going to ask you, 'Michael, do you know what time it is?' And that is your clue that you are intruding on an important conversation."

This should also tell you a few things about our family dynamic. Instead of just directly saying, "Michael shut up for a few minutes," or "Michael, we are trying to talk to John, sit there and be quiet," my mom came up with a "code" that would signal an attention-seeking eight-year-old boy to bite his tongue. You can imagine how this went down. That night, over and over, my parents would ask John, "So, honey, can you tell us about German class?"

And over and over I would say something stupid like, "You guys think the moon is big?" and over and over my mom would kindly and patiently turn to me and say, "Michael, do you know what time it is?"

I would shut up for ten seconds and then the cycle would continue. Finally, after my mom had asked me what time it was for the tenth time, my sister Kristy blurted out, "Mom, you've asked him that a hundred times—it's six-thirty p.m.!"

Twenty-five years later, at John's bachelor party at Oktoberfest in Munich, Germany, my brothers, dad, and I laughed about this story. John may have been terrible at German in high school, but right then it was his terrible German that was keeping us fed and drunk with our German-speaking waitress, which we were thankful for.

We were and still are a close family. A family that did a lot of things together. Even if that thing was finding out why John was shitty in school. One characteristic that sets my family apart from others is that my family was and still is fun. We had fun together and frequently it was funny to be around my family. We were the funny family.

Humor was a huge part of our connection with one another. Whether it was watching my dad almost have a heart attack from laughing so hard at a family viewing of the 1988 film *A Fish Called Wanda* or Todd and me putting on lip-synching performances of Michael Jackson for our grandparents (they were terrified) or my mom creating a Valentine's Day dinner structure called "Love Mountain" where a giant table centerpiece sat with strings connected to presents that trailed to each place setting, it was fun to be a part of my family. One time a shy friend of mine from middle school came over and after an hour he pulled me aside and said, "Your family is hilarious . . . and I'm exhausted," and he promptly called his mom to pick him up.

The one activity we took pretty seriously that wasn't always funny was tennis. We loved tennis. Before John McEnroe's US Open matches, my dad would pop popcorn and we'd all sit down to watch, yelling at the TV after each point. My parents hosted Breakfast at Wimbledon parties for the women's and men's finals, and I remember eating homemade strawberries and cream watching Martina Navratilova win many of her Wimbledons while trying to avoid awkward conversations with our neighbors because I wanted to watch the tennis. Yearly, the whole family would get in the station wagon and drive to Detroit to watch exhibition matches (the most memorable was Andre Agassi vs Jimmy Connors). One year I snuck down to the court and asked Jana Novotná for her racket and as she handed it to me, a bigger kid took it out of my hands. That wasn't funny at all. All the way home down 94 west I sat in the back back and cried into my arm. But more importantly, tennis wasn't just observed as a family, it was played as a family, together. Something we called "Kosta Family Tennis" (creative) and we did this at the local Ann Arbor tennis club, Racquet Club of Ann Arbor (creative).

Chapter 3

Kosta Family Tennis

IF YOU HAVEN'T figured it out by now, the Kosta family unit was taken very seriously by my parents—so if they wanted to play tennis, that meant we all were going to play tennis, whether we wanted to or not. It never crossed my mind that I could choose to not do the family activity. Because it wasn't an option. Once my dad threw the word "family" in front of the activity, it was one hundred percent mandatory participation. Some real examples: Family Mother's Day Car Ride, Family Putting Flyers on Parked Cars Promoting Dad's Business, Family Cleaning the House, Family Making Chinese Food, Family Mom's Chorus Night, Family Drywall the Basement, Family Todd and Michael Clear All Shrubbery from the Front Yard (this was a three-week job), Family Grocery Shopping, Family Six P.M. Dinner, and of course Family Tennis.

Family tennis happened at a wonderful tennis and racket club called the Racquet Club of Ann Arbor. It was a former horse farm and apple orchard. It's fancier now, but back then, the family membership cost $600 per year. I know that because my dad reminded us all the time when we complained about being bored: "Stop complaining and go down to the Racquet Club, I paid $600 for that!"

For $600, it was the greatest value in town: eight hard courts, four clay courts, a backboard, a swimming pool, and a grass yard.

The Racquet Club was where Kosta Family Tennis went down. We'd get two courts, one court of doubles and one court of singles, and we would rotate. One thing I love about being in a big family is that anywhere you go, you have a party. No matter what, there are already six people there. I always felt bad for only children because the only people they got to hang with were their parents—gross. And they couldn't even play doubles!

The atmosphere was always laid back and supportive. There was a lot of laughing and yelling out "Great shot!" and "Where did you come up with that one?!" type bullshit. Thinking back on it now as a parent, I realize it was a little bit about connecting with the family but mostly about just running around and making us kids tired so we would easily go to sleep later. I would see some of the other dads down there with their kids putting lots of pressure on them and feeding them balls and screaming at them to move their feet, and it never looked like fun. Kosta Family Tennis was fun.

I think that's why I love tennis so much. It was fun, and as a little guy, I wanted to be a part of the fun. As I got better and better at tennis throughout the years, I started meeting better and better tennis players, and I noticed that without a doubt the ones who succeeded the most were the ones who genuinely loved playing. I saw so many wonderfully talented players slowly fade out of the sport, due to pressure from parents or coaches. Stop doing that, parents. Make it fun and the kid will enjoy the sport forever.

Here's another thing I vividly remember about Kosta Family Tennis: my mother did not enjoy playing doubles with my father. Yet, somehow, it always happened. My dad loved to give advice, offer "help," coaching, strategies, etc. It's truly remarkable. He was so analytical that it actually sabotaged him, but he didn't realize it. One year, when I was in high school, we decided to play a father-son doubles tournament together. For bonding, I think. Before the first point of our first match as I was getting ready to serve, my dad wanted to talk strategy.

"OK, son, I watched this guy during the warm-up and I think you need to serve the ball toward the inside right elbow because his forehand has a slight wrist angle that appears to be a weakness. Once you do that, I will shuffle my feet to cause him to look away from the ball and that's when I will pounce. Now, his partner is left-handed, and I think his backhand grip is too loose—"

All this before the first point of the match. I stopped him. "Dad, Dad, stop, I'm just gonna serve it as hard as I can and we'll win the point."

And that's what happened. My dad can't not overthink things, it's in his DNA. This can have value in other parts of life, but in tennis, it's detrimental.

My mom, on the other hand, is naturally not a competitive person. She's a social worker. She is kind and sweet and maternal. One anecdote sums up my mom perfectly. Living in a home comprised primarily of males, one year my mom was worried that the household was getting too competitive. Maybe it was the pool tournaments in the basement that led to fistfights and crying, or the Ping Pong games that led to me and Todd not speaking to each other for weeks on end, or the hole in the wall that one of our friends punched after losing a game of Nintendo. Whatever the case may be, she wanted us to get more in touch with our "empathetic sides." So, she bought the Ungame. It was a board game, but there was no winner and no loser; the point was just the "journey," if you will. We would roll the dice and hop around the board. Occasionally we would have to answer a question from a card. "Oh I get it, like Trivial Pursuit," you might be thinking. But then the question would be "Name three things that you're thankful for," or "Can you name a time in the last week that you helped someone?"

As you can imagine, my brothers and I really hated the Ungame. I think even my dad hated the Ungame, but he could never admit it to my mom. There we were, in a highly competitive household of male bravado, in "We are #1," capitalistic, USA! USA!, sitting around our family table in athletic gear having to figure out the last time we . . . helped someone?

So when my mom played doubles with her husband—who is so competitive he used to race his kids up the stairs each time we went up them—they had two completely different competitive mindsets. And they didn't mix well.

The big issue with Mom-Dad doubles was always the same: Dad wanted Mom to poach. "Poaching" is exactly how it sounds. It's a doubles play, an assertive move by the server's partner to run across the center service line right as the returner returns the serve and the servers partner then attacks their shot. All you really need to know is that it's an aggressive move and my mom and the word "aggressive" have never gone together. Unless you are describing her strategy in helping others, like "Jan is aggressive with her volunteering." Even that doesn't sound right.

So, Dad would tell Mom to "poach" and then he would serve and my mom wouldn't poach. Then my dad would yell, "Why didn't you poach?"

And my mom would yell, "I don't want to poach!"

On occasion, some tears might fall. Then we would rotate and change the teams. I remember one time my parents signed up for the mixed doubles (men play with women) tournament at the Racquet Club. They drove to their first match, and then a few hours later I remember my dad coming home, alone. A few minutes later, my mom got dropped off by someone else. Not only had they lost the match together, but they had nearly split up the marriage. To this day, no one knows what happened, but I would bet a lot of money it involved poaching.

One thing I remember about Kosta Family Tennis distinctly is that my sister, Kristy, had serve issues. Serious ones. She could double fault literally four times in a row. That means that if you were her doubles partner, you would stand at the net and basically collect the balls from the net for her so she could miss some more and you could lose faster. It was sad, really. I'm so happy that Kristy is now a successful person because sometimes Kosta Family Tennis was hard on her. You double fault once, your partner says, "Hey don't worry about it." You double fault twice, maybe they say the same thing. But three or four times in a row, shit, that's hard on everyone. By the end of her service games, people on other courts would chime in and tell her what she was doing wrong: "Hey, I noticed you're serving terribly, you should keep your head up more." Or "Hey, I know you don't know me but you are rotating your right hip too much . . ." Kristy never asked for anyone's advice, but the Kostas—and tennis players—love to give it.

Like golf, tennis is a highly technical sport overwhelmingly played by rich, educated people that think they know a lot about it just because they took a lesson once from an "expert." It drives me insane. Few other sports have such notoriously entitled participants. Can you imagine a stranger at the playground basketball court pulling you aside, saying, "Hey, I think you'd have more success with your jump shot if you pronated your wrist a little more"? They would get beat up. Also, when you're performing badly at something, you don't need other people to point it out, you already know.

To her credit, Kristy gracefully and kindly listened to everyone's advice (Dad's included, even though he was sometimes her opponent) and tried her hardest. Knowing what I know about tennis now, I see that Kristy could have done a few easy things to help her serve. She had the wrong grip and her toss was way too high. Today, I could fix her serve in ten seconds, but then I was eight and didn't know shit. Kristy is a nurse practitioner and the most educated person in our family, so I think she got the last laugh. Also, she hasn't played tennis in over twenty years.[1]

Even as the youngest, I was good at Kosta Family Tennis. I don't say this to sound cocky. In life, you remember when things click, and when I played tennis, it just clicked. It seemed easy to me. If my brain thought of something on the tennis court, my body could make it happen. If I needed the ball to be over in the corner, I could just hit it and it would go over there. There I was, as a little kid, watching my sister double fault or my mom afraid to poach or my dad unable to hit a topspin backhand, and I just did all those things and I did them fairly well. I was surprised that it was so hard for them. I guess it's what you call "being a natural." As time went on and I moved up the tennis ranks, I realized that there were a lot of kids that had the same ability, some even more so than me. But in the beginning, when I was still grouped in with everyone, it was safe to say that I was better than most.

The only other time in my life when I felt something click like that was when I first got on stage as a comedian. It just felt right, it felt natural. A fish in water. So, for me, it's tennis and comedy. I wonder if the "click" will ever happen again. If not, that's OK, these are two extremely amusing activities and I'm very thankful for them.

...

Despite having natural abilities as a tennis player, and plenty of exposure thanks to Kosta Family Tennis, there was also something the Racquet Club offered that helped me get a lot better: The Backboard.

---

1   It should be noted that it couldn't have been easy being the only girl with three brothers in our house. Here's an example: one evening my brother Todd was trying out his new karate kicks on my sister. The game, as he saw it, was to try a roundhouse kick and see how close he could get to Kristy's face without actually kicking her. Eventually he got so close that Kristy put her hands out to protect herself—in which case Todd kicked her hand and broke her finger. When Kristy complained to our dad that her finger was broken because Todd karate kicked her, my dad said to her, "Well, you shouldn't have tried to block it."

A fancy way of saying a "wall." It was an ugly, giant, green cement wall, roughly thirty feet by thirty feet. It had the lines of a tennis court on the ground and a slanted white line across the wall—the "net" so to speak.

The Backboard was where shit got real. Tucked behind the tennis courts and underneath a busy Ann Arbor four-lane highway, the Backboard was where all the serious tennis players at the Racquet Club would hang. I would hit alone on that wall for hours. I'd drop the ball in front of me, hit it against the wall and see how long I could continue the rally until I missed. I can still hear the sounds. Tennis is a wonderful sport of sounds: the ball on the racket (*whack*), the ball against the wall (*thud*), the ball bouncing (*plop*), *whack, thud, plop, whack thud plop* over and over again.

Every activity has its Backboard. Basketball players spend hours shooting free throws at the park; hockey players skate alone on shoddy homemade hockey rinks in their backyard; boxers famously have some of the roughest and most awful training facilities on earth; musicians practice for years in gross padded-wall rehearsal studios. These spaces are where the work goes in, where the progress is made. And it's done *alone*. It's so important to have that bonding time with yourself, to push yourself and challenge yourself, *alone*.

It's exactly the same with comedy. When my friends come into town, they always want to join me as I run around LA or New York doing spots at night. They want to peek behind the curtain of what they think is a sexy glamorous showbiz life. Then we do it and it's inevitable—every time, at some point, they ask me, "Dude why are you doing this to yourself? There were only eleven people at that show. They didn't even speak English."

I tell them that small crappy audience, in a poorly lit, damp comedy club, that's my backboard. It's practice, so it seems easy when there is a real audience of a thousand people that do speak my language. Hours alone spent working on your craft give you the confidence of knowing that you are ready and prepared when you need it most.

A coach once told me, "Your life is what you pay attention to." Damn, that's real, isn't it? You can't escape that. Our lives are what we look at. It seems a lot more complicated now with responsibilities like rent, jobs, family, car payments—but at the end of the day, life is what our eyes are looking at. (Think about that the next time you scroll through Instagram. Is this what I want my life to be? A woman in a bikini pitching beauty products?) At that important moment in my life, smacking the ball against the Backboard over and over was what I was paying attention to, it was my life.[2]

Kosta Family Tennis ended after the sun went down. We would play into the dark, and I remember bats would start flying around. We would then all sit around on the grass, and our parents would drink beer and we would talk about the matches and laugh (sometimes tears needed to dry). I still think about those times on certain nights when the weather is the same, or I see a bat flying around at dusk, or when I see a very sweaty middle-aged man. My dad was always so sweaty and gross after Kosta Family Tennis—and this was the eighties, so men were wearing these thin-collared shirts with fabric that mimicked lingerie lace. He always needed help taking his disgusting, soaked, and see-through shirt off, and the job usually fell to me and Todd. We would each grab an arm and he would bend over and we would help him pull his drenched shirt over his head. He would make those weird noises that dads make "*argg ardf grughh*" that I find myself making now. Dad would then drive us home with his shirt off and I remember him putting his half drunken beer between his legs, taking sips as he drove.

---

2 The garage door of our house also served as a nice backboard. And when you turned the outside floodlight on, I could hit on it well into the night, infuriating most of our neighborhood I'm sure (*whack, thud, plop*). One time, there were too many cars parked in our driveway for me to use our garage door, so I ran over to our neighbors' house and hit on theirs. It had a few rectangular windows, one of which I promptly broke with an errant forehand. A few hours later, when I casually mentioned this to my parents, they quickly walked me over to the neighbors' house and I had to announce to his whole family while they watched TV that I had broken the window and that I was sorry.

Chapter 4

Ann Arbor Junior Open

AS YOU NOW know, a lot of my life has consisted of me trying to get attention. First from my family, then from my peers, and now, as an adult and a stand-up comic, from the world. I don't know why. Was something missing in my upbringing that caused me to need more affection, attention, and recognition from others? Or was everything fine and I was just born wanting to be the center of the universe for no discernible reason?

I tend to think it's the latter. As I get older and talk to therapists and analyze my behavior, it's pretty clear that I simply like and desire attention. Maybe it's because Mercury was in retrograde when my mom was pregnant; maybe it's because our family dinner table was too crowded for me to be singled out; maybe it's none of these things. Maybe acceptance is the strongest emotional connection we can have with other humans and I'm just a victim to needing it, like everyone else. I certainly don't think there was anything significant missing from my upbringing, parents, or home, besides, you know, not having a baby scrapbook or that one time Mom left me at baseball camp for three extra hours because she had the times mixed up. But I'm clearly over that.

I know what you're thinking: "But Michael, aren't the people that constantly want attention and recognition really annoying to be around?" You nailed it. They are . . . ah, we are. Always interrupting, acting out, making jokes. We're the worst. Teacher evaluation after teacher evaluation read: "I enjoy having Michael in class but when he is gone we get so much more done," or "I really like Michael, but he seems to have a compulsion to disrupt our progress and thinks he is the only important student in class."

Look, I'm not proud of this. Many times in my life I've heard words coming out of my mouth and my brain has said loud and clear, "Don't say this, do not say this thing," and it still comes out. My dad would yell at me: *"You have to think before you speak!"*

It's just an instinct, an impulse, and it's very hard to control. Much like an addict hates their behavior but continues to do it, I cannot let a good joke—or at least what I think is a good joke—pass without blurting it out. This has caused frequent pain and trouble with girlfriends ("Your brother is a pothead, everyone knows that"), bosses ("Let me drive, you're too short"), my wife ("If we are being honest, no, I do not enjoy your stir fry"), coaches ("How much longer are we practicing because if we keep going I'll go get my night vision goggles"—this one got me in a lot of trouble), teammates ("Alex, is your bad one-handed backhand so bad because of your lazy eye?"), friends ("Your sister's breasts got much bigger in college"), you name it. I have made a joke or said something inappropriate to every single person I know, and looking back I think, "Why in god's name would you ever say that?" I don't know.

All I know is it happens, and it happened a lot more before I started doing stand-up comedy. I remember watching Robin Williams do an interview on TV one time, and I said, "God, this guy is so annoying, always trying to make jokes." And my sister goes, "That's what YOU DO!"

• • •

So, I wanted attention, and as an eight-year-old I didn't exactly know how to get it. Until 1988, when our family friend John Long won the Ann Arbor Junior Open Boys' 10 and Under. You can tell how important it was to me because all these years later it's still an easy memory to recall. John was nine and was in the finals of the Ann Arbor Junior Open, which was played at the Racquet Club. It was a small-time tournament; there were probably sixteen to twenty-four kids under the age of ten playing for the championship trophy to find out who was the best ten-year-old in the region. But I had lived my whole life up to that point within a one-mile radius, and everyone I knew and socialized with entered the tournament. It was our Super Bowl.

I entered the Boys' 10 tournament and lost somewhere in the opening rounds. John, a year older and a year better than I was, made it to the finals, which was exciting because he was our friend and this was our home club. Watching John play in the finals was a big event. Parents drove down from their homes to add their support, the kids lined up court side, older brothers and sisters were all there, the local pros were all pulling for John. Some details elude me. I remember John's match being on Court 10, I know John used the original Wilson Pro Staff, and I feel like he might have been wearing the Stefan Edberg shirt with his signature on it. Most clearly, I remember the attention John received. Every point with the *"oohs* and *ahs,"* the claps and sounds of support; it was a tremendous match.

At some point John won the match (and because this was the finals, he won the whole tournament) and we went nuts. We picked him up and carried him around, throwing him up and down, cheering and screaming. We headed to the pool, and his mom made us take his new shoes off before tossing him in (how Midwest is that?) and then we dunked him in the water with his clothes on. The absolute thrill of victory! It was wonderful. Looking back thirty years later, it's still wonderful. Winning. Winning is awesome. And this was the first time in my young life that I realized it. I know we're in the age of participation trophies and ribbons for trying, but let me tell you, when you're nine years old and you beat out twenty-four ten-year-olds for the trophy, it stays with you for a lifetime. It stuck with me and I didn't even do it, John did. (When I started writing this chapter I texted John, "Do you remember the score for your Boys' 10 AAJO Final, 1988?" Immediately, I saw the three dots on the screen and he responded, "6–1 7–6" . . . next text: "vs Matt Hagan" . . . next text: "Court 10").

John accepted his trophy that day in soaking wet clothes, and we all had smiles on our faces.[1]

Besides being happy for John, I was extraordinarily envious of the attention he received for winning the Ann Arbor Junior Open Boys' 10. It feels silly to write that but it's true and I'm trying to give you guys the truth, OK? High fives, slaps on the back, trophy, picture in *The Ann Arbor News*. He was #1 and it looked like that was the best number to be. I saw that being a champion got you a lot of love and a lot of attention and I remember thinking, "Well, that's what I'll do now. I'll just win the same tournament next year." I wanted my picture in the paper.

One year later, I'm a year older, a year better at tennis. Same

---

1   Now, as a seasoned competitor, I look back and wonder: Where was his opponent? Did we ever congratulate him? That probably wasn't a very fun moment, losing and watching the entire club celebrate like the moon landing just happened. Kudos to that guy, I hope he is happy and successful.

tournament, same category, Boys' 10 and Under, and I'm in the finals. I played a kid named Bradley Adams, a left-handed kid from the Detroit area. I saw him earlier in the tournament, and he looked a little chubby. I wasn't even nervous before the match. I really thought it was a done deal. I was assigned the same court number that John had a year earlier, Court 10, a little sign from the tennis gods that this would be a walk in the park. A nice big crowd formed to watch me win, friends (John Long was there), family friends, *girls* even. I saw a TV reporter taking pictures. My dad took the afternoon off work to watch his son slaughter Bradley Adams like the cow he was. Here's the most embarrassing part: I remember packing extra shirts in my bag so after I won and got thrown in the pool, I would have something dry to change into to accept my trophy. The last thing I was focused on was the actual match and playing against the crafty lefty that was Bradley Adams.

You see where this is going? Quickly, I lost the first set 6–4. Not only was he good, he was really good, and he was better than me. His lefty serve was super annoying, his backhand wouldn't break down. He actually moved really well and covered the court like a pro. He made tight calls, he had a little swagger when he walked, he came to win. He was prepared to do battle and I was prepared to have my picture taken. It all hit me at once, and tennis is not a forgiving sport when you have a mental breakdown. No teammate to rely on, no helmet to hide your tears, no timeout to take a break. Add all that to the fact that I was also nine years old and didn't know how to control my emotions at all.[2] In tennis, it's just you, all alone, standing in the middle of the playing surface, figuring out if you're going to sink or swim; or, in my case that day, slowly and painfully, publicly, die.

I started crying at around 3–0 in the second set. That nice crowd

---

2 I still don't. The last time I played tennis in LA, it was at a friend's private court, and I was so angry I threw my racket over the fence and it landed in their pool.

of supporters? I saw them slowly disperse, and I remember hearing some whispers. My brother John, my hero, the person who gave me the Roddy racket as a Christmas gift five years ago, the racket that I was still using at this moment, ran out onto the court to tell me that I had to keep it together and just try my hardest and that I was doing great. How embarrassing is that? A member of the crowd ran into the match to help dry the tears of one of the players. My world crashed down hard that day. Bradley beat me 6–4 6–4.

I can't remember much more after the match. I have some vague memories of crying through the awards ceremony, watching Bradley accept the trophy, seeing his parents really happy for him. But for me, it was a sad day. I cried for days after that match. It hurt so bad. Not only did I not get the attention I wanted, but the attention I did get was because I was a pussy on court, crying because I never considered that my opponent in the finals might be good at tennis.

Bradley went on to piss me off for another 5–6 losses in the years to come. The last time he beat me was at a tournament in a public park in some very poor Detroit suburb. I was twelve and after another humbling defeat, through even more tears, I smashed my racket on a dumpster. I hated Bradley Adams so fucking much. This was before sponsorships and free rackets. Smashing a racket meant that I would have to work around the house for my mom for free until I earned the $150 I needed to buy another racket. I also remember watching a homeless man with a shopping cart picking up my broken racket afterward. What a strange dichotomy: spoiled child loses tennis match, breaks racket, poor older homeless man sees the broken racket as some kind of resource (what could he possibly use that for?) and takes it. I hope he put it to better use than I did.[3]

In retrospect, it's clear that Bradley Adams showed up at just the right time. He was there to toughen me up and prepare me for higher

---

3 Bradley Adams is currently the head mens' tennis coach at Villanova University.

levels of tennis. Through his many victories and my many tears, he eventually bitch-slapped me into shape.

In the years to come, I started getting the attention I was looking for on the court. I won the Ann Arbor Junior Open in the Boys' 12 and the Boys' 14 pretty easily. I can't tell you anything about those matches. I must have played well and beaten some good players, but I don't remember because these victories didn't affect me the same way that goddamn Bradley Adams did.

Slowly—very slowly—I learned that in tennis, much like in many other aspects of life, setbacks can serve a purpose; if you try to learn from them, and if you keep working hard, more opportunities will present themselves.

I remind myself of this all the time as a comic. If you're bombing, don't pull a Michael Kosta vs. Bradley Adams and cry on stage. Instead, cry off stage, take some time to collect yourself, and get back out there. It may still suck, but you'll be better and stronger. I've done thousands of comedy sets, most of them good, but there are some really terrible ones in there that I can't forget. I call them my Bradley Adams sets. I've played and won thousands of tennis matches, most of which I can't tell you a single thing about, but the losses—I'll never forget those.

Pain always prepares you. Sometimes it's preparing you for something you don't even know about yet. When I started doing comedy, older more experienced comics would comment on how resilient I seemed after failing to get a reaction from the crowd or a bad set.

Never in a million years would I have thought that weeping on Court 10 at nine years old while my older brother consoled me would make having a few jokes fall flat in front of strangers feel easy, or that it would make me a better and more savvy stand-up comic. Life is weird, man.

After the Boys' 10 Under Final, I can't say that I never underprepared again, or that I never thought about the result of winning before actually playing the match. But I know that day, that tournament, that Adams did ultimately make me better at tennis and now comedy. Perhaps most importantly, I learned that if I wanted the attention that I so desperately sought, well, then I needed to get a lot better at tennis.

Chapter 5

Junior Tennis

ARMED WITH THAT attitude, I dove headfirst into the world of junior tennis and my next six to seven years, through a lot of trial and error, I learned that what determined my success was less about forehands and backhands and more about my overall attitude and my effort, both of which would be consistently tested in the cesspool that is USTA Junior Tennis.

What is "junior tennis" you ask and why is it a cesspool? Junior tennis is the never-ending calendar of junior tennis tournaments, sponsored by the United States Tennis Association, that revolve around the country (and now world, but not when I played). Junior tennis consists of the top one hundred to two hundred junior tennis players in your age group whose parents pay for their kids to compete against each other (often at the request of the kids, mind you). At the end of the year the USTA would release the rankings based on the calendar of results. For a year that ranking number was *your* number, and that number was your ranking in your age group in the entire country. Numbers that I carried over the years: #47, #31, #127, etc. Sometimes you would play the same kid three times in a row in three different cities. Junior tennis was meant to be fun, but in retrospect, it was a pressure cooker, and as far as we knew it was the only way to consistently compete and to see where you stood compared to the other players in your age group in the country. Adults, now, speak of having "tennis trauma" from playing junior tennis and I get it. The nerves, the pressure from parents, the travel, the age groups, the heat, the injuries, the cost, the equipment, the losses, the cheating, it can add up and it can break you. And it does break kids, sadly.

Knowing all this, even now, as a forty-something-year-old father of two daughters, I'd still like my kids to play tennis: tennis prepares children to be responsible and well-balanced adults. When you play tennis, you're the one solving your problems. Team sports are great for other reasons, but I think it's important for kids to learn how to handle life solo. Later on, they can partner up and get some help, but when they're small children I like the idea of making it hard on them. I mean, the mother bird pushes her babies out of the nest to see if they can fly, right? I wouldn't necessarily want my daughters to go through all the emotional ups and downs of junior tennis that I went through, but also I remember very clearly *asking* my parents if I could play those tournaments. They weren't forcing me. I was doing it to myself. Here's a good example of that.

Around 1992, I was in the finals of a big regional tournament. A tournament I begged my parents to play. My mom even said to me before she sent in the $35 entry fee that accompanied every junior tournament entry form, "You sure you want to play this one? You've played a lot of tournaments this summer."

"Yes, Mom, I want to do it."

I was the first seed in the draw and I won my first four matches easily, and made the finals. The day of the finals I woke up very nervous. Being the first seed, I was supposed to win, the pressure started to really wear on me. The tournament was an hour south of our home in Ann Arbor and I made my mom stop twice on the way down US-23 because I had severe stomach problems. I remember sitting on the toilet, in a grungy Ohio rest stop (for the second time), overcome with dread and tension and asking myself "Why do you do this to yourself? Is this fun? OMG what happens if you lose?" In the car, I was curled up moaning like an injured fawn. My poor mom was watching me suffer and would try to comfort me, putting her hand on my back. "Honey, just try to have fun. It's just a tennis match, etc. It's gonna be OK no matter what happens." But it was so hard for me to actually grasp that.

I walked on the court depleted and exhausted. After the first game, I took a deep breath and realized I was so much better than this player and won easily (6–1 6–0). It wasn't even a contest.

I still think about this match when I get nervous now as a comedian, "Relax, it's gonna be OK." I think "Your mind is making this much harder on you than you need it to." That's one of the reasons I like the junior tennis for kids, it helps you (forces you?) to manage the emotions of life.[1]

A less obvious reason: you are constantly learning how to deal with opponents who cheat. In junior tennis—matches where all players are under eighteen years old—most tournaments don't have lines people (also called line judges), so who do they naturally put in charge of deciding if your shot was "in" or "out"? *Your opponent!* That's right, the person who is trying to beat you. It's like that TV show about the beauty pageant kids, but not as civilized. All the while, you have some sleep-deprived mom or dad who remortgaged the house for tennis lessons pacing up and down screaming into their fists as they watch their kid get "hooked" (cheated) out of a match.

I have lots of memories of parents yelling at me through the fence, yelling at their children through the fence, yelling at other parents behind the fence—lots of memories of yelling. When you watch tennis on TV now, the cameras always cut to the parent sitting in

---

1   The kid I beat 6–1 6–0? He's now a DJ.

the players box, politely clapping, wearing a Nike hat. But for every one of those that exists there are ten thousand parents who threw punches at each other, tried to fight the tournament director, refused to stop coaching, and totally tried their best to win a tennis match for their child even though they weren't the ones on the court. You know that guy you work with who loses his temper sometimes and drinks way too much at the holiday party and has a twitch? I bet he played junior tennis and had a psycho parent. Parents, stop doing this to your children! The success isn't the outcome of the match, the success is playing and competing with class. That's it. That's the lesson. I'm sorry you missed the free throw for the state championship in 1975, but helping your son win this quarterfinal match in the Boys' 14 Bay City Indoor Championships isn't going to change the fact that you lost an important game.

Fortunately, I had wonderful tennis parents. They had the energy, excitement, and money to support me and help me become a better player. I have countless memories of them sitting outside in the heat, all day Saturday and Sunday, cheering me on. They got fresh shirts from the car, filled up my water bottle, drove me to practice courts, arranged practice partners. Both of them tried to help me with strategy and tactics even though they really didn't know anything about the sport. They were always happy when I won and sad when I lost.

There are, however, a few examples of times when my parents did get really mad at me during my matches. It was rare but warranted. My mom once screamed at me inside our minivan after a match because I had treated my opponent so poorly. I was trying on a new on-court personality, a cocky, assholey, swaggery personality and my mom, the social worker, was furious about it. She felt I had disrespected my opponent, a boy who wasn't particularly coordinated and struggled athletically. She was right and I never pushed it that far again.

Then there was the time my dad lost his shit on me in the ten-minute break between second and third sets at a tournament in St. Louis (junior tennis players are granted a ten-minute break for coaching, hydration, orange slices). He screamed at me inside the locker room for the entire club to hear. I was being lazy and crabby and whiny on court. He had taken time off work to travel with me and thought my attitude and effort were shit and he told me so. Once again, the parent was right. I adjusted, won the match, and then waited for him to come back to the courts and pick me up because he had left to prove a point (point taken).[2]

Most memorable was the time when *both* of my parents freaked out. Double whammy.

I was eleven, around 1991, and I was playing doubles with my friend and former 1988 Ann Arbor Junior Open Boys' 10 and Under champion, the legendary John Long. John was one of six kids, and his parents weren't as nitpicky as mine. He liked to push the boundaries when it came to his behavior. And in a sport where there is no defensive lineman to smash you into humility every once in a while, these attitudes could occasionally escalate.

As he was my doubles partner and older role model, I definitely looked up to him and mimicked his behavior from time to time. In tennis, even if you had good parents with good coaches who would check your ego occasionally, it only lasted so long. Eventually we, as gifted junior players, would be back on the court whupping our less skilled opponents and our egos would start growing again like mold.

---

2   It should be noted that both of these parental reactions happened after I won. I hated losing so much that if and when I lost, my parents saw that as enough of a punishment. After I lost a match, I would stay in my room and sulk and basically ground myself. I'm sure on more than one occasion my parents were actually rooting for me to lose. Think about it. Once I lost, the tournament was over. No more driving for hours to a hot, humid cement tennis parking lot, no more sleeping in crappy hotel rooms, watching me cry and yell and scream. We went back to our nice lives, where the family's happiness wasn't determined by an eleven-year-old boy hitting a yellow ball over a net. So, of course my parents wanted me to lose. Wow. It just hit me now.

It wasn't until we started competing nationally against other punks like ourselves, who were better than us, that we realized maybe we should focus more on the tennis and less on the attitude.

I was eleven, John was twelve, and we were the best in the region for our age. We were playing doubles together in some local tournament and were just crushing everyone. We were winning sooo easily. We were bored, frankly. It was the finals and we were cruising to victory and John had this wonderful idea at one of the changeovers. It went something like this:

John: We're killing these guys. This sucks.
Me: Seriously these kids suck, this isn't even hard.
John: Let's play left-handed. Let's beat them the last game left-handed.
Me: Great idea.

So that's what happened. We went back out there and played the last game left-handed (we're both right-handed). We won easily. Looking back, I'm thinking, "How bad were these kids if we could beat them with our opposite hand?" That's not easy in tennis. Tennis takes a lot of coordination and timing and to just switch over to the other hand is tough. Anyways, we won, we laughed about it, we made a big stink at the trophy ceremony, telling everyone that we were so good we won left-handed. You know, the way assholes behave.

I don't remember the ride home, I just remember sitting at the kitchen table with my parents afterward. I vividly recall the trophy that I had just won was nowhere to be seen. Mom and Dad were beyond upset. They were so mad that their anger had turned into disappointed silence. Do you remember doing that to your parents? Shit that was bad. "I'm not mad at you, I'm disappointed in you"— that phrase stings and one I only heard when Mom and Dad thought I really messed up.

It had never crossed my mind that playing left-handed would be considered disrespectful to my opponents. It still seems like a bit of a stretch, come on, we just wanted to be challenged, am I crazy? I thought my parents were blowing this a little out of proportion, but what was I supposed to do? Go back and not play left-handed?

My dad picked up the phone and handed it me and said, "Call them. Call your opponents and apologize right now."

"Dad, call them? I'm not calling them. Who calls their opponents after they beat them? That's insane."

My parents did not budge. They lectured me about respect and kindness and effort and how those kids were trying their hardest to beat us and we just rubbed it into their faces that they weren't as good as us. I thought, "Yeah, exactly, that's sports. It sucks to lose and I've been there also. Aren't you supposed to win easily?" "You can win easily but you have to win with class," my parents said.

Argh. That word "class" is so annoying. I mean, winning and losing is hard enough. Now I know, class on a tennis court consists of being respectful to your opponent at all times, trying your hardest, accepting that you will lose sometimes, winning with composure and humility, being fair, treating people with kindness around the tournament. Exercising these behaviors is difficult for me *now*. As a kid, this seemed like some bullshit extra test on top of the original test. I thought I did the thing I was supposed to do (win) and now you add *another* test (win with class)?

My dad handed me the wireless phone (not cell phone, wireless landline) and we looked up my opponents' phone numbers in the phone book (ask your parents what I'm talking about). I asked, "Does John Long have to call and apologize?"

And they said, "We don't know, we aren't his parents." Classic parent line.

So I called my opponents a few hours after beating them. It might have been the first time this has ever happened in sports. Did Michael

Jordan call Reggie Miller after embarrassing him in Game 7 of the 1998 Eastern Conference Finals?

First I called Eric Famet's house. Years later we became friends and won a state championship together as teammates on the Huron High School tennis team, but we weren't friends when I called. We were just awkward eleven-year-olds. His dad answered and put Eric on the phone. My dad stood over me and my voice trembled, "Hi Eric, it's Michael Kosta, I just wanted to say sorry . . . eh, sorry for playing the last game today left-handed."

The words felt like bricks tumbling out of my mouth. Eric seemed a little taken aback and just said "OK" and then I said "OK," and I hung up. *Yikes.* Can we be done with this now? Nope, they made me call the other player. For some reason I didn't feel like Pelé's parents made him do this shit when he was a kid.[3]

Same situation, same trembling voice, the dad answered and put his son on the phone. I can still feel the nerves. I said the same thing, "Hi, it's Michael Kosta, I just wanted to say sorry for playing the last game today left-handed." The voice on the other end started laughing, "I don't care, you guys played good." Click.

I have mixed feelings about those phone calls to this day. I absolutely acted like a cocky son of a bitch, and my parents did what they thought was right. Half of me thinks that what happens on the playing field happens and you never need to apologize for it because all is fair in competition. The other half of me understands why my parents made me do it. Besides the fact that they had to socialize with those kids' parents, it was not cool of us to rub it in that we were so much better.

---

3 Yeah, I just compared myself to Pelé, obviously that's a stretch but at the time I thought I was the greatest tennis player on earth, which is how we got in this situation in the first place.

Many years later at a Future[4] event in Godfrey, Illinois, I was on the other end of some cocky behavior by my opponent. My partner and I were losing badly to two highly ranked professionals and one of them started mocking us and talking shit. These two guys were highly coveted USA national team players who had been sent to junior Wimbledon and the junior French Open when they were kids. They had their hotel rooms paid for by the National Team and they traveled with a coach. They had matching outfits and all their expenses paid for by the USTA. They were hot shit and they acted like it. My partner and I slept anywhere we could afford, strung our own rackets, and made sandwiches to save money.

The tides had changed, one team was far better than the other, and I was on the team that was considered weaker and not as worthy. And I remember thinking, "This sucks. These guys don't even think we're worthy of sharing a court with them." And that stung. It stung to be disrespected and treated like shit just because we were losing. So we started to fight back. We started to talk shit back to them and get in their faces. Our opponents thought we were being too "energetic" for a team that was losing badly. We were. What we were trying to do was change the course of the match because we were getting beaten so badly.

And it worked. We clawed our way back and won the second set. We hated the way they were treating us and we used it as motivation to play better. It did make me wonder if my parents overreacted by protecting those other kids all those years ago. I mean, if they were so pissed, maybe they should have played better.

---

4   A "Future" is the lowest level of a pro tournament with the least amount of money and ranking points. From lowest to highest it goes, Futures, Challengers, tour level tournaments, and then the Grand Slams.

Chapter 6

Cheating

JUNIOR TENNIS, BY definition, is exclusively populated by young teenage boys. Boys who think they're men but are actually emotional toddlers who want to win more than anything. This meant there was a lot of cheating—really creative, art-form-type cheating. My favorite cheating story happened at a local qualifier. It was 1993, and I was thirteen years old. This was peak cheating time in junior tennis. My friend Nathan O. (I'm abbreviating his last name to protect him) was playing Steven Chang (fake name, I tried to publish his real name but Legal wouldn't let me . . . yeah, lawyers). Steven was a good tennis player but an even better cheater. This motherfucker was a *smart* cheater. He knew the right times to cheat. There's a joke in junior tennis: "A bad hook cheats on the first point of the match, a good hook cheats on the last." Because once the match is over, there isn't a whole lot you can do about it. Steve was a smart hook. He used to keep a tennis ball in his pocket, and if he found himself in a difficult situation in an active point and he thought he might lose the point, he would quietly reach into his pocket and throw the ball into the court. He'd yell "Let!" and the point would have to be replayed.[1]

---

1   In tennis, a "let" means you replay the point. A "let" can be called for various reasons: a ball from another court interrupts play; a chair gets blown over into the court; a dog runs onto the court (this happened at one of my matches); etc. It's a judgment call and certainly up to interpretation. Basically, a "let" is a do-over. I love that tennis uses this system.

Back to Chang. The Steven Chang ball-in-the-pocket trick was one hundred percent not allowed under the Let Rule. It's actually a code violation and could have gotten him disqualified from the match, but this was junior tennis and the volunteer lines person/Harvey probably wasn't completely up to date with the rules or how to best enforce them against a snot-nosed eleven-year-old who had studied the rule. So, this kept happening to Nathan O. Steven Chang would throw a ball into the field of play when he was about to lose a point, to replay it, or he would call a ball out when it was in (a more traditional form of cheating). Steven eventually elevated his cheating so much that he did the unthinkable, he changed the score. He simply said the score was different than it was. Just like when you play UNO with a five-year-old, he changed everything to be in his favor.

This is pressing the nuclear button. Nathan just stood there saying, "What? That's not the score!" The bottom line was Steven was a cheat, and to make it worse, he was also pretty good at tennis. So his opponents had to beat him *and* beat his cheating, extra tough.

How do you prepare to beat someone who just changes the score?! It's almost an unbeatable play. So Nathan O., in all his composure and "class" said, "That's it, Steven, you are such a cheater I am getting a lines person." He grabbed the balls and his backpack and walked off the court to the tournament headquarters to request a lines person.

It should have been obvious what was going on. Never in one hundred years would you take all the balls and your stuff with you to get a lines person, you would just walk to the tournament center and then walk back to the match with a lines person. But Nathan O. had a different idea in mind and we didn't realize it until about twenty minutes had passed. Nathan O. did not return to the court. Instead, two female players showed up with their rackets and asked what was going on.

"We're waiting for an umpire," Steven said in his gross cheating voice.

One of the ladies replied, "Huh, not sure, but this match is over and we have ten minutes to start on this court."

"What?" said Steven. "It's not over, we are in the middle of the match."

Just then the tournament director came over and yelled, "Let's go, Steven, we need the court for the next match."

The realization hit Steven like a ton of bricks and slowly trickled out to the spectators. Nathan O. had not asked for a lines person, he had simply reported that the match was over and that he won. I see your cheating and I raise it one thousand percent. As you can imagine, Steven went insane. Screaming and crying and screaming. Straight up full body meltdown. The cool, calm cheater on the court lost his shit like I had never seen. I have a vivid image of his father (who fully knew about—if not coached his son on—his cheating antics) also going insane. Those two were screaming at the tournament director, threatening her, calling on their giant car phones (who were they calling, the president of tennis?).

Nathan O. went full double nuclear and gave Mr. Steven Chang a little taste of his own medicine, and not a small taste, for that matter. Meanwhile we were in the corner smiling a little and looking for Nathan O. He was nowhere to be seen. Like my father in St. Louis, he was gone. And one of the best things about the nineties was once you left somewhere, no one could track you down. No texts, no emails. For all we knew, Nathan was hiding in the bathroom, but he was *out*.

A few things changed that day. Steven Chang slowly drifted away from the junior tennis circuit. I don't know if tournaments stopped accepting his entry, or if his father was so embarrassed by what happened, or if Steven was, I don't know. We didn't see much of him after that. Also, Nathan O. got mad respect. He was like the guy in prison who comes in on the first day and punches out the main honcho (that's how prison works, right?). People knew that

Nathan O. was not going to take anyone's shit and he was revered for putting an end to Chang.

If you ask anyone who played competitive junior tennis in any region in any era, there was always a Steven Chang. A very good tennis player who cheated and cheated and caused massive amounts of pain and difficulty. And eventually they drifted away. My guess is that these players are usually under immense pressure from their parents to win and eventually they break and their tennis comes crumbling down. Who knows, maybe Steven is a politician now, I don't know. Nathan O. works for a pharmaceutical company, which doesn't surprise me.

Chapter 6A

My Cheating

I DEFINITELY CHEATED more than once in my tennis career, but if I had to grade my cheating level, I would say it was pretty low. For the most part I called the ball fairly and honestly. And as you get to a higher level of tennis, you can no longer call your own balls, anyways (full lines crews call all the balls)—and for good reason, there are ATP ranking points and money on the line and with such high stakes, everyone would cheat. People want to win, and these aren't just normal people we're talking about. These are high-level athletes and they are some of the most competitive, winning-obsessed people known to man. If you take a poor kid from Russia whose only way out is to make it on the tennis tour, and you let him call his own balls, guess what? He isn't going to care about class or integrity. He is going to try to win. This isn't just Russia, this is everyone. This goes for all sports, everywhere. The stakes are so high and athletes value winning so much. Back when I was playing, if someone had offered me a performance-enhancing drug and told me I would not get caught, I would one hundred percent have taken it. No doubt. My guess is that the same goes for ninety percent of athletes. Athletes will cheat because nothing is more important to them than winning. To think otherwise is naive.

When it comes to my cheating, one memory haunts me to this day. It was shitty and I'm not proud of it. What I now know: the best players don't cheat. They don't need to cheat. The ones with class and integrity may lose on occasion to a cheater, but in the long run, the players who play with class advance higher and farther, because they are focused on the quality of their play and the respect of the sport. That's what you want to aim for.

I say this now as a professional comedian. Someday you will be a professional something else (maybe tennis player, but most likely not) and the match you played seventeen years ago at a tournament will not be important, it really won't, but the way you conduct yourself sets you up for life and what's ahead. That being said, here's how I cheated.

We have to jump ahead a few years to a college match. It's not that there wasn't cheating in the juniors, but this one sticks out because it was so blatant. I played at the University of Illinois and we were playing Duke at home. Who doesn't hate Duke? I mean it's such an elite, wealthy, pompous university, easy to hate and easy to make fun of. I really hated them and their coach had never recruited me like I wanted him to, so I felt slighted. It was a home match and I loved that these rich Duke kids had to play us next to the cow pastures of Champaign-Urbana.

It was my junior year, and I was playing Andres Pedroso. Andres was an old friend from junior tennis and was a class act for as long as I had known him. He always played fairly and with integrity. He was ranked considerably higher than I was at the time, and I felt like I had something to prove before we faced off at home in Illinois. This time the match was indoors, just how we liked it.

I cruised through the first set and was leading in the second set. At one point I remember thinking to myself, "This is easy, what should I do tonight after I win?" Apparently, I like to do this to myself. Instead of staying focused on what's important, staying in the present moment, I like to think ahead, exaggerate the situation, let my mind wander. All of which are the complete kiss of death to any athlete. You think Tom Brady is thinking about his dinner plans during the two-minute drill? In other sports if you let your mind wander, someone will tackle you, throw a baseball at your head, or check you into the glass. Not tennis; tennis lets your mind wander for as long as you are stupid enough to let it. (Obviously, no sport lets your mind wander more than golf—I've played entire rounds that I can't remember.)

As expected, my lead over Andres started to fade. My confidence was suddenly gone and I started feeling tighter and more stressed. And to make it worse, my opponent was starting to gain confidence. It was 3–3 in the second set and it was break point for Andres. I came into net on a backhand cross court approach shot and Andres hit this unbelievable running backhand passing shot that zipped past me and landed very safely inside the sideline (emphasis on safely). Maybe a good foot inside the sideline. Point Duke, game Duke, 4–3 Andres (Duke).

But, not so fast. Before I could really think about it, I yelled "OUT." Sometimes in tennis, what you want to have happened comes out of your mouth instead of what really did happen, also known as the truth. (Much like an inappropriate joke that I one hundred percent should not say will still make its way out of my mouth.) I wanted the ball to be out, so I yelled "Out." I remember hearing a few gasps in the audience. Like "WTF" gasps. Like "ha, good joke" type gasps. I mean, this ball was so clearly in I even surprised myself that I had the balls to call it out. Athletes are sometimes described as courageous; well, me calling this ball out took a lot of courage, that's for sure.

We had an umpire on our court—he was in a chair, overlooking the match, and his job was to intervene when someone made a bad call, like, for example, now. I, of course, could also correct my call and give the point to Andres, a friend of fifteen years, but I was too hung up on winning and I didn't feel like following the rules of tennis.

So Andres, knowing we had an umpire and knowing how the sport worked, simply said, "Sir, there is absolutely no way that ball was out, everyone here, including Michael, knows it. Do what is right and give me the point, please."

Then the umpire said something I will never forget: "Sorry, I didn't see it."

What transpired next was one of the greatest meltdowns I have ever witnessed. Andres went batshit. He absolutely lost his mind. It was like lightning struck his emotions and they exploded in front of me. He jumped and screamed and started yelling at me in Spanish. I mean, I couldn't blame him:

First, I made a terrible call. Really bad. I cheated him. He was right, I knew it.

Second, the umpire saying "I didn't see it"? I mean, how could you not see it? Everyone saw it. You had the best seat in the entire tennis facility. The only thing you get paid for is "to see it." You literally sit in a high chair overlooking the court, and the ball that I cheated on was roughly fifteen feet from your nose. If you didn't see that, not only should you *not* be a tennis umpire, you are probably blind.

I attribute my bad call—and letting it go uncorrected—to a few things. The less selfish reason is that Andres played for Duke, and I hated Duke, and I wanted our team to beat them very badly. The more selfish reason was that Andres carried a high NCAA singles ranking, and I wasn't ranked at all. I was good, but my teammates at University of Illinois were really, really good, so I played lower in our lineup—in this case, I was #4 of the six spots. I always felt like I was being punished for playing on such a great team. If I had played on a worse team, I probably would have played #1 or #2 and would have had more opportunities to play—and beat—other nationally ranked players. Because I was #4 on my team, I rarely got to play ranked players except when we played other very highly ranked teams (like Duke). Essentially, playing Andres was a huge opportunity, and I also believed that if he got his confidence up and I started to get tight, I would lose the match. These aren't good reasons, but these are the reasons.

To make matters worse for Andres, the temper tantrum he threw after he got cheated was so bad that he got a point penalty. The umpire was able to see that. His coach ran over from the sidelines and had to restrain Andres from further escalating the situation. At that point the match was as good as over. Andres had blown a fuse and couldn't even hold his racket any longer. I won easily after that. Andres refused to shake my hand, refused to shake the umpire's hand, and walked off the court and into the Illinois cornfields like a character from *Field of Dreams*. I can't blame him, he got cheated. I did play better than him and there is a world in which I didn't cheat and still would have won the match, but once the tide started to turn, I cheated to make sure that it would turn back toward me.

I'm forty years old now and I swear to god I still dream about this match. It really bums me out that I did this both to Andres and the sport. I love tennis so much and I think the unique beauty of the sport is that it relies on the cooperation of the competitors. Like golf, tennis gives considerable power to the actual athletes to determine their success or failure. I abused that. The other thing that really disappoints me in all this is that I had been playing great. I was playing really beautiful tennis, beating an opponent who was highly ranked, showing what I believed to be my true potential on the tennis court, and then I went and dirtied it up by being a classless bitch.

Andres was a friend, someone I had practiced with and known for a long time before that match, and I certainly ruined that. Any friendship that we had was over. Sports are tough and friendships come and go, but the fact that I treated a friend like that is bullshit. And the fact that I still think about it shows that it wasn't worth it. It was short-term thinking and short-term gratification over something that should have been treated with more respect.

Also, and this part doesn't help either, the next week we were in Seattle for the National Indoor Championships and as we walked into the practice courts on the first day, I saw that Duke was just wrapping up their practice. Andres and I locked eyes and I quickly looked away, embarrassed and reminded about my cheating.

Then Andres walked over to me.

"Oh shit," I thought. "Is this gonna go down again? Do I have to fight him?"

I grabbed my teammate's arm and told him to stay put as I might need help defending myself (I don't know how to fight, duh). Andres approached and said, "Hey, Kosta, I just want to apologize for my behavior last week. It was rude and I reacted very unprofessionally, and I treated you and your coaches poorly. Please accept my apology."

My jaw dropped to the floor. I didn't know what to say. I felt completely disarmed and vulnerable. He was apologizing to *me*? I should be apologizing to him. I mumbled something back like, "Yeah, OK, cool," and we went our separate ways.

Andres went on to play professionally and had a lot of success, he got ranked Top 300 in the world in singles and doubles. He is now the head coach for the University of Virginia Men's team. I wish him the best of luck and want to formally apologize for my line call to him back in the year 2000.

. . .

Cheating is a shitty part of the game. Processes are put in place to try to keep it at a minimum—in the pros, players aren't even allowed to make their own calls—but it still happens, and it sucks when it does.

In comedy, the equivalent to cheating is stealing someone else's joke[s]. It's the one rule of comedy: don't steal.

Comedy is hard. It takes a long time to come up with a funny take on a topic (weeks to months to years). Stealing someone else's hard work is wrong and shameful and those comics should be killed painfully and publicly.

But Michael, you just admitted to cheating in tennis, what's the difference? You're right, but also, hear me out. In the average tennis match, there are roughly 150 points. When you decide to cheat, you are making one of those 150 points yours. Yes, some points are more valuable than others, but that's the gist. The ball is moving at ninety miles an hour, it lands, you have a split second to decide if a two-inch ball touched a quarter of an inch of line, and *poof*, it's over. Twenty-five seconds until the next point. That, to me, is a lot different than sitting in the back of the comedy club listening to another comic (who is killing it) and deciding to take his/her joke, or alter it just enough to make it yours (this is the most common) all because you suck at comedy or are unoriginal. I'm proud to say I have never stolen a joke in my twenty years of stand-up comedy.

That being said . . .

About ten years ago while on stage in Appleton, Wisconsin, I performed one of my friend's jokes (something about a calculator watch, "who is doing so much math?"). I was watching a video of his before the show and then I got on stage, and it just came out. The audience laughed. I was mortified. I called him after the show and apologized. He said, "Thanks for letting me know, it's OK, it happens."

But it doesn't happen. Great comics don't do that. I felt terrible. I have never done that again. I don't want to be labeled a "cheat," but I also learned from tennis that when you do cheat, you will be haunted with that decision for the rest of your life.

Chapter 7

Grandpa's Probably Dead

ONE BEAUTIFUL SPRING morning during my senior year in high school, my dad busted into my room, shook me awake and said, "Michael, wake up. Grandpa's . . . probably dead," and then he did the move where you take your own hand and slowly mime cutting your neck to show that someone is dead.

Let me back up just a second. It was the end of the school year, 1998. I was eighteen and about to graduate with honors from Ann Arbor Huron High School. I mention "with honors" because twenty-five years later it still makes me laugh. I was a member of the National Honor Society (approx. 3.5 GPA) but part of graduating "with honors" is that you had to be of service to your community. A few days prior, the NHS had notified me and my parents that I had never been of service and therefore, because I hadn't reached all of their criteria, I would not get to wear the yellow sash on my graduation gown that NHS members get to wear, and that my mom wanted me to wear so badly. I would not graduate with honors. At that point in my life, I had no clue what "being of service" meant and thought being a great tennis player was a great service to my community (was it not?).

My grandparents had driven in from Goshen, New York, to support me at the Michigan High School State Tennis Championships in a few days, but also, and more importantly to them, watch their youngest grandson graduate, and even *more* importantly watch him graduate "with honors" which, on graduation day, was communicated by wearing, on your gown, a stupid fucking yellow sash.

When my mom learned that I wouldn't be graduating with honors and that she would have to explain that to her parents, it became a bigger problem. Anyone that has ever had a mom and a grandmom knows that the dynamic between those two is complicated and mysterious. Nothing would have hurt my mom more than having to tell *her* mom that her son was a big idiot loser who wasn't of service to his community. Long story short, I called the local NHS chapter and asked them what I had to do to prove that I wasn't a dope, so I could wear the yellow sash on graduation day. Thankfully, it felt like they had dealt with this type of phone call before (they probably get them every year when the grandparents arrive in town), and they said to me, "Well, our garden needs a lot of weeding, how quickly can you get down here?" So I grabbed my dad's gardening gloves and pulled up weeds for four hours. You'll be happy to know I was photographed on graduation day wearing my yellow sash with honors.

Before graduation, though, was the state tennis tournament. "States" as we called it. I was the #1 singles player, a senior, and one of the captains. It had become a tradition that the night before the team leaves for States that we would all get together at the Kosta house, Jan and John Kosta would make dinner for the team, we'd have a team meeting and then, as cliché as it sounds, ten young men would sit around the Kosta family room and watch *Rocky IV* as loud as the TV would allow. The tradition started two years prior and we won the tournament, so we had to keep it up. My grandparents, who were accustomed to a quiet and grandparenty life, alone in sleepy Goshen, New York, were thrown right into the mayhem and energy that existed around their eighteen-year-old, competitive, hyperactive, social grandson. They sat in chairs behind the team, watching the movie at the kitchen table (there was no way they could have gone to sleep, the volume was too high). Once the movie was over, Burt and Doris said goodnight to my tennis team, I gave them each a hug, and as they walked up the stairs to their bedroom I remember thinking "That was cool of these eighty-year-olds to be a part of that."

• • •

When my dad jolted me awake early the next morning with the highly effective combo of *"Michael, wake up. Grandpa's probably dead"* and the slit your neck move, he really couldn't have communicated the message more clearly or efficiently. But word of advice to any parents out there: this is not the best way to (1) wake up your child and (2) deliver that kind of news. That's a memory that sticks with you.

Now, in my father's defense, he was a probably a little discombobulated himself. Just a few minutes earlier, his mother-in-law had woken him up telling him that her husband wasn't breathing. By a wonderful stroke of fate my mother (it was her father that wasn't breathing) was out of the house walking the dogs.

I hurried out of bed and went into Grandma and Grandpa's room, where I saw my grandmother in her nightgown standing, quietly staring at her husband of sixty years lying still with his mouth wide open. Holy shit. My dad was right, it looked like Grandpa was dead. My father rushed in with the phone on his ear talking to 911. He nodded at me the way a father nods at his son when he needs something done. I sat Grandma down, got her a glass of water, and held her hand. She was remarkably calm and kind, as always, and really just scared. My grandpa had struggled with heart problems for roughly ten years, but that didn't make it any easier. My grand-mother described what happened to the 911 operator: "I woke up to him gargling, trying to breathe, and then he just fell silent."

I stood next to my dad and we just stared at my deceased grand-father. Mom was outside somewhere enjoying her morning walk; I was the only kid still in the house.

The lady on 911 recommended that we try CPR. She talked us through it step by step. I'll never forget her voice, how steady it was, how sure she was of her instructions. The people who answer the phone when we call in an emergency are so helpful and objective and calm—we should give them all the medals and honors. I immediately regretted all the times as a kid that I called 911 and hung up (it was a lot). What transpired next might have been payback for that.

My grandpa was lying on his back, in his pajamas, under the covers, with his mouth open. It sounds harsh but the best way to describe it was that he looked dead. It's hard to pinpoint exactly but an alive body looks alive and what a dead body looks like is just . . . dead. Eerily still and frozen. It looks like the life is gone. Now I get why those kids in *Stand by Me* wanted to see one so badly. It's unlike anything I had ever seen before. We went through the CPR and mouth-to-mouth re-suscitation. The woman on the phone counted us through the steps, I pressed on Grandpa's heart over and over again, and then we took a break and dad forced air into Grandpa's mouth.

When you blow air into a dead person's mouth, the lungs fill with air and when the air releases the person seems almost alive. The body moves with the air, sounds come out of the mouth. My dad put his lips on Grandpa's and forced air into his lungs. I will never forget the sound of the air leaving Grandpa's mouth. *Whooooooosh.* Long, dead air, escaping. Grandpa's body jerked and his lips fluttered. It was not going to work. Dad hung up when the ambulance arrived. Grandpa was gone. It was all very sad and frightening.

Two generations of Kosta's doing CPR together on an eighty-eight-year-old man in his PJs. I didn't think of it at the time, but so much changed then. So many things needed to be figured out. What would Grandma do? What about their house? His will? How could we tell Mom? It was one of those moments in life where you understand that we are fragile and mortal. Everything we know and love will die. Dad was now the oldest man in the family, and someday it might be me doing CPR on him. It was a moment of growing up, becoming more responsible. I was in high school, everything was looking forward. Plans for next year, college, tennis, everything was always in front of me, but at this moment all that stopped. Death has a way of doing that. This wasn't tragic, this wasn't horrific. It was a wonderful man wrapping up his life, with his family and his wife, in the most peaceful way possible. But death still changes everything.

I remember my dad standing out in the street looking for my mom. I sat inside with Grandma, looking outside. We weren't sure which direction Mom would be coming from. There was an ambulance and firetruck in the driveway and she eventually walked up with both dogs on a leash. I remember watching Dad embrace her and tell her what happened. It was actually a beautiful moment to watch, my dad breaking the saddest news possible to my mom. It was a private moment and a moment that showed how much they care for each other. It was really sad and authentic and heartbreaking to see. I'll never forget it.

The house was busy. Lots of medical personnel, the phone started to ring, family calls, neighbors started to stop by. Dogs still needed to be fed. I remember hugging my mom and trying to console her.

"What time do you have to leave?" she said.

"What? I'm not going anywhere."

"States," she said. "You have your state championship."

I had forgotten all about it—we were supposed to leave in a few hours, oh yeah Grandpa and Grandma were in town to watch me play tennis! It was typical of my mom; her father had just died and she was still concerned with whether I had my bag packed for States.

I stayed around for most of the day, helping when I could. Eventually I did make it up to Midland, Michigan, to join my team for the State Championship. I remember feeling so absolutely relieved to be back on the tennis court. Just to hit the ball and grunt and feel the racket. It all felt so wonderful. Much more wonderful than the day before. Let me repeat that I absolutely did not go through anything extremely difficult, this wasn't war or a tragic death by any means. I cannot compare to that. I hope I never have to. But waking up one morning and giving your grandpa CPR with your dad and helping move his body out of the bedroom was also not a normal day for me. Stepping on the tennis court made things feel normal again.

The tournament was a blur. I don't remember much. I do remember that our team (Huron High School) finished a disappointing second place. I remember winning the individual championship 6–0 6–0 in the finals. In a weird accumulation of events, I finally played my best when it mattered most and absolutely destroyed my opponent. I know his name and I can type it here right now, but no one deserves to be identified when you lose 6–0 6–0 in a final. Even just typing out the score now makes me feel bad for him. But he didn't stand a chance—I had too much emotion on my side. Even after everything, my parents and grandmother were there, cheering me on. Tennis became a nice distraction for us for the moment. We knew that once the weekend was over we'd have to head to New York and take care of everything you need to take care of after a death.

After winning my final match, I walked off the court and snuck away to be alone in a quiet corner in the men's locker room, and for the first time in three days, it all hit me and I cried. My grandfather loved watching me play tennis, so at the funeral I took the ball from my championship match and buried it with him.

• • •

Shortly after all of this, in May 1998, I graduated (with honors ☺) and reached the end of my junior and high school tennis days. I had a lot to be proud of. At the highest and most competitive division (Michigan tennis was divided into divisions based on school size), I had won two Michigan State Singles championships (I should have won three, but my junior year I blew it), and was considered a Top 30 national player in the country.

Over the last ten years of junior tennis, I had acquired hundreds of tennis trophies. Literally. The entire upstairs of our house was so filled with them that periodically we'd have to move boxes down into the basement just to make room. Not bad for a little skinny kid from Michigan who learned to play tennis by hitting against his parent's garage door.

All of that was meaningless to me, though, as that summer I was consumed by one thing, getting my body and mind ready for college tennis at the University of Illinois.

Let's go back a year, to the fall of my junior year, 1997, and explain how I ended up wearing the Illinois hat in the first place.

GUN + $ = COMEDY
(1999)

PART 2
College (Mostly)
1998–2004

FACILITATE
FUN (2000)

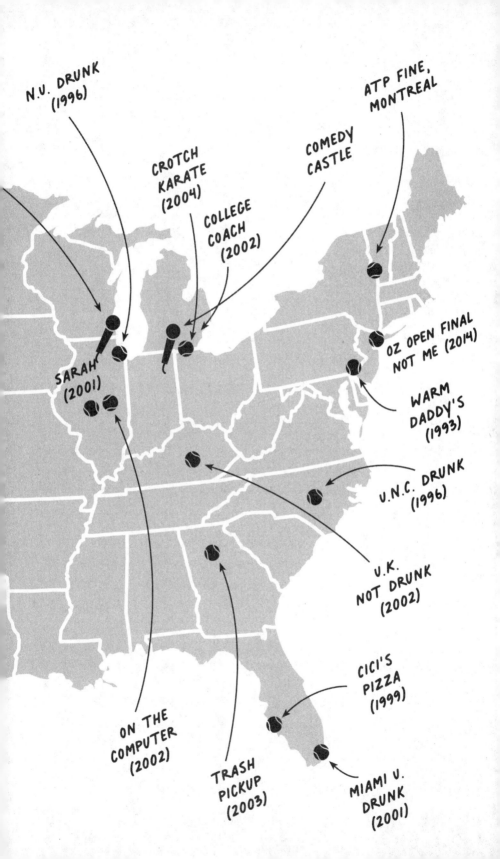

N.U. DRUNK
(1996)

CROTCH
KARATE
(2004)

COLLEGE
COACH
(2002)

COMEDY
CASTLE

ATP FINE,
MONTREAL

OZ OPEN FINAL
NOT ME (2014)

SARAH
(2001)

WARM
DADDY'S
(1993)

U.N.C. DRUNK
(1996)

U.K.
NOT DRUNK
(2002)

CICI'S
PIZZA
(1999)

ON THE
COMPUTER
(2002)

TRASH
PICKUP
(2003)

MIAMI U.
DRUNK
(2001)

Chapter 8

College Recruitment

IN THE FALL of 1996, as a high school junior, I was recruited by a bunch of colleges. This means that universities pay for you to come to campus for forty-eight hours while they give you the sales pitch hoping you pick their school to attend. It's great. All these adults fawning over you, a seventeen-year-old kid, lying to your face. I struggle with how much I should reveal about my official recruiting visits to the colleges that wanted me. Should I share with you that I got drunk at a football game at Northwestern, and also got drunk at a football game at Michigan, and got drunk at a frat party in North Carolina, and at a college bar, with a borrowed ID, at Miami? Should I share with you that I didn't get drunk at Kentucky and wondered why anyone ever went to school there? No, I don't think that would be appropriate.

What I do want to share with you is that from the moment Craig Tiley, the head coach at the University of Illinois, picked me up at the airport, I knew that's where I wanted to go. It was immediately clear this was a classy guy who ran a very competitive and professional program that would win. Everyone in high-level sports is competitive, but what was different about this guy was that he had a plan. Without a doubt, Champaign-Urbana, Illinois, was arguably the *worst* city of all the places I looked at. The tennis courts were in the cornfields. Tractors would drive up and down the main roads. The school's pride and joy was the Morrow plots, an acre of land where they experimented with new ways to grow corn. They even built the library underground so it wouldn't shade the cornfield. The week before my visit, I was in Miami watching models sunbathe at the beach, this week I'm smelling the manure from the central Illinois farmlands.

But they had a great tennis team. Coach Craig was a South African transplant who had no preconceived notion of what any university was good or bad at, because he didn't even know the American university system at all. He was the perfect guy to disrupt the entire college tennis world. He quickly and efficiently recruited very tall, very cocky, decent tennis players and taught them how to play an aggressive and unapologetic style of tennis that pissed off most of the tennis world. I loved it. His players played with a chip on their shoulders, they acted like they were overlooked by major colleges and played like underdogs trying to prove a point. As each one of the players told me their story of how they ended up there, I began to see that these guys were just like me. Great athletes who hated to lose but needed a leader to help them put it all together.

A team is only as good as its coach. The head coach determines everything and without question, in my opinion, Craig was the best coach in the game. The fact that he wanted me on his team made it a very easy decision. Oh, and also Sarah.

I'll never forget Sarah. Saturday night of my recruiting trip, I got drunk with the team at someone's apartment and we drove to Kam's, the worst best college bar in the world. If you like toilets overflowing and your feet sticking to the floor, you'd love Kam's. I'll never forget the guy who drove us there (who hadn't had any booze yet) parked illegally and as we got out of the car a security guard came over and said, "Hey, you can't park there!" Then realizing who it was he said, "Oh hey, it's the Big Ten Champs. Have fun, I'll watch your car."

Maybe this city wasn't so bad after all. That kind of special treatment certainly wasn't happening in Miami.

We got into the bar and I immediately noticed this stunning, sandy blond-haired, dimpled woman. If you haven't figured it out yet, I liked women. I was seventeen and my hormones were going absolutely insane. It's not fun; it's like having a terrible superpower.

It became evident that I had been staring at this woman for a long time because she eventually came over and asked me to dance. WTF. Ah, yeah, let's dance. We danced and flirted for a while. She even kissed me on my neck during a Ludacris song, and squeezed my hand a few times. She smelled great, she had the longest, hottest legs and green eyes. Wow. I was totally gonzo. There I was, not even old enough to drink, enter a bar, or vote, and I just pulled the hottest girl on campus.

Members on the team were like, "Holy shit, Kosta, nice work!"

"Sarah is into Kosta, hell yeah!"

I felt like a Big Ten champ myself. This was a great place.

I flew home the next day. Craig had given me a binder of materials to look at about Illinois. Academic rankings, business school pamphlets, tennis schedules, handwritten notes from the team, charts and graphs about my own tennis game, etc. I looked at all of it but all I could think about was Sarah. Those legs. I kept thinking about what they must look like without those jeans on. Yikes!

After all the visits, it was time to sit down and make a decision about which school I wanted to go to. Essentially it was my decision, but my dad played a big role as well. Money was a factor. Some schools offered full scholarships, some schools offered partial, some schools offered nothing. In NCAA tennis, women's tennis teams are granted eight full scholarships, men's are granted four and a half. So male players rarely receive full scholarships, unlike the women. Not exactly "equal" and a part of Title IX implementation that rarely gets broadcast.

Illinois made a very nice offer, one that my dad loved as well. Michigan offered me a full scholarship and Northwestern made me a nice offer, too. As we sat down and went over the decision, I have to admit I thought about Sarah and those green eyes and those legs. I should have been thinking about which academic program was the best, but instead I was fantasizing about Sarah asking me to wash her body after a long day.

My decision came down to Northwestern and Illinois. Both great schools, great programs, with fantastic head coaches. I hate to admit this but it's true: I remember thinking about the girls I met when I visited each school. All those hours the coaches spent recruiting me, talking to me on the phone, analyzing my game, talking to my dad about development, ordering me sesame bagels because they knew I liked them, arranging visits with professors and academic advisors, and the only thing I could think of was which girl at which school I liked better. And even more laughable, it was really about which one I thought liked me more. At Northwestern I had met this really cute sophomore; we kissed, and I emailed her but never heard back. That was a long time ago, months. I wondered if she'd even remember me. I didn't even remember her name. At Illinois I met Sarah, she kissed me, the team was impressed, that was last week. Still fresh in my brain. Those legs. I could just imagine them lying on my twin bed in my dorm room after a night out together. Maybe she'd be wearing my T-shirt.

I picked Sarah, I mean, Illinois.

. . .

The next fall I was a freshman on campus, part of the same team that had embraced me on my visit the fall before. The sales pitch, however, was over. Craig and the team weren't catering to me anymore. Shit was real now. It wasn't that anyone was mean or difficult, but it was time to get to work and that's exactly how it felt. Recruiting is very important because it determines who is on your team. It's taken very seriously, and should be, but it paints an unrealistic picture. The other fifty-one weekends of the year, the team is working hard trying to get better. That was the reality now.

Eventually, I ran into the woman who had been festering in my brain for nearly a year. I recognized her hair and her smile and her eyes. Those green eyes. She looked taller and more beautiful than I had even remembered. Don't forget, we were young adults who hadn't reached our peak yet, which meant that was the time of our lives when people age *better* after a year.

There I was, in the same bar, staring at this beautiful woman who, whether I want to admit it or not, played a role in my decision. I had been thinking about her for a year. She barely looked at me. She looked at me the way you look at a car driving by. You see it but you don't really care it's there. I walked straight up to her, figuring she just needed her memory jogged. Certainly she had felt the same connection that I had a year ago. How could she not?

"Hey, Sarah, remember me? It's Michael," I said. I'll never forget, I was wearing black dress shoes and white socks and shorts. No joke. I thought that was OK.

"Ah, hi," she said. "I think I remember."

Just then one of my new teammates came over and put his arm around her and whispered something in her ear. She laughed and moved in closer to him under his arm. They had a history.

She said, "I remember, Gavin paid me twenty dollars to flirt with you . . . I guess it worked?"

In a weird way, I wasn't that hurt. It was funny. It was so obvious. I don't know why I didn't think of it, but there was absolutely no chance this woman would have liked me. She was stunning, she was twenty-one, she was perfect. I was seventeen wearing cargo shorts with a Supercuts haircut. Gavin was a dick for doing that, but as my relationship developed with the team, I understood it all better. These guys wanted to win. They wanted to win so badly that they were willing to do whatever it took. Gavin liked me and thought I was going to help the team win, so he used the resources he had available to him. One of those resources was a twenty-dollar bill and a beautiful woman named Sarah.

Chapter 9

The Coach: Craig Tiley

LIKE ANY GOOD coach or teacher, Craig has a way of getting into your brain and sticking there. I haven't played competitive tennis for twenty years, and I still frequently find myself thinking, "Craig wouldn't like that," or "Craig would love this." Last weekend I walked into a comedy club in upstate New York and the place was filthy—litter in the greenroom, dust on the vents, and I immediately thought, "Craig would hate this."

In the four years I played for him, we had our ups and downs, but by the end, I can at least say with certainty that I got to know him, very, very well. The way he coached and the standards he held his players to were reflective of who he was as a person. And somehow, in the process of making us a better tennis team, he was instilling values and a code of conduct I still follow today—both as a stand-up comic and person in the world.

Here are some of my favorite memories from my time playing under Craig that I think also illustrate the type of person he is and the standard that he held his players to.

Ownership

Craig had a deviously effective strategy that he used every year to basically get us to do whatever he wanted. Later as a coach myself, I stole this strategy and used it on the players at the University of Michigan. Now, as a comic, I'm too afraid of it to use on myself. Every fall, as we all arrived on campus, excited to be back at school, thinking about all the parties and girls that awaited us, Craig would call a team meeting and ask what our goals were for the year. "Once this year is over, what is it that you want to have achieved?"

He would pass out paper and pens (not pencils) and have us write down three team goals and three personal goals.

Here are the goals I wrote down for the year 1999.

Team Goals
- Win the NCAA team championship.
- Win Big Ten Team championship.
- Achieve #1 NCAA team ranking.

Personal Goals
- Play #3 or higher on the team.
- Win Big Ten singles championship.
- Develop my forehand into a bigger more consistent weapon.

Now, you might be thinking, wow, those are some lofty goals. But I was a confident young man with decent tennis skills and those goals were, I felt, within reason. Mine weren't the worst. We had one player whose #1 Personal Goal was "Win the US Open." That gives you an idea of the kind of athletes Craig recruited. (For the record, that player never won the US Open or even qualified for it, sorry Royce.)

Craig would place our goals on a master board and hang them in the locker room as little reminders of what we were trying to achieve.

We quickly learned that writing down the goals was the easy part. Achieving them, or even twenty percent of them, was the hard part. And that's what Craig would take advantage of. Craig knew the type of people we were: high achievers, highly competitive, hated to lose. He knew our goals would be lofty. He knew we could never look at ourselves in the mirror if our #1 Team Goal was "place top 5 in the Big Ten." And once we turned in those goals, he had ownership over us.

Because if we actually wanted those things, then we had to commit and follow Craig's plan. Freshmen year after we turned in the goals, I remember Craig leafing through them and saying, "OK, nice job guys, these look like wonderful goals. You'll be happy to know I booked up six courts tomorrow at eight a.m. for anyone who wants to start working on these goals first thing."

We all looked at each other like, "Oh shit . . . isn't Cary's party tonight?" Not anymore. That's how you get ownership as a coach.

All year Craig would say, "Hey, I'm just here to help you achieve your goals, I'm just doing what you said you wanted." Damn that was annoying!

Craig took these goals very seriously. He saw them as a blood oath and acted as though he was hired to get us to achieve them. One winter, we played Purdue, and we lost the doubles point (we went down 1–0) and had a ten-minute break before singles started. Craig was absolutely furious, like bonkers mad. He didn't think we should be losing anything to Purdue. We had heard from the upper classmen that a few years earlier, after consecutive bad practices, Craig had taken their goals off the wall and set them on fire. Yup, you read that correctly. He had pulled a lighter out of his white tennis shorts and set the players' team goals aflame in the middle of the locker room. Would I be so lucky, right now, to witness such a powerful and completely insane coach reaction?

Unfortunately, no. Instead, Craig stormed into the locker room, sat us all down, and ripped our team goals off the corkboard. He started yelling out what we wrote: "Win the NCAA!" (rip through another page); "Win the Big Ten!" (rip through another page, actually tearing up our goals in front of us); "Win the Team Indoor!"

Then he hit us with it: "How do you expect to achieve these if you can't even beat Purdue at doubles!? A team that finished seventh in the Big Ten last year."[1] Even without our coach committing arson, the point was made and we went on to beat Purdue 6–1.

Trash

Everywhere we went, Craig picked up trash. My father used to say, "Leave a place better than you found it," but Craig took this shit to another level. I remember after a brutal travel day our flight got canceled and we had to stay in a crappy Atlanta airport hotel, the kind of hotel that has Domino's pizza ads on the keys. As soon as we got into our rooms, exhausted, the phone rang. It was Craig: "Michael, you're in charge, get everyone down to the lobby, now."

The lobby was a mess, trash and food wrappers everywhere. Craig hit us hard with it: "Growing up in South Africa I always heard that

---

1 It should be noted that Purdue didn't finish seventh in the Big Ten, they finished third, and they were a very good doubles team.

Americans were lazy and fat and would leave their trash everywhere, but I didn't realize that was true until now."

Ouch. Here's the best part: it wasn't our trash. It was trash from another team that was staying there. I know that because I had helped pick up *our* trash before we all headed up to our rooms, so Craig wouldn't be mad at us.

As a leader of the team, and an advocate for my teammates and someone who knew Craig liked when his players stood up for themselves, I swallowed hard and spoke up: "Craig, this isn't ours, Jeff and I picked up our trash. This was that other team's."

Craig stared at me for what felt like a long ten seconds, and then smiled, "Good, I didn't think my team would do that. OK, now pick up that team's trash."

So the twelve of us, half asleep, picked up the trash of another school's soccer team. The manager of the hotel came over and thanked us and told Craig he was a great coach. This happened all the time.

Recruiting

Craig was a master at recruiting, at getting high school tennis phenoms to want to play tennis at Illinois. I didn't entirely understand how he did this until I arrived at Illinois as a freshman and found myself on the other side of his recruiting brilliance. That team that made me feel special and cared for on my recruiting visit? I was now a part of that team. I needed to make recruits feel the way I had.

That fall, the first round of recruits came in for a football weekend. When I spent a little bit of time with them that Friday and Saturday, I noticed the upperclassmen were really monopolizing the attention. Then Monday practice came along and Craig started by passing out pens and paper. "Alright, let's take a little test," he said.

"For every answer you don't know or get wrong, as a team, we'll run a suicide.[2]"

What could this test be? Probably match strategy, I thought. Something to do with doubles and the stats he told us last week relating to first serve percentage. Boy was I wrong.

"First question," Craig said. "Write down the first and last name of each recruit that was here this weekend."

Ah, OK. I think I know that.

"Next question, write down if each recruit has a sibling and how many."

Oh shit. Now that I definitely don't know.

"Next question, write down what their parents do," and the questions kept coming.

"Write down what city and state they are from."

"Write down their style of play."

"Write down what other schools they are looking at."

Damn.

We ran for half the practice that day.

The next recruiting weekend I spent all my time hanging with the recruits. Out of nowhere I would blurt out, "So, you got any siblings? What are their names and hobbies?" Did it make recruiting feel like a job? Yes. Did it help make the best players feel special, cared for, and important? Yes. Did that help *me/us* win more tennis matches? One hundred percent. Is that why Sarah flirted with me on my recruiting visit? Sadly . . . probably. But these recruiting skills help me, today, with being an adult and working at an office and trying to be a likable, inspiring person.

As you can imagine, I really excelled at recruiting. Once I realized I was just playing the Tennis Ball Game, something my mom taught

---

2 A suicide is a series of sprints designed to make you feel so awful that you contemplate suicide.

me fifteen years prior, it was easy. I can't say the same for everyone. A few of my freshmen peers didn't even know the first name of some of the recruits.

Shaving

Craig was and still is a big fan of shaving. He believed a clean-cut guy played better tennis, followed rules more closely, and overall was a winner. And if you dared have scruff on your face, well, you were a loser. He told me this on my recruiting trip (although he definitely sugarcoated it a little more) but I didn't realize how much he really meant it until I actually showed up on campus.

One fall day my freshman year, I forgot to shave. I grew up in a house where my dad would sometimes shave, sometimes not. He was his own boss, so he could do that. So naturally sometimes I shaved, sometimes I didn't, just like Dad. It seemed like life had worked out pretty well for him. I had some scruff, went to practice, thought I had a decent one, grabbed some dinner, and went back to the dorm.

As soon as I sat down the phone rang. I didn't even know we had a phone, much less who could be calling, since I'd only been at school for four days. I hesitated for a moment, then cautiously picked it up.

"Hello."

"Hi, Michael, it's Craig." My stomach dropped, Craig sounded serious. But maybe he was just calling to see how I was settling in?

"Oh, hi Craig, how you doing?" I said, trying to sound casual and happy.

"Not great actually. I noticed that you had a pretty awful practice today."

My heart sank. "What?" I said, confused. "I did? I thought I played OK. I beat Sean in a set."

Craig kept going, "Yeah, well, I'm not talking about the score, am

I? I'm talking about your footwork, your serve needs lots of work, your forehand isn't strong enough."

Oh shit, was this some kind of test I was supposed to know how to pass? Because I didn't know how. So I said, "OK, well, I guess I need you to educate me on this stuff, maybe we can work on it together tomorrow?"

He ignored that. "You looked very sloppy. Just a total mess. Your face isn't shaved. It's affecting your whole game."

"My face?" I echoed, more confused. "It's affecting my game? I don't understand."

Craig, like only Craig can do, kept going: "Sloppy face. Sloppy footwork. Sloppy game. If you look like shit. You play like shit. You act like shit. This isn't the player I recruited."

Yikes. He was really taking me down. He continued, "When you watch the US Open and Wimbledon and the players hold up their trophies, do you see a bunch of bearded champions, or champions with scruff on their face, Michael?"

I thought about it. "Well, actually Pete Sampras usually had some scruff—"

He cut me off. "Your ugly beard one hundred percent affected your game today."

Ugly beard? I pushed it a little bit, "Craig, tell me how whiskers on my face affect my footwork, I mean, I don't see the relation."

Craig wasn't buying it, "Shave your face or don't come to practice tomorrow. And that goes for you, for the other freshmen, and for the rest of the year."

That night, after I hung up the phone, I shaved my face, and that's what I did for the next four years until I graduated.

Now, as a comedian, I go weeks without seeing someone who has shaved their face. Hell, I go weeks without seeing someone with a clean shirt. I wonder if those comics know how much it affects their performance.

The Coach: Craig Tiley

. . .

On Craig's bookshelf in his office he had a three-ring binder that was labeled "Ten year plan to win the NCAA's." Well, just as he planned, in his tenth year as head coach, 2003, Illinois went undefeated and won the NCAA championship, as if simply following the binder's contents. Unfortunately for me, I graduated in 2002, so I missed getting a championship ring by one season. I was, however, at the championship match in Athens, Georgia, and as I ran around the courts hugging my former teammates and celebrating with Craig, it did cross my mind how clean-shaven everyone was.

Even as a freshman, it didn't take me long to realize that being a part of this team was special. Like-minded, similar age, similar backgrounds, hungry to compete, men, all focusing together on an agreed upon goal: win. The happiest I have ever been on the tennis court is when I am with people I care about. First my family (Mom, Dad, John, Kristy, Todd) and then, what became my second family (Craig, Bruce, Carey, Gavin, Nathan, Jamal, etc.). It was quickly apparent that the Illinois tennis team, to me, was just family tennis. A more competitive, much higher level with much higher stakes (and more expensive), family tennis. Craig, the Dad of this family, might have been the reason I went to Illinois in the first place, or even could find Illinois on a map. But my teammates, my friends on the Illinois tennis team, were the reason I loved playing tennis at Illinois, the reason I gave every single ounce of my energy and focus to Illinois tennis, and these men are still present in my life today, many shoulder, knee, and back injuries later. Craig built that team and found those people and for that I am especially thankful.

Chapter 10

Red Clay in "Amsterdam"

BY JUNE 1999, my freshman year at Illinois was over. We lost in the quarterfinals of the NCAA, which was disappointing. But by most standards, I had a successful year, finishing the season playing #5 singles and winning some big matches when the team needed it. Heading back to Illinois before summer break started, I had some decisions to make about what I was going to do with my summer. Remember the days when that was the big decision? Tough life, huh? Should I go home to Michigan and drink with my high school buddies or should I stay on campus and drink with my college buddies? Well, one quick meeting with head coach Craig and I realized I wouldn't be doing either of those things.

"The summer, Michael, is where good tennis players become great." Shit.

As per usual, Craig was right. When you play a Division 1 sport, your summers are actually important. It's when you can improve your game and make strides past the other competitors who aren't choosing to practice twice a day in the summer heat. So, despite my desire to drink beers in the sun and chase girls around, I figured it would be smarter and better for my tennis if I filled the weeks with tournaments (and an occasional beer).

One of my older teammates, Jeff Laski, shared my desire to mix tennis with fun. He also had an ATP doubles ranking and was kind enough to offer to play doubles with me, which would drastically improve my chances of getting into the doubles main draw of any low-level pro tournaments we played.[1] This meant I would be able to play in a pro doubles event and earn my own world ranking points, which would be very helpful. It was classic Jeff Laski generosity and I certainly appreciated it. Jeff was a teammate and friend and the idea of traveling together sounded like a lot of fun.

A note about the level of tournaments: These were the minor league, the lowest level, of pro tennis tournaments. Still filled with great players, but the draws were mixed with both unranked players who were trying to get on to the world ranking computer (high-level junior, college players, washed-up pros) and also players ranked as high as Top 300 in the world trying to "level up" to the next higher rung on the pro tennis ladder. Besides the main draw, they also had a "qualifying" where anyone, truly anyone, could sign up and try to play their way into the main draw. Because I was unranked, I would have to play the qualifying.

For some perspective, if you won your singles match in the main draw, you won around $150 and earned one ATP ranking point, if you won the whole tournament you won around $2,000 and ten ATP points. Almost always, you spent more money than you earned at these

---

1   The college season was over, so if you wanted to play high-level tournaments in the summer, you had to play in the pros.

level of tournaments. But playing low-level pro tennis was a great summer opportunity for college players. You got the opportunity to play against some of the world's best tennis players, you could earn valuable ATP points (that would help you after you turned pro), and you could travel the world, not just play at American universities and towns. The idea of testing my game against other world-class players, on different surfaces, and seeing how I fared was really appealing. I always wanted to be a pro, and the summer was a unique opportunity to dip my toe in on the action and see if I could hack it. For me, winning a few matches against ranked players, and earning a few ATP points, would have been a huge win. That was my goal this summer.

I liked Jeff a lot. He was a calm, kind person, who was an incredibly talented athlete. He was a Chicago kid and I had known him and his family for many years and had always connected with them. Jeff's dad was a truck driver, far from the norm of the common rich tennis kid whose dad worked at Goldman Sachs or IBM and had unlimited money. Jeff was grounded, laid back, and valued fun, which was important in a world travel partner.[2] Jeff and I were teammates but I wouldn't say we were close friends yet, and the idea that I would get to know him better on this trip was very appealing.

Jeff and I sat down and looked at the world schedule. Where exactly did it seem fun to play, but also wasn't so popular that it would be crowded and filled with a bunch of tough players? Three weeks of hard courts in California? No, too popular. Four weeks of clay/dirt in Nigeria? No, too far away—and we heard horror stories about traveling there. Six weeks of Indoor carpet in Russia? It's summer, who wants to be indoors in Russia? Four weeks of red clay in the Netherlands?

---

2   Once, in Scottsdale, Arizona, after a very long practice when our assistant coach, Bruce, denied our request to take the next morning off, Jeff told Bruce that he didn't "facilitate fun." Bruce immediately told us to put our bags down and sent us back on the sunny court to run suicides. After fifteen minutes, as we lay on the hot asphalt court unable to breathe, Bruce said, "How was that, Jeff? Was that . . . *fun?*"

Sounds interesting. Where exactly in the Netherlands? Twenty minutes from Amsterdam? Yes? Book it, we're going to Amsterdam.

Jeff and I boarded our flights with nothing but our rackets and a sense of adventure. We felt like we were making a smart choice. We could tell our college coaches we were going to Europe to work on our game, which would make them happy, and we were also going to Amsterdam, deemed "the most liberal city in Europe." Let's not say we were going there because they had legal prostitution and weed; but let's also not say we weren't going there because of those things.

Before the trip, we had probably played about two hours on clay, which is not enough practice time on a totally different surface. That would be like if you were a chef who specialized in grilling meat and you were going to an international vegan cooking competition, so you spent two hours one day getting to know a few vegetables. I called a bunch of European tennis players before we left and got their advice on playing on red clay over there. I was used to green American clay, but red clay was slower and grittier. How different could it be, I thought?

Apparently very different, because the second person I called said, "You aren't playing that Dutch red clay circuit are you?"

"Yeah, we are. It sounds like fun to us."

"Well, good luck," he said and hung up.

...

From my journal on this trip.

SFTHT (SOMETHING FUNNY THAT HAPPENED TODAY):
Before boarding our flight the customs agent asked me, "That man over there, is he trying to get on your flight?"

Me: Which man?
Agent: The one holding the hammer.

Red Clay in "Amsterdam"

The first point I played in the qualifying on the slow red Dutch clay was unlike any other point I had ever played in my tennis life. I was playing a local Dutch kid, smaller and skinnier than me. When we walked onto the court, he had two rackets in his hand and an empty cup to put water in. I figured this would be the perfect warm-up match. I had a twelve-racket tennis bag, two pairs of shoes, and enough equipment to climb Mount Everest. I remember packing four shirts for this match. My opponent had one shirt and it was on his body.

To start the match, I served a slow slice ball out wide to his forehand. The red clay spun the ball even further and wider than I had wanted, but greatly appreciated. "Wow, what a serve," I thought. My opponent was well off the court, so I decided to run into net (as you would on a fast American hard court). I figured I would get his weak attempt at a return, volley the ball into the open court, 15-Love. Book us a table for dinner, because that's a wrap.

Instead, as I sprinted into net, my 140-pound opponent, with rips in his T-shirt, casually and gracefully slid across the court like a Dutch speed skater, wound his body and racket up fluidly, and lobbed a forehand return over my head. *LOBBED*. A goddamn lob return. I watched the ball soar over me and land three feet inside the baseline.

"Love-15," the umpire called out.

In my twenty years of competitive tennis, no one had ever lobbed a return of serve over my head. I was shocked. Not only did this Dutch child lob my ass, he lobbed my ass for the next two and a half hours as I clawed, grinded, fought, and scraped my way to a 6–2 6–3 loss. I got killed. Welcome to red clay European tennis. Holy shit.

The thing we didn't realize was that red clay court tennis wasn't a fun option to these kids, our opponents. In the USA, people play on clay as a fun little summer activity. For European competitors, red clay was the *only* option. They grew up on clay and they will die on clay. They have clay in their socks, in their underwear, they probably sprinkle it on their croissants in the morning. They know how to move on it because that's how they learned to play tennis, on red clay. I figured all this out over the course of two hours losing to a Dutch seventeen-year-old who dressed like it was laundry day.

To make matters worse, Jeff and I tried to sign up for doubles like we had planned to do, but so many highly ranked players showed up that our combined ranking wasn't going to get us in the draw. So Jeff had to ditch me and sign up with some stranger with a higher ranking. Not Jeff's fault, but certainly not ideal either. So, despite my excitement for playing overseas, I was now out of the singles draw, sitting on the sideline watching my travel partner play doubles with a random German kid who spoke zero English.

As a player, I hated watching. As a comedian, I hate watching comedy. I want to be the guy on the court, on the stage, not the guy sitting in the crowd watching people I believe I am better than. But that's one of the biggest differences between comedy and tennis: reality.

Comedians often sit in the back of the room and refuse to laugh at other comedians because they think they are better or funnier. Comedy, of course, is subjective. It's an art form. "I'm funnier than him" or "That's a great joke" are all just matters of opinion. With sports it's the opposite. I can sit on the sidelines watching a tennis match and think "I am better than this guy," but the bottom line is that I'm out of the tournament and he is *in* the tournament. It's hard to argue with that. He, for the time being, is a winner. And I am a loser. Comedy is very vulnerable to overpromotion, comics lying about their performance, buying social media followers or publicity. I miss this so much about tennis. Even if I spent $100,000 on a publicity team and had millions of Instagram followers, I couldn't change the fact that a kid who still lives with his parents beat me 6–2 6–3 today. Sport is brutal and honest and it's wonderful because of that. Most things in life seem to be the opposite: diplomacy, politics, networking, etc. All those words are irrelevant when you have a scoreboard.

Back to the Netherlands. On top of it all, Jeff and I were staying at a bed-and-breakfast in the Dutch countryside, in a town that—upon further review—wasn't twenty minutes from Amsterdam, but actually a five-hour train ride. Somebody (me) had spelled the Dutch city name wrong when searching for it. This is easier to do than you'd think. Sardaam, Sardemm, Sardaanm, and Sardamm are all different places in the Netherlands. This wasn't like a hotel bed-and-breakfast, this was the home of a woman who happened to, on occasion, let strangers pay her for a bed. There was a rose garden in the front, quaint shuttered windows, and a field full of daisies on the side. Super cute, but there was also a nine p.m. curfew.

So, there I was, out of the singles, not in the doubles (zero ranking points, zero money earned), five hours from Amsterdam, sleeping next to my college teammate who was still in the tournament. It's these memories I think of when people stop me now and say, "That must have been so much fun playing on the pro tennis tour." I'm sure the pro tour they are thinking of *is* more fun. London, Moscow, Buenos Aires, ball kids, nice hotels, big prize money. But the pro tour I played was nine p.m. curfew, no TV, red clay, losing to a kid only halfway through puberty, and as far as I could see not one pretty girl anywhere in the Dutch village, however you spelled it.

The bed-and-breakfast owner was a really sweet woman who spoke zero English and, paired with our zero Dutch, this made communicating a little difficult. Jeff and I certainly liked to sleep, as most athletes do, but every morning at eight a.m. she would walk up the stairs and wake us up screaming "Brekker! Brekker!" I assumed it meant "breakfast," but I still don't know. Maybe she was asking for help. Jeff and I would slog down the stairs and sit quietly while this woman served us a Dutch breakfast, which was essentially an English breakfast with a few different cheeses and a soft-boiled egg sitting in one of those cute little saucers. Neither Jeff nor I had ever seen an egg served this way—all we saw was this egg, with a shell on it, sitting on this tiny little throne. It made us laugh every day, because it seemed so important and so purposely placed there. We didn't have any idea what to do with it or how to eat it, so, when a moment became available to us, we would grab the egg and place it in our pocket. Then on the twenty-five-minute walk to the courts each day, we would take our eggs out and try to hit this cow that was grazing nearby.

By the end of the week, Jeff eventually lost in both singles and doubles, and we decided to go out and do what we had really wanted to do this whole time: get drunk.

The only problem was, this was a small Dutch village in the countryside, meaning: (1) There was one bar. (2) It closed at ten p.m. And (3) ten p.m. was after our curfew. Considering it was our last night we said fuck it, let's get drunk and deal with the consequences of being late to our B and B. What's the worst thing that could happen? This was before AirBnb reviews (a much more fun time). We were never going to see this woman again after we left this town.

We hopped on a tram and made our way to town. We found the bar, it was next to the church in the center of town, like in every European village ever. The bar had first opened in the 1300s, which we tried to wrap our heads around but couldn't fathom. This wood-floored, dimly lit drinking establishment was roughly four hundred years older than our country. There were booths open but we drank at the bar, looking for "action," as I like to say. There was none. The most "action" we saw, was a few bicycles riding by. At nine fifty-five p.m. we realized another issue: transport. No cabs, no bikes, trams stopped at nine p.m. (WTF). We were alone and drunk and far from our beds in this old medieval Dutch town. When the bartender locked up the door he handed us a few beers on our way out. "For the walk," he said as he pedaled off to his home in a tree or whatever.

We had quite a walk. About an hour. It's a good memory, though, walking with beers through the Dutch countryside at night with my friend Jeff. As we talked and drank and walked, we laughed about me getting lobbed on the first point of my match, we laughed about Jeff and his doubles partner not being able to communicate, and we laughed about not understanding how the Dutch eat their eggs. We also laughed when we finally got home and the old woman opened the door for us in her nightgown and hairnet and yelled at us in Dutch. What a strange set of decisions we must have made to be at this place, with these people, in our lives right now.

Chapter 11

DTF

FROM MY JOURNAL on this trip.

SFTHT (SOMETHING FUNNY THAT HAPPENED TODAY):
Not knowing if our taxi driver speaks English, Jeff and I show
him the address of our hotel on a slip of paper, he looks at it and
says, "You two are going to a fucking farm."

Tennis is a forgiving sport. You can make so many mistakes in a
tennis match and still have the opportunity to win. It's not like gym-
nastics or figure skating or boxing, where one wrong move knocks
you out. This is because of the scoring system. Four points won, new
game, clean slate, start over. Six games won, set won, clean slate, start
over again.

This also applies to the yearly calendar. With fifty-two weeks a
year of tennis on the pro tour, you can always redeem yourself. Bad
week? Don't worry, there's a new tournament Monday. You have time
so don't panic. The challenge is staying sane when you have down-
time, when you lose early in the week and you have six days to kill
till the next tournament. One of the things I did to help me relax
and not overthink my losses was I started to write jokes. I would
take an hour or two a day to write stand-up jokes or things that I
thought were funny, this helped me detach from the stress of my

results. Once I left tennis, I took those joke journals and used them to organize my first five minutes of stand-up comedy.

So when Jeff and I hopped on our Dutch train and headed to our next week of tennis, I was happy that I had a new week and new opportunity and that the last week was behind us. New courts, new hotel, new restaurants, new everything. This was particularly helpful when you lost. Not only did you want to have a fresh start, you were required to. Unfortunately, though, if your forehand sucks in Rotterdam, it usually sucks in Manchester. And if I haven't been clear about this yet: my forehand did suck.

We arrived late into another tiny Dutch village. The hotel was, as one would expect, inside of a windmill. I can't think of anything more Dutch than that. In this tiny town, there was one hotel and that was it. Which meant that everyone was staying there: players, coaches, girlfriends, umpires. If you were even loosely affiliated with the tennis tournament you were sleeping in the windmill.

Thanks to a flyer posted at the front desk, we all knew that there were two shuttles going to the courts from the hotel each day. One at seven a.m. and one at noon. Almost seems like they randomly picked those times out of a hat, huh? Unfortunately, no one knew their match times because the tournament director never posted the draw or times at the hotel. And the internet—well, it was the year 2000 and we were inside of a Dutch windmill—so let's just say the WiFi was spotty. Many of us tried calling the tournament director in his room the night before the first matches (I led the charge on that), but there was no answer. It was later revealed that he came back to the hotel later that night drunk with a lady. Yeah, the guy in charge of the match times and the tournament was out getting drunk and picking up a woman.

Match times usually started at ten a.m., that was kind of the international standard. It was quite possible that Jeff and I would play at four p.m., but it's also possible we would play at ten a.m. We had no way of knowing and neither did any of our opponents, who were also staying in the same dilapidated hotel that worked as a graining mill for much of the 1700s (also posted on a flyer at the front desk).

We had a choice to make. Sleep in and take the noon shuttle and possibly miss our match and get defaulted despite flying all the way to Holland for said match, or wake up at the ungodly hour of six a.m. and take the seven a.m. shuttle so we could make our match, though we didn't know when it was anyways. (For some reason I don't feel like Roger Federer and Rafael Nadal are dealing with these same dilemmas at Wimbledon.) As expected, all the tennis players chose to go on the seven a.m. shuttle. There really was no choice unless you were a raving lunatic, which I was close to becoming.

As expected, the seven a.m. shuttle provided to approximately seventy-five tennis personnel was a twelve-seat van. I remember the look on the driver's face as he turned the corner and drove in to see seventy-five large males with tennis bags and coolers standing outside, waiting to get into his van. "Maybe we should have just gone to California, Jeff," I said.

Like the Swiss and the Canadians, the Dutch really like to follow the rules. And in particular, this seven a.m. hotel-to-tennis-courts-shuttle driver. This dumbass only had twelve seat belts and the law said you couldn't transport more than twelve people, so that's all he was transporting. Exactly twelve people buckled up and off he went. Returning thirty minutes later for another twelve people. All we needed was one Mexican bus driver and this thing could have solved itself in one trip, but no, rules are meant to be followed even though nobody seemed to follow the rule about posting the draw or the match times the night before, so that's what he did.

Nine times out of ten the level of tournaments I ended up playing in sucked like this. Hotel problems, draw problems, court problems, shuttle problems. Just problems all the time.

As I learned later, this is exactly how the beginning of a pro comedy career works, as well. Maybe it's just any profession that people think is cool, but playing shitty comedy clubs and bar shows really wasn't that different from being stuck in a windmill in Holland. More drinking, but that was the only difference.

The people and places treat you terribly. Lucky for me, when I went through this kind of bullshit in comedy, I remember feeling like I knew how to handle it. I knew the only way out was working my ass off to get the hell out of that level and move on to a higher level. These tennis tournaments sucked and they could make you feel really shitty about yourself and your life choices, and even though I didn't know it at the time, they one hundred percent prepared me for my next profession.

It's a good lesson and I think back to it often. Maybe your life sucks right now. Maybe you are going through some nonsense, and I'm sorry about that. But maybe also, all this BS is preparing you to thrive and be successful in your next endeavor. This isn't a self-help book, but I just felt like writing that. I can do what I want, I'm the author.

As you can imagine that week of tennis sucked ass. More ass than the first week where I lost to the Dutch kid with holes in his shirt. I did finally get on the shuttle and arrived at the courts around nine a.m., only to find out that I was the last match of the day, approximately five p.m. start time. I was reading *Theodore Rex*, at the time, an eight-hundred-page biography of Teddy Roosevelt's US presidency. I felt like I finished half the book that day at the courts. I remember lying in the sun reading the book, learning about the tragedies of his life: losing his mother to typhoid fever and then eleven hours later losing his wife after she gave birth. I loved the story of how he got shot before a campaign event and he continued to give his speech while bleeding. I remember reading all that, on that day, and thinking, "This still isn't as bad as this week of tennis." That gives you a sense of where my head was at. And the week of tennis hadn't even started yet. It was just the hotel and transport situation. But again, this is exactly like comedy. If the hotel and the city you are in suck, usually your experience there sucks, too. Even if the comedy club is tons of fun and the shows are hot, if you have to go back to a hotel with bedbugs and eat Popeyes chicken every day, you don't want to go back. I'm talking to you, Comedy Cafe in Milwaukee, Wisconsin.[1]

My memory of my match that week in the Netherlands is a little fuzzy. I know I lost. I know that Jeff lost as well. We signed up for doubles and didn't get in. So officially our first two weeks of European pro tennis were over. I was 0–2 in singles, having not won a set, and hadn't played a single point of doubles, which was the reason I went there in the first place. I had, though, almost finished *Theodore Rex*.

The best news was that Jeff and I were still getting along, and if anything, were becoming closer friends. He suggested we ditch Netherlands and head to France, where we had a French teammate who was living there for the summer. "Arnaud is in Paris and says we can go there and play in some money tournaments and stay with him," Jeff said.

"OK, but what about the tournaments here in Netherlands that we signed up for? What do we tell Craig?" I said, like a little bitch.

"Stop acting like a little bitch," Jeff said. "I just said let's go to Paris. Who gives a shit about Craig? It's the summer."

This was the kind of upperclassman leadership I needed and valued. We packed our bags, hopped on a train, and headed to France.

---

1 The first time I played there, when I got paid the "owner," who claimed to be in a motorcycle gang, pulled a handgun out and placed it on the desk pointed at me while he counted out my money. "I keep this here just in case the comic isn't happy with his pay," he said as he paid me $600 for four shows.

Chapter 12

Americans in "Paris"

I'LL NEVER FORGET that train ride because there was this dumbass American kid sitting in front of me. There were a lot of dumb American kids on that train (ourselves included), it was the summer in Europe and there were a lot backpackers, etc. But this one kid was especially annoying because he had a giant rain stick. Do you know what that is? Google it. It's basically a heavy stick with pebbles in it. This thing was about five feet long and was decorated like it came straight from Africa. Why this white kid wearing a "Penn" T-shirt had a giant fucking rain stick with him on the train from Rotterdam to Paris was beyond me. His rain stick took up the entire overhead compartment, so I had to sit on most of my bags so dipshit's thirty-pound souvenir didn't get moved or scuffed.

But it was hard to stay annoyed for long—as an American, it's truly spectacular riding through Europe on the train. I drifted off to sleep on top of my luggage, watching all these places I'd only heard of in books and movies, flashing past me outside the window. Antwerp is just right outside. I had no idea that was a real place. Brussels? That's Brussels? Holy shit, it looks terrible!

My dad owned a travel agency and he instilled in us a great excitement and appreciation for travel. Not by forcing us but just by taking us. Seeing how excited and appreciative he was of new places, different cultures, new adventures inevitably wore off on us. Also, he didn't exactly ask us if we wanted to go on these trips, much like baby Michael strapped into the car seat not knowing where I was going, you just went where he went.

One year my dad's annual trip to the Philadelphia Flower Show had a few spots left. "Michael is coming on the trip," he announced over family dinner.

"What?" I said, "I'm coming on . . . what? The Philadelphia Flower Show? Ah thanks, Dad, but I'm good," I replied.

"No, you're coming. It will be good for you."

So off I went to the Philadelphia Flower Show. Me and about eighty seventy-year-old women. I met and talked to all of them. While sitting on the bus together they would slowly (emphasis on slowly) show me their scrapbooks and picture books of their orchids, tulips, and hydrangeas. Working in the entertainment industry I know some self-centered people, comics and actors that will talk and talk about their successes for hours, but no one, I mean *no one* will talk longer than an elderly woman bragging about her orchids, that's just a cosmic truth.

You know what? It was good for me. That's what's so annoying about my dad. He's usually right. Doing what you don't want to do does build character. It does make you a better person. That being said, it's super annoying. As I found out later, I think the reason my dad wanted me to come to the Philadelphia Flower Show was because after the first day (I learned a lot about perennials) we got back to the hotel and my dad announced to my mom, "Jan, Michael and I are going to the blues bar." And what my dad says is what happens, so that's what we did. Keep in mind I was thirteen years old with braces and no clue how this was going to work.

We took the suggestion of a hotel employee and went to Warm-daddy's, a famous blues bar in Philly. It was packed. My dad said something to the host along the lines of "This is my son and he has never been to a blues bar before."

We got a table next to the stage. My dad ordered a scotch on the rocks and I sat there, looking around astonished. I had never seen so many black people in one location in my life. I noticed that they were also studying us—a few snickers and laughs and pointing. If I had to guess it was probably "Why does that kid have braces," or "What is this white family doing here?"

After a minute the drinks came, the music started, and any nervous energy that existed was over. We, as a people, do have differences. We have race and economics and height and religion, but once a good song comes on, who gives a shit? We are all human then. The music was tremendous. One after another blues hit after blues hit. The singer was getting sadder and sadder each song. "My momma kicked me out" and "My wife's cheating on me again" and "I can't pay the rent" and "I'm drinking too much." Holy shit, what was this place? I had never heard such honest, beautiful music before. I was thirteen, I didn't have any problems, but I certainly liked hearing about this guy's problems. He had so many.

As the scotch started to course though my dad's body, he started to talk to me about life and his choices. Now that I'm a grown man, I know that Dad was drunk, but at the time I remember thinking, "Huh, Dad sure is being talkative and honest about his life." I also now know that this is the product of listening to good blues. It just gets inside you and you can't help but be honest about yourself. I mean it's pretty easy to admit that you made a wrong choice when the man on stage is singing into a microphone about his wife cheating on him with his best friend.

My dad moved in closer to me and started, "Everyone will tell you you can't. Everyone will give you a reason about why you can't do something, and they might even be good reasons. But it's bullshit, Michael. Do you hear me? Are you listening?"

"Yes, Dad, I'm right here." (I was sitting directly next to him, looking at him.)

"People talk themselves out of everything. They say 'I can't do that' or 'No that's a silly idea,' but it's not a silly idea, Michael. *It's not a silly idea, Michael.*"

"OK, Dad," I said.

We sat quietly and listened to music for a few hours and eventually we walked back to the hotel together. It was a nice moment and one I think of often. Roughly fifteen years later when I started to tell people I wanted to be a comedian, I heard "You can't do that" or "That's a silly idea" and I thought about my dad screaming to me at Warmdaddy's in Philly and, well, here we are. Thanks, Dad.

Wham! I woke up from my train slumber with a giant aching head. The rain stick. Goddamn it the rain stick. We had finally stopped in Paris, and the rich kid's PhD prop rolled off the overhead rack and landed directly onto my relaxed and sleeping head. And thanks to having to lie on my bags, my head was propped up just perfectly for maximum surface area to be hit. "*OW!*" I yelled.

"Ah sorry, I thought I had that tied down . . ." Penn boy stammered.

I mean, who carries a stupid rain stick around Europe all summer? My head hurt. It hit me hard. Jeff was a few cars down, so he missed the whole thing, but upon hearing me yelling at the Ivy League dope, the conductor came over and boy was he excited. I didn't know a Dutch guy could even get that excited. He immediately checked on me and pulled out a long official-looking notepad and wrote the kid a ticket. It hurt to laugh, but it was still funny.

...

Paris was something else. As soon as I walked out of the train station it hit me in the face. The best way I can describe it now is a French New York City. The same intensity, the same amount of people, just more French speakers and more people who really don't give a shit about you. Arnaud had told us to meet him outside of the train station, so Jeff and I stood outside for a while. We should have come up with a better plan. Jeff dug into his tennis bag and found a phone number for Arnaud's house. It took us about forty-five minutes to figure out how to make a call from a French public phone, we didn't have the right money or language or country code. When we finally got his mom on the phone she said in French, "Gare du Nord, Gare du Nord." Turns out there is more than one train station in Paris. There are five. Why Arnaud didn't tell us this, is beyond me, but it does give you a pretty good indication of the kind of person he was. Nice, generous, and totally oblivious to details or basic life skills.

A sidenote: Six months prior, the Illinois tennis team had a secret meeting behind Arnaud's back to discuss how to handle what was becoming a major problem: Arnaud's body odor. The team voted that someone had to tell him how to use deodorant and they voted for me to be the one to tell him. Something about how I had a friendly way of being an asshole or how he already didn't like me so what did it matter? It took me a few days to tackle the task but eventually after practice one day, after everyone left the locker room I handed him an Old Spice deodorant and said as kindly but directly as I could, "The team wants you to use this, once in the morning and once after your post practice shower." He looked at me kind of perplexed and said, "But I don't shower after practice," and stormed out. I put the deodorant in his locker and it was never spoken of again.

Jeff and I hopped into a taxi (turns out we were at Gare de Lyon train station) and took the twenty-minute ride to Gare de Nord, where we immediately found Arnaud waiting for us. "You know there are five different stations in Paris," he says. We finally got to Arnaud's house and right before we got out of the cab he said to us, "I am sleeping at my mom's house. This is my dad's place. He is asleep now but you two sleep in the living room. I will come get you in the morning, OK?"

"Ahh what? We don't know your dad, Arnaud. How do we get in? What? Your parents are divorced?"

Arnaud slammed the door and the taxi zoomed off. Jeff and I were left standing on the side of the road in the middle of Paris (I think?) in front of a total stranger's door.

"I guess we go in," Jeff said.

The door opened, we walked in, and if Arnaud's parents were divorced, it was clear by the look of this apartment that they *just* got divorced. Arnaud's dad's place (we think, I mean we didn't really know whose place we were in at this point) looked like total shit. Empty boxes everywhere, cigarettes everywhere, empty beer bottles on the floor. It smelled like a divorced guy's house if that makes sense. There was a small bedroom door and we put our ear up to it and could hear a guy snoring. We laughed, "I guess that's Arnaud's dad?!"

We grabbed a few beers out of the fridge and sat on the one tiny gross couch and looked at each other. "Let me tell you about the rain stick dude," I said. I shared the story with Jeff and we laughed. Eventually Jeff took the couch and I fell asleep on the hardwood floor. I don't remember there being sheets or covers or towels or anything. There was a very good chance that two American men were going to sleep in a complete stranger's home in Paris. Weirdly, I had no problem falling asleep. Maybe it was the concussion.

The next morning Arnaud walked in and woke us up. Apparently we had the correct apartment after all. He also told us, "My dad is gone, he left this a.m. for the South (pronounced "souss"). You have the place to yourself."

The morning light didn't do much for the apartment, it was clear now how terrible the place was. But it was a place and it certainly beat having to pay for a hotel room. Supposedly, we were in the area of Paris called "Mulan," that's what was told to us.

Arnaud then led us to the French Open Stadium, Stade Roland Garros. The French Tennis Federation was there and if we wanted to play in a French money tournament we had to be evaluated and ranked by the French tennis system, which was totally separate from the ITF and the ATP, the two international ranking systems that every single country in the world follows . . . except, of course, the French.

Jeff and I walked into the grounds, saw the beautiful red clay courts from a distance, and then entered the French Tennis Federation offices and got our rankings. The rankings weren't an exact science. Arnaud led us into a dark, messy office, spoke French for a few minutes to an official, and then the guy handed us a card. My ranking was minus 2.8. Jeff, because he had an ATP point at the time, carried a ranking of -15. How in any system someone could be ranked minus 2.8 and -15 is beyond me, but Arnaud reassured us that these were good rankings. He also explained that he signed me and Jeff up for a tournament and we had matches tomorrow. Normally it took at least two weeks to enter a tournament, we had matches in eighteen hours. Wow. OK.

"Arnaud, what about you, are you playing?" I asked.

"No, I take the summer off," he replied, which was absolutely hilarious. There wasn't one Division 1 collegiate tennis player in the United States who took that much time off. But the fact that Arnaud took three and half months off from tennis explained a lot of things. Like why he always showed up in the fall looking like he hadn't played all summer, and it also explained why he never really got any better. And why he usually had a smile on his face and better stories than most of us.

The French Tennis Federation holds these monthslong tournaments and depending on your ranking, you get entered into the tournament toward the beginning, middle, or end of the draw. How it all works, I have no idea, but it really is a wonderful system to get all types of different levels of tennis players playing in the same tournament. And reflective of their name, at these money tournaments, the players win money. Now, Jeff and I were amateur athletes under the strong supervision of the NCAA, so the rules stated that we weren't allowed to earn prize money, but considering the NCAA made billions of dollars off the practically free labor of its "student athletes," Jeff and I decided, very happily, that we would take the money and just keep it secret.

I remember the French tennis guy pulling out a giant paper draw that spanned across an entire office wall. It looked like the biggest family tree I had ever seen, turned on its side, and he showed us that based off our ranking (that he literally just gave us after talking to Arnaud, never actually seeing us hit a ball) we were entered in the quarterfinals of the draw. Not bad.

We had not even hit a single ball in the country of France, Jeff had slept on a couch filled with cigarettes, and I was still concussed, and we were in the quarterfinals of a money tournament. This certainly beat fighting our ass off to win a few games against a Dutch teenager on the red clay, for no money. We found some hard courts[1] at a nearby park, hit for a few hours, and went back to Arnaud's dad's divorce pad to shower. We had matches in the morning.

Arnaud had us over to his mom's house for dinner—and it's a night

---

1   The French money tournament was on hard courts, two weeks of red clay was enough for us; in fact, I have never again in my life stepped foot on a red clay court.

that still makes me laugh, all these years later. It was a real house, with furniture and a patio and a family and a dog—not a disgusting man pad with one towel hanging over the door frame. We sat outside in the French summer sun and Arnaud's mom was very sweet to us and served us a great meal and we played in the yard with the dog and Arnaud's younger brother. It was very pleasant and really the first time we had a slow, friendly, family-oriented meal since arriving in Europe. These small exchanges, even though they are only two hours, really resonate with you when you are on the road, bouncing from place to place, packing and unpacking, losing and losing, eating shitty train station food and having rain sticks drop on your head and never really connecting with anyone intimately. A nice family dinner can recharge your batteries for a little while. So I was thankful for that.

That, however, is not what still makes me laugh. There was a moment during dinner, when Arnaud's mom brought out a loaf of bread on a cutting board with a knife. Arnaud asked his mom something about the bread, and she replied "oui" and then he picked up the loaf of bread and threw it in the trash. Just picked it up, threw it in the trash, and then moved down to his plate for more food. What the . . . Arnaud's mom threw her hands up and said "Oh Arnaud" and walked away.

Shocked, I turned to Arnaud and said, "Arnaud, what was that about?"

Arnaud simply explained, "I asked my mom if she microwaved the bread, I hate microwaved bread . . . and she said yes, so I ruin the bread."

I mean . . . what?

It was further evidence that this guy Arnaud was absolutely out of his mind. Even the way I remember him crossing the street when we'd walk to class in college—he would just walk across the street, not at a crosswalk or anything, just wherever he felt like, and he would put his hands up like "everyone stop, Arnaud is crossing the street" and the cars would screech to a halt and he would cross the street. The first time I saw it I thought, "Holy shit, the French are insane." But it wasn't the French that were insane, it was Arnaud.

Watching Arnaud throw the bread in the trash remains one of my go-to thoughts when I need a good laugh. But it was also totally inappropriate and completely disrespectful. *His poor mother,* I kept thinking. And maybe this is a stretch, but if our behavior mirrors our parental role models, then it started to make some sense as to how and why Arnaud's parents were divorced. I mean, I have no idea what the issues were, but if Arnaud feels comfortable throwing his mom's bread into the trash in front of guests, I have a feeling he learned that behavior from his dad, right? Am I looking into it too much here?

Whatever the case may be, Jeff and I had only been in France for eighteen hours and it was already wildly insane and totally different from the Netherlands. This is why you travel. Even now, having been to France a few more times as a real adult, I can't say my experience with the country is any different. It's beautiful and messy and a pain in the ass and disrespectful and passionate and amazing and absolutely a shit show.

• • •

The day—the first day of the tournament—Jeff and I woke up earlier than we needed to because the apartment would get really hot and start smelling like Arnaud's dad once the temperature rose. We also had, more or less, no idea where we were. I mean we knew we were in Paris, but we weren't sleeping next to the Eiffel Tower, so we needed time to figure out the trains and plan on mistakes, etc.

It won't come as a surprise that Arnaud told us we didn't have to pay for the Paris Metro. He said, "You are American, you don't have to pay," and showed us how to just jump the turnstiles.

We knew this was bullshit but somehow hearing it from a real French person gave us all the permission we needed. And considering figuring out the ticket situation was almost impossible, we decided that it would be a lot easier to just steal train rides for our time there. So that's what we did. And it worked. Now, whenever I get a speeding ticket in upstate New York or a parking ticket in LA, I always think it's payback for the hundreds of dollars of free French train tickets I got in the summer of 2000.

Jeff and I arrived at the tennis center to find that it was a much bigger and more serious event than we had expected. There were crowds, tickets being sold, concessions, a bar, etc. It was wonderful. The French people really got behind their tennis and it was such a pleasant surprise. We were expecting the Dutch feeling, which was let's do the absolute least amount possible to get through this week of semi-pro tennis. In the Netherlands, the tennis club had to argue with its members to allow a pro tournament to come through and you could feel that every time you stepped in. But here in France it was as if they *built* the courts for these events.

Jeff turned to me and said, "This might actually be fun."

To which I responded, "Yeah, until you play me."

When we checked in, the tournament director said, "Oh, you are the Americans."

He sent us out to our courts with our opponents and we were off.

At the start of my first match, I remember my opponent shaking my hand and introducing himself, very pleasantly. I was thrown off. Is this guy trying to get in my head? How dare he? But as we warmed up, it quickly became clear that this was a friendly situation. Yes, we were playing for money (no ranking points), but the vibe was fun and supportive.

Jeff was playing on the court next to me and we chatted a few times at the back of the fence. "This is hilarious," he said. "My opponent is a wonderful guy."

Considering it was the quarterfinals of a giant national tournament the level of play was . . . pretty bad. I played a French gentleman who was well dressed and equipped but couldn't really make a forehand. I knew I had a bad forehand, but this guy made me look like Andre Agassi. And I should be clearer, my forehand was generally sufficient, but when you put it next to top pros, it was a puppy dog. Now, that day, though, my puppy dog forehand was looking pretty sweet, probably because my opponent's forehand was a mosquito.

I remember saying to Jeff on one of the changeovers, "Maybe we just move to France and play money tournaments the rest of our lives."

Jeff and I both won easily, 6–2 6–2. We grabbed our stuff, thanked our opponents, and left for the train station. Semi-final matches the next day.

Somehow, we ended up again in one of Paris's five major train stations, even though we managed to avoid it on the way there coming from "Mulan." There were cops and patrolmen everywhere, so we thought it would be a good idea to stand in line with the five hundred other tourists to buy tickets from the one customer service agent available.

We probably should have realized something was wrong when our tickets cost 375 francs, instead of the more familiar 12 francs, but what was a franc anyways? After we got on, I noticed this train had fancy seats and a bar car and families dressed nicely with suitcases and fancy paper hats. Travelers know that occasionally you have a feeling that something is wrong. It's good to trust that feeling. That feeling is there for a reason. The train door closed.

"Huh, Jeff, this doesn't feel like the right train, does it?" I said.

Jeff was tired and didn't care. He was generally way more laid back than I was. This usually helped him. I was typically the one stressed out while he was happy to lie on a suitcase and take a nap while the situation figured itself out. The situation usually got figured out because of me (you know that's true, Jeff).

The conductor started to make some announcements; we were getting ready to move. I looked at our tickets and couldn't see anything helpful, just French words smashed into more French words. I started asking the passengers around me, and as the train began to crawl along, slowly leaving as trains do. "Excuse me, my friend and I are trying to go to Mulan, is this the right train?" "Oui, Milan," he said. "OK . . . This. Is. The. Train. To. Mulan?" I said real slow and annoying as I handed him the tickets.

"Mulan?" he said. "Milan something something in French . . . Milan." And he started laughing.

"We are trying to go to Mulan, Paris."

He kept laughing and pointed somewhere else. A woman came over and said in beautiful oh so beautiful and nice to hear English. "This train is going to Milan. Milan, Italy."

"Jeff!" I yelled. "THIS TRAIN IS GOING TO ITALY" and for the first time in two weeks, including his on-court movement, I saw Jeff really move.

It could be argued that our most impressive athletic achievement in this entire trip was Jeff and I getting off this train. The conductor was nice enough to open the door for us and we jumped out of a moving train, just like in the movies. Jeff, like a cowboy with his bank heist money, threw his racket bag first and then jumped out, I think I was dumb enough to jump while holding my bag. We landed, just the two of us on the totally empty Parisian train platform as the very nice, comfortable train took off for the nine-hour trip to Milan, Italy.

Jumping off a moving European train with fifty pounds of equipment on your back doesn't seem like it should be one of the requirements of being a professional tennis player, but it is. Comedy has this, too. As a professional stand-up comedian people say to me all the time, "It must be so nice, only having to work for an hour a day" (that's typically how long I perform on stage). It's an ill-informed thing to say to a comic—if you say that, stop. It is true, though, that comics *perform* for an hour. That's the best part, the performance. The rest of the day, though, is filled with stand-up comedy business bullshit, stuff that you have to do and do well to continue to be able to perform: five a.m. flights, morning radio appearances with DJs that hate you, relying on a drug-addicted-money-laundering-comedy-club-owner to pay you, terrible and clingy local comics who try to bully their way on to your show, gigs getting canceled because someone more famous (and less funny) wants the same date that you were booked on for six months, social media obligations, fake ass conniving "friends" who will stab you in the back to advance themselves, paying taxes and organizing taxes for each state/country that you got paid in the last year, auditioning for TV shows/movies that you never get, getting fired by your agent because your TV show got canceled, auditing your manager to make sure he isn't taking more money than he is supposed to (he is), missing all your friends' weddings because you have to work on the weekends and you can't pay rent this month, missing a gig because Canadian customs doesn't like the way the comedy club in Calgary filled out your paperwork, seeing billboards everywhere displaying smiling pictures of more successful comics than you, begging/pitching comedy networks to watch your comedy/read your show script/not cancel your meeting, I could keep going with this but I think you get the point.

I'm not saying being a comedian is harder than your job, I'm saying being a comedian is the *same* as your job. You could make the same list of obligations for your job, I'm sure. I bring this up because being a minor league pro tennis player is the same. The match is the equivalent of the comedy performance. It's fun (especially when you win) and can be short. It's the one time that all the bullshit goes out the window and you get to *just* focus on that. It's the best. BUT . . . being a pro tennis player has, just as many, if not more obligations than just the match. Yes, I won my match that day 6–2 6–2 and it was easy and fun. That was one hour. The other eight hours of that workday involved getting to and from the courts, having equipment prepared properly, managing meals and hydration, managing injuries, etc. (Recovering and rehabbing from an injury can literally be a full-time job in itself.) That day, one of the parts of the job that was most difficult and most annoying was jumping off a moving train with all our bags, after already playing and winning a tennis match.

· · ·

I don't remember much about my semi-final match the next day. I googled it, but nothing seems to show up as far as results go. I was also googling in English and this was a French money tournament. There are two things that I do remember about it, though. (1) I remember that I won in three sets. (2) I remember that I lost the first set because I was drunk. Let me explain.

When Jeff and I rolled into the courts, I immediately checked in for my match and the tournament director said, "You have a friend here waiting for you." And the director nodded to my opponent from the day before.

Mosquito forehand walked over and said to me, "In France, after you play, you have a beer with your partner." Pretty sure he meant "opponent"—but I got it. "You left yesterday. I was waiting for you at the bar."

Jeff laughed and slapped me on the back, "Good luck" (his opponent from yesterday wasn't hanging around). I followed yesterday's opponent to the bar and had a few beers.

It was wonderful. It was so European and I loved it. He asked about my life and my tennis and my family. I did the same. It was like we were on a date. In fact, part of me wondered if we were on a date and I didn't know it. But that was just my American gay paranoia taking over. The French, after all, are a lot more comfortable with same sex friends, and sexuality in general. After three beers, his wife showed up and he introduced her to me. "This is my partner from yesterday," he said in English, like he had been bragging about me to her. And then he turned to me and said, "OK, have fun and good luck."

We shook hands one more time and then he left. Just like that. How cool is that? I mean, American tennis clubs don't even have a bar.

Americans are so wrapped up in winning and losing. We rarely focus on the journey, the action, the process. It's all results. This man, my opponent, tried to win, but he didn't really give a shit. To him, winning was playing. It was getting out of the house, hitting a few balls, having a few beers with his "partner." So, when I won the match and then got the hell out of there, he wasn't happy. I had disrupted the process. This also explains why the French can't win a Grand Slam, but now that I'm older I've started to reevaluate my life and what makes me happy and what I would want to teach my children—holy shit, it's this. It's my opponent waiting to share some beers with me and discuss life and be friends even if for just a brief moment.

Those beers, also, are the reason I lost my first set. Back to being American. Jeff and I were on courts side by side again and he noticed that I was moving a little slow and that I wasn't striking the ball as well as I usually was. I mean I did just finish three 1664 Lagers. I don't remember anything about my opponent; this was an internal battle, really. Jeff was winning easily so he was paying quite a bit of attention to me and my match. I have a vague memory of him bringing me some Gatorade at one point, as if that would sober me up or something.

I got down early in the first set and by the time I sobered up, my opponent was serving for the set and held to win it in a close game.

At this point Jeff had already won, so I had his full attention now, which included a little back-fence coaching. At this point in our lives, we had been around a lot of tennis and a lot of coaching and our knowledge base was pretty solid. Jeff would say something like, "His backhand can't pass, approach and come in." Pretty simple stuff and information that you as the player usually already know. But it was nice to hear Jeff tell me what he thought I needed to hear, and it says a lot about Jeff that he was trying to help me win, so we could play each other in the finals.

I won the second set easily and remember winning the third and final set handily as well.

Afterward, Jeff and I grabbed a beer at the bar; both of our opponents had left. So maybe it wasn't French tradition after all, we didn't care, we were in the finals the next day and if we got a little drunk, it didn't matter, we were playing each other!

We had a decent amount of money at stake. The winner got 780 euros and the loser got 340 euros. Not exactly f-you money but that's roughly US$1,000 to the winner and when you're about to be a sophomore in college and you steal muffins from the Whole Foods buffet to save four dollars, it feels like a lot.

Jeff and I talked over the beers and decided that playing each other for that amount of money kind of sucked. So, we decided to play for $100 and split the rest of the money. This was classic Jeff: fair, fun, and easy to work out. Also, we were competitive people, it's not like either one of us was going to not try our hardest to beat the other. You didn't get to our level if you didn't hate losing.

· · ·

It had been a while since either of us had played in a singles final, so it's safe to say we were a little nervous at the start of the match. After a few official-sounding announcements in French where Jeff and I both recognized our names, and nothing else, the match started. I would estimate that there were around five hundred spectators, including a few pretty girls in attendance, which was always enough to get my juices flowing, to use a disgusting phrase.

There were a few clouds in the sky and I remember the air being cool and heavy and I felt like that helped me. If the air was heavy it slowed the ball down. Jeff had an enormous serve and forehand. *Huge* weapons. Inside, he was a nightmare. But we were playing outside, thank god, and the air was thick. My game plan against Jeff was to try and take his serve away from him and to attack his backhand.

Once the match started, everything went according to plan and I got up early. I was returning great, Jeff was giving me a lot of second serve chances, and I was coming to net on his backhand successfully.

When I started winning, Jeff started to get pissed. His frustration wasn't aimed at me, but it was a little hard to not take it personally. "Oh, you didn't think I could beat you?!" It just made me want to beat him that much more. I stayed focused and won the first set and felt like the match was very much on my racket. I was playing great, the conditions were helping me and Jeff was acting like a bitch and getting in his own head.

Maybe I would just walk out of here a champ and get to talk to some of those French girls I noticed. We sat down on the changeover and I was up 2–1 in the second set, about to serve. And then . . . Jeff's prayers were answered. Clouds approached, darkness arrived, and the skies opened up and started pouring rain. I believe Jeff even started laughing and said something like, "Well, this certainly gives me a second chance."

It was funny but also certainly annoying because even he knew that if it had stayed going the way it had been, I would have won.

It was expected to rain for the next four hours, and the tournament officially decided to move this party indoors. My juices were forced to stop flowing, due to weather, and now I would have to get them flowing again—inside (just doubling down on the disgusting phrase).

Jeff is an amazing indoor player. He knew it, I knew it.

We hopped in some tiny tiny French cars and drove off to what appeared to be a barn with one tennis court in it. I remember our driver smoking a cigarette while he drove us. Maybe hold off on the smoke while you have the two athletes in the car? Just a thought. The fans got in their tiny tiny French cars and drove to the barn as well.

The atmosphere was wonderful. Five hundred fans packed into a barn somewhere in France. People were laughing and smoking and drinking wine and clapping after each point. If I could remove myself from the fact that I was watching my lead slowly disappear, it would have been a fun environment to play in. It would have been an even more fun environment to *win* a tournament in.

Jeff won in three sets, and the tournament threw us a party afterward. Everyone came onto the court and made a trophy ceremony, handed us our money (cash), popped open some Champagne (you know, from Champagne), and we got drunk among our new friends. Someone drove us home after the match, it was dark and Jeff and I had a little buzz on. We got home, cracked open some beers, and laid out all the money on the table. It looked like a lot of money. Pretty cool considering we earned that playing tennis, a silly little game with a felt ball and baseball bat with strings in it. Jeff counted the money out and then ceremoniously gave himself the extra 100 euros we played for. He earned it. We both felt good. If we stayed outside I would have won, I'm sure of it.

We've both now moved on to greater things, we both make more money now than we did then, but I'll never forget Jeff counting out that sweet crisp euro cash that late evening in Paris. I think they paid us in twenties so it meant even more bills to count, which added to the drama. I remember saying, "I wish they paid us in fives so this would never end."

Jeff laughed and had to start counting all over again, which was the point. Getting rewarded in cash is always so sweet. Way better than a stupid trophy with a frozen gold man serving on it. It feels dangerous, it feels gratuitous, it feels like a privilege to handle that much cash. I remember checking the front door to make sure it was locked during the counting process. As if we were counting hundreds of thousands of illegal drug money and at any moment some gangster would bust through the door and pry it from our hands. It was only 1,000 euros but it felt like a million.

Chapter 13

Red Light District

WITH CASH IN our pockets and a successful week of tennis behind us, Jeff and I had a week to kill before we needed to get back to the Netherlands (where we were supposed to have been playing tournaments this whole time) and catch our flight out of Amsterdam back to the US. Some players may have looked into different training centers, or tried to find other French players to practice with, but how fun does that sound? Plus, France was playing Italy in the Euro 2000 Soccer championship that week, so we decided to take full advantage of what can only be described as absolute insanity.

By the time Jeff and I got on the train out of Paris, we were ready to leave—France had beat Italy in dramatic fashion, we were hungover and exhausted, and I was looking forward to getting out of Arnaud's dad's divorce pad. I don't remember why, but when we got back to Amsterdam, Jeff and I split up. Maybe Jeff hopped on an earlier flight, or maybe we just decided to do our own thing, I don't know. But from what I can piece together, I had two nights in Amsterdam on my own.

From a tennis standpoint, I would say our experience was pretty subpar. For me, four weeks of travel, five singles matches played, two won, three lost. Zero doubles matches played. Zero books finished—I left the Theodore Roosevelt book somewhere and never got to finish it. But from a life standpoint, I would say it was pretty special. I didn't realize it at the time, but twenty years later, I'm writing and reminiscing about the trip because it affected me so much. Also, now, as life becomes filled with responsibilities and expectations, it is becoming even clearer how few responsibilities and expectations I had during those years. Yes, Craig and Bruce, our two coaches, would be mad that we didn't have a productive tennis summer, but besides running a few extra laps during conditioning, I could get over that. It's not like I had a bad tennis summer so now my baby can't eat or whatever.

On the night before my flight home, I remember playing cards with some new friends at Bob's Youth Hostel in Amsterdam. It's still there to this day and I know that because while writing this book I went to Amsterdam and found it and it appears to be exactly the same. As soon as I saw the iconic blue sign with white writing, the emotions and memories came back like a wave. This place must have carried some significance for me to react that way. Hostels are all about new friends. I can't tell if they are real friends or if everyone is just so lonely and bored that you partner up to make your travels easier. Actually, isn't that kind of what marriage is? I mean, love also, of course.

We were playing cards, drinking Heinekens, having a good time. It was fun to meet new people, although they certainly were always a little surprised when they asked me what I was doing in Amsterdam and my answer was "playing in a pro tennis tournament." Which, to be fair, was a bit of a stretch because I played in two (low-level) pro tournaments, weeks ago, not in Amsterdam. But whatever, I was trying to impress the cute Australian girl (did not work).

The Heinekens were roughly $2 each in the hostel lounge. Not a bad price considering down the street a beer was $6 at a fancy restaurant, but I was such a cheap-ass at the time that I actually walked down the road and bought a twelve pack of Heineken (trying to match the exact same can the hostel was using) so I could drink those in the lounge and not spend the exorbitant price of $2 a beer. After doing the math I realized I was saving about 75 cents a beer. Score. After a few of my own beers, I became a little less cautious about sneaking them in. "You want a beer?" I asked my new friends, "I bought these down the road because it's cheaper."

As I finished my sentence I felt a tap on my shoulder and I looked up and it's the older (thirty-five?) bar keeper/hostel manager, who had clearly seen this racket before. He seemed like the type of guy who thought it would be fun to work at a hostel during his younger life travels but somehow ended up here, managing the exact people he once was.

"Did you buy those down the road?" he asked, pointing at my beers. He clearly knew I did because he had just heard me say, "I bought these down the road."

But of course I was drunk and cocky and cheap so I said, "No, I didn't."

Thankfully, he cut to the chase or else we would have kept doing this game. "This is your warning. If you cause any more trouble, you will be asked to leave. Do you understand?"

I replied, "Hey, it's not like that, look, I apologize . . ." and just like the Dutch train conductor didn't want to put up with any bullshit from the Penn rain stick dipshit, this guy wasn't putting up with me.

"Do you understand?"

"Yes, I do. Sorry about that."

I turned back and all my new "friends" were gone. I was all alone. Somehow the cool tennis guy who snuck his own beers into the hostel wasn't as cool as he thought. Well, I guess the Australian girl had to go somewhere? What makes me laugh about this now is that I got a warning. I'd literally left the tennis world twenty-four hours ago, a world where umpires give out warnings for poor behavior. I thought I was in a place where there were no rules. Amsterdam is called the most liberal city in Europe. Prostitution, pot, mushrooms, it's all legal and all good here. Well, as I learned this trip and as I saw many other people learn on my most recent trip, Amsterdam doesn't mess around with the rules. They are liberal, they are forward thinking, but if you act like a douchebag, they have a system in place to punish you.

Considering I was now all alone, I decided to go grab dinner alone somewhere, the man yelled out to me, "Don't forget, we have a strict one a.m. curfew."

"Excuse me?" I said.

"We have a curfew, one a.m., you must be inside by one a.m. If this doesn't work for you, I am happy to check you out," he said all dick and assholey.

"One a.m. curfew, OK, no problem at all," I said. Meanwhile I'm thinking "What the shit is a one a.m. curfew? Can a hotel even have a curfew? Funny how they didn't tell me that when I checked in" (they probably did).

As I took a walk looking for a cheap gyro, I proudly decided that I wasn't going to let a one a.m. curfew ruin my fun. If by chance I was out that late, I would just stay out all night and return at nine a.m. *Or,* really worst-case scenario, my bedroom was along the front wall of the hostel, by these big open windows. I could easily jump up there and sneak into bed no problem.

Five hours later I found myself sitting on a curb drunk, alone, and exhausted. I don't know where I ate, I don't know what I did. Most likely I bought beer and walked around, as you are allowed to do that in Amsterdam. And it's really such wonderful people watching, you could do it for hours. From a group of fifteen African men popping whippets out of balloons to a group of nine women celebrating a bachelorette by getting stinking drunk, there was always something fun to look at. I sat on the curb in my jeans and white buttoned-down shirt. When I returned to Amsterdam twenty years later, I saw many, many American boys wearing the same outfit, drunk, sitting on the curb. Goddamn it, I hate that I was one of those guys.

It's a good reminder that even though I now have way more responsibility and important life stuff to worry about, I really appreciate not being twenty. Now that I'm in my forties, I understand how things work and can, more or less, figure out people's motivations, how systems operate, why we are where we are. I can anticipate problems that others might not see coming. It's nice not being totally lost. For example, now, if someone told me I was staying at a hotel with a one a.m. curfew and I had one night out in Amsterdam, I would know that I should change hotels, or change my evening plans (realistically, now, I would be in bed by ten-thirty p.m. because I booked a bike rental at eight a.m. the next day). Youth has youth, but they don't know shit. As I sit back and think about these years and my experiences, I am going to chalk one up for experience, maturity. Also, some of that stuff that I learned, I learned because I made the mistake. Mistakes are important, keep making them.

This night, sitting on the curb alone in Amsterdam, is an example. I looked at my watch: one thirty-five a.m. Shit. I was tired, drunk, and still pissed off about this one a.m. curfew thing. I was also defiant enough and my judgment was bad enough that I remembered my idea about climbing up the side of the wall and sneaking in through the window. Not only am I a better athlete than anyone staying there tonight, I told myself, I'm probably the best athlete that has ever stayed there.

As predicted, the second-story window of my communal bedroom was wide open, leaving a nice breeze for all the losers who decided to make the curfew and be in bed by one a.m. in Amsterdam. I looked around a little bit, there didn't seem to be anyone around. I checked the wall for foot placement, there were a lot of good options. I unbuttoned a few buttons on my shirt, placed my leg on the ledge, used my pro tennis triceps to push myself up and like a thoroughbred horse jumping a fence I scaled the wall and easily got both hands inside the window and room. It was so easy that I actually wondered if maybe this hostel had a "curfew" because it was a weird old law or something that they had to have and this was their way of winking at everyone and saying, "Hey, don't forget we *have* to have this curfew, but as long as you have an open mind you can come home whenever you want."

As I moved my leg inside the room and placed it on the floor, I congratulated myself on a job well done and further admired my athletic prowess. Did I mention that I was probably the greatest athlete to ever stay at this hostel? Then, light from a flashlight hit me in the face. The manager, who wanted to be a travel writer but instead landed a hostel management job, was sitting in a chair by the window. Waiting up for me, apparently, the same thing my mom used to do with my older siblings to make sure they weren't drinking.

To his credit, he was remarkably composed (possible he had done this little douchebag mouse trap before?). "I packed your bags, they are downstairs. You can come inside and go out down there."

I have to admit, for the first time in my life I was rendered speechless. Did he just say he "packed my bags" for me? Like a dog being caught in the act, I slowly followed this guy's hand down the stairs and out the door. I tried to make a joke on the way out just to help defuse the stress I was feeling and also because I wanted to get the last word. "I guess I'll just sleep here," I said referring to the front stoop.

"If you sleep here I will call the police," he said.

And I believed him. Why wouldn't I, this man has effectively done everything he has ever said to me at this point The door shut behind me and I heard a good two to three locks engage. For a brief moment I thought about climbing back inside the room just for fun, but I didn't and I'm thankful for that.[1] He probably would have tased me or I would have ended up in a Dutch prison, whatever that is.

There I was, drunk, tired, dressed like a thirsty clubgoer, holding (and this was the part I underestimated) a giant twelve-racket tennis bag and a duffel bag worth of clothes and shoes for a small family of four, standing in the middle of a dark Amsterdam street. Now what? It was roughly two a.m., I had a flight back to the USA around noon. Seven hours I needed to kill. Tomorrow I would be home, back to mandatory practices, back to obligations of school and tournaments, back to grocery shopping and doing the right thing. It became pretty clear what needed to happen: this was the perfect time to visit the Red Light district.

Prostitution was never my thing, I always felt like for the same amount of money I could have sex with a woman who also wanted to have sex with me. Now I was usually wrong about that but call me a romantic, I thought prostitutes were for losers who couldn't get laid, not me. That being said, my first stop was to where the prostitutes were.

If you haven't visited the Red Light District in Amsterdam, it is worth a visit. I've never been anywhere that is so open about sex. It is remarkably honest and, I believe, wonderful. Mankind's long turbulent history with sex is something that fascinates me. I grew up in an attempted Catholic home—thankfully we all ditched that terrible religion once Grandma died—but it baffled me that there was so

---

1   For the record, it should be noted that Bob's Youth Hostel now has these boards that go over the outside windows. It would be remarkably hard to sneak into the room with these boards up. I'm gonna go ahead and think that they ordered these after I was there. Was the manager still there?

much shame, guilt, rules, and regulations surrounding not even just sex, but even *thinking* about sex.

Every single person on this planet is a product of sex. Not only humans. That dog you love? Sex created it. Those orchids you planted? Product of reproduction. That pork chop you are eating? Pigs had sex and now you can eat. Everything is sex. People need to chill about sex.

It took me ten seconds of Catholic Sunday school before I turned to my brother and said, "Wow, these people really have some issues with sex." I was ten.

Despite that awareness, shame and guilt and secrecy about sex still snuck into my conscious. So, having reached the end of both my trip and my rope (getting kicked out of my hostel gave me a new-found I-don't-give-a-fuck-ness), I finally had crossed over into the underworld and I allowed myself the true pleasure of stepping foot into the mysterious darkness that is legal prostitution. The Dutch, in their infinite wisdom, knowing that prostitution has long been the oldest profession, has long been a cesspool of illegal narcotics, sex trafficking, slavery, and much more, decided that instead of fighting it and arresting the women (and men, to be fair, but mostly women) decided to legalize it, regulate it, tax it, and protect the people involved. What a wonderful decision!

I gave myself this wonderful pep talk as I walked through the canals and corridors of Amsterdam at two-thirty a.m. with my tennis rackets and duffel bag. "I should buy a prostitute and help the Dutch economy," I told myself.

It was pretty quiet out there. Any time I walked by a woman (who was neatly tucked away into her small "apartment" with a full-size window where people on the street could look in and decide if they wanted to talk further) she would wave or do the "come here" with her finger move. I nervously approached a few, they would quickly open their door and do their best to convince me that I should join. This usually involved something along the lines of "How you doing, baby? Aren't you cute, want to play?" Or the one I kept getting, "Why don't you come say hi before you head to airport?" The beauty of prostitution is that they don't care if you are drunk, sweaty, carrying bags, and still dressed like you struck out at the bars. They want your business and I certainly looked like a man who was desperate to give them mine (business).

I had previously decided that I had $50 to spend on this. That was way more than I really wanted to spend but it was my last night and I was going balls to the wall, to use another disgusting phrase. At first, I stopped in at the women that I thought were beautiful. They were too expensive. They were well over $200 and this was twenty years ago. Then I started going to the women that I thought seemed nice. I mean if I was gonna do this, let's at least do it with someone that was kind? Right? I don't know and I still don't know. But sadly, even the nice-seeming prostitutes were too expensive. So then, and I believe this might be how a lot of men go about this important decision, I went with the women I thought I could afford. The prostitute that you can afford when your budget is $50 is—and how do I say this nicely?—not the most attractive lady. She is a lady, so that's good.

The professional sex workers that work for $50 have a different type of skill and that's the skill to get you to say yes. The same way that a used car salesman gets you to buy a banged-up 1998 Honda Accord? That's what these ladies were good at. The beautiful woman with the perfect hair, body, and face sets her price high enough so she doesn't have to deal with the guy who has a hundred-pound duffel bag on one arm and a backpack tennis racket case on both shoulders.

So I get called over to this woman, this 1998 Honda Accord woman, and I can't tell you much else about her other than she had big breasts. Huge Dutch apple pie breasts. I think everything was big. She seemed nice though, so that was good. We spoke for a moment and she told me that for what was roughly forty US dollars I could "suck and fuck." That seemed to be the preferred term that these ladies used. How it all worked I wasn't quite sure. I mean are you telling me that you suck my dick and I reach orgasm and then we fuck? I was twenty but I wasn't Hee-Man. Or are you telling me that part of fucking is that you also suck my dick? Or are you just saying two words that every young male wants to hear, to try and make the sale?

Let me just put it this way: everything was awkward. It was awkward from start to "finish." It's still awkward thinking about it. I was so nervous, so out of my league, so unsure of how this whole buying sex thing worked, so filled with Catholic nonsense, that it was very difficult for me to have a good time.

I would say half of her job was getting me to just relax, but there was also just some business stuff that needed to be taken care of. Like a doctor visiting a patient before surgery, she had to explain this process to me, a clear novice. She was going to take my money, I was going to take a shower, then we would move to the bedroom. I listened intently, sitting in this prostitute's apartment that was also her place of business. I had known her for three minutes but she had all my respect. I gave her the money and, as expected, she handed me the crunchiest, roughest towel I have ever known. I remember taking my clothes off, about to hop in her shower, thinking, "How can I just get out of this?" Well, I could just leave. "Just grab your shit and leave," I kept thinking. But no, the penis that was guiding me, was telling me to stay. So I stood in her kitchen, which was also the bathroom, and briefly showered. I remember looking out through the plastic door and seeing Ramen noodles stored on a shelf. This is an image I won't forget. Showering in a prostitute's kitchen/bathroom, seeing her noodles, moments before we "suck and fuck," whatever the hell that means.

Once I was done showering, I sat on her bed and she started to "massage" my shoulders and legs. She was wearing lingerie of some kind, I was in my crunchy rough towel. There was limited room because I had all my bags with me as well. Her place was so small we had to keep moving my duffel bag and tennis racket bag. I wonder if she had ever had a giant tennis racket bag in her sex apartment before? I figured I was probably the best athlete that has ever been in her apartment, right? Right? She appeared to be comfortable. She knew how to move, how to help me relax, she had a good energy. Just like a pro comic makes performing seem easy and comfortable on stage, a pro prostitute does the same.

Eventually a slight bulge appeared under my sandpaper towel and let me tell you, this was chum in the water for this lady. Once she saw indication that this was going in the direction toward it being over, she pounced. You know how they say great athletes notice the smallest of moments where they have an advantage and they capitalize on those moments immediately? Well, call this lady Tom Brady because she had an opening and she took it. Before I could say "Can I have some noodles, please?" she had put the condom on me (with her mouth) and had started the "sucking" portion of the "suck and fuck." Being a twenty-year-old who had only received a handful of blowjobs, I had certainly never received one with the full power, double protection, ten-gauge latex condom that a professional sex worker uses. I mean this thing was like wearing a Goodyear tire. I vaguely, vaguely felt the littlest of tingles. Imagine putting all your winter clothes on, snow pants, winter jacket, hat, scarf, boots, and then someone very coyly, lightly, tickling you with a feather. That's what it felt like. Like if I tried, I could pretend it wasn't happening.

The problem with this situation, though, is that it *was* happening. She was very much doing her job and she was trying really really hard. And I was just sitting there looking at her thinking, "Oh shit, this is going to take a long time . . . and this is just the

'suck' part." The more effort she put in, the louder the noises became. And the louder the noises became, the more awkward it was.
After the noises came the body movement. Like a fireman trying to
loosen a stingy fire hydrant she started to use her body, and there
was a lot of it to use.

I'm on my knees on her single bed, my back is to the window (cur-
tains are shut), I'm wearing a military grade latex condom, she is on
her knees, wearing some Dutch lingerie, facing me, going down on
me, effort and noises are full one hundred percent. I remember looking up at her apartment while this is happening and I see facing me
tacked up on the wall a monthly calendar. And each date had some
stuff written on it in Dutch. So I'm trying to orgasm but I keep looking at this woman's to-do list for tomorrow. What did it say? Dentist
appointment, grocery shopping, visit Mom? I wondered if the $200
prostitute had the same type of thing going on.

My erection level was anywhere between forty and sixty percent. It
would fluctuate between barely able to hold a condom on, to "Hey,
not bad little guy." Of course this made her job even more impossible.
I have to say, though, she was not letting up. It's hard not to think
about what she was thinking about during that time. Does she recite
her favorite poem in her head? Sing "Stairway to Heaven"? Think
about what she has to do tomorrow? I commend this woman, and all
sex workers for that matter. This was not an easy situation and she
handled it like a true professional.

Eventually I closed my eyes, thought about an attractive woman
that I liked at school (Sandy) and barely, with an emphasis on barely,
dribbled a little bit of orgasm into the UN-approved Health Hazard
Hazmat suit that was this condom. *Phew.* It was a relief. And not
a sexual relief, it was an awkward-situation-is-over relief. She said
something nice like, "You're cute, that was fun" or whatever she says
to everyone, and I grabbed my clothes and bags and ran out of there.
Not sure if I still had the "fuck" portion of the "suck and fuck" avail-

able to me but I certainly didn't want it or care. How anybody could have sex after that is beyond me.

I took my bags and started the long walk to the train station. I slept the rest of the night on a couch at the Schiphol airport. The next day I boarded my plane and flew back to Chicago. My first international tennis tour was over, and it went out with a bang. Well, not a bang, but you know what I mean, a dribble.

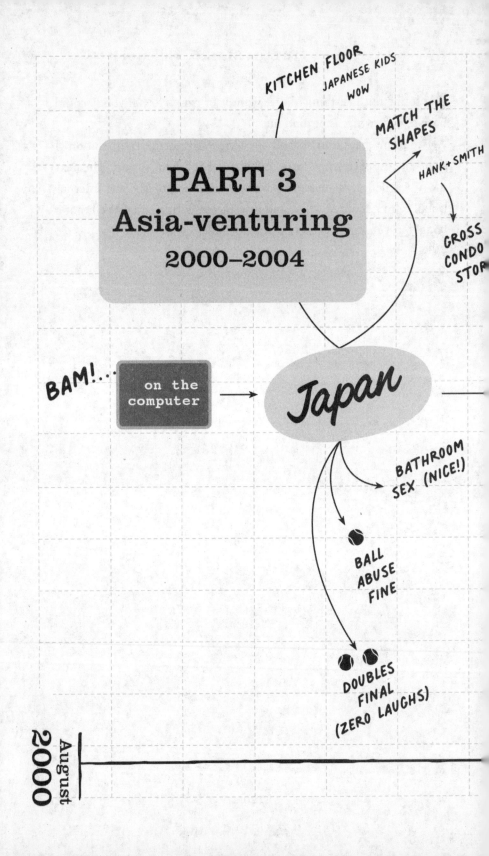

KITCHEN FLOOR
JAPANESE KIDS
WOW

MATCH THE
SHAPES

HANK + SMITH

PART 3
Asia-venturing
2000–2004

GROSS
CONDO
STOR

BAM!....

on the
computer

Japan

BATHROOM
SEX (NICE!)

BALL
ABUSE
FINE

DOUBLES
FINAL
(ZERO LAUGHS)

August
2000

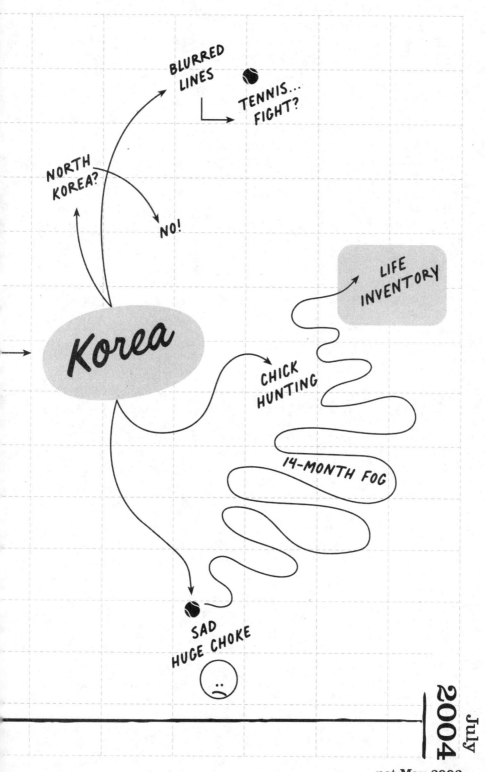

July **2004**

not May 2003

Chapter 14

First ATP Point

"POINTS." THE ONE definitive lesson I learned (tennis related) while playing overseas was that if I wanted to be a pro, I had to have some "points." More formally identified as ATP ranking points. With at least one, I would be able to often bypass the ridiculously difficult qualifying rounds where every match was a battle, and you have to win four in a row to make it in the main draw. With some points I could just start off in the main draw, where the matches were tough as well, but if you win just one match you are already in the points and the money. It was July 1999 and I made a goal that in a year, with another twelve months of college tennis under my belt, I would get at least one "point," which would put me on the formidable ATP computer. Once there, my chances for more pro success would increase tremendously.

Getting that first ATP point is something every world-ranked tennis player will always remember. It's very difficult.[1]

---

1   Think of it this way: The latest ITF Global Tennis Report states that there are 87 million tennis players around the world, roughly 1.1 percent of the world's population. When I was playing tennis there were about 10,000 male tennis players that had earned at least one

Firsts are always a big deal. First kiss, first day of school, first paycheck, first time getting punched, first marriage, etc. After the first, everything changes. Earning your first ATP point in tennis carries equal value. Your name, in the draw, will have your world ranking next to it. It sounds silly, but that's nice. "Michael Kosta #1250" is better than "Michael Kosta" (unranked). It's a badge of honor.

True to the goal I set for myself, my first ATP point came in the summer of the year 2000. I had just finished my sophomore year at Illinois, and I was staying in Champaign to practice and play the summer Futures Circuit in the Midwest. It was so hot you could barely think. The tournaments were played in public parks, with little shade, huge asphalt black parking lots, where you would park your car and have to leave it there all day. No players lounge, or locker room to hang. I have many memories of sitting in my car blasting AC trying to stay loose for a match. It was brutal. And because I didn't have any ATP points, I would have to win all four qualifying matches to make it into the main draw. Losing in the main draw wouldn't earn me any ranking points, but I could get a bit of a payout (maybe $111). If I lost in qualifying, I earned nothing.

Because of the heat, there was an ambulance *on site* that just kept its motor running because the players suffering from heat stroke would get carried over and dropped off.[2]

It was, during those super-hot days, a lot less about tennis and

---

ranking point, meaning they were on the ATP computer. Basic math: 10,000 ranked players out of 87 million means to be on the ATP computer you are in the 0.0001 percent of all tennis players in the world. Not in the USA, or North America, or Atlanta, but the world. Here's another illustration: think of the best tennis player that you know personally, odds are, that person was never even close to earning one measly ATP point.

2   Carried is the correct word. Oftentimes a player would first have cramps on the court (it was definitely well over 120 degrees on a hard court in the sun), try to play through a few cramps, they would get worse, take an injury time out, until eventually the player would collapse on the court, unable to move. Volunteers along with the one tournament-supplied athletic trainer would literally pick up the player, in his tennis clothes, and carry him like a wounded soldier to the ambulance. This was usually accompanied with lots of screams and groans as the player's muscles would cramp again during the carry.

mostly about physical endurance and mental toughness. This ended up playing in my favor. I didn't have the forehand, I didn't have the overhead, I didn't have the amazing coaching my whole life like some of the kids I was playing against. To make up for all of this, I focused on fitness. I worked my ass off. I figured if I could keep a match close, my fitness usually was a big reason I could win.

Looking back now, the summer of 2000 was probably the fittest I've ever been my entire life (earlier that year I ran an 8:04 mile and half, which is a 5:20 mile—as a fun experiment, I should time my mile and half now to see how many hamstrings I pull). I signed into qualifying for the tournament in Decatur, Illinois, which was a 15k Future. That's $15,000 total prize money. 128 Qualifying draw meant I would have to win four matches to make the main draw.

Decatur is roughly an hour west of Champaign, where the University of Illinois was and where the whole team would stay during the summer to practice and play in tournaments like this one on the Futures Circuit. We would hop in our cars, drive an hour on I-72, and get to the courts. I remember joking that the drive was so straight and so boring that you could take your hands off the wheel for the majority of it and the car would not turn for an hour. Cornfields to the left, cornfields to the right, mixed in with a few pro Second Amendment billboards. Classic rural Illinois.

For this tournament, the USTA was experimenting with a new scoring system, so each set went to 4 and you had to win 3 out of 5 sets. If you don't know what that means, all you need to understand is that it was fast-paced and you were rewarded for taking chances; ultimately it played well to my strengths. Things were in my favor—the courts were close enough that I could stay on campus, I was very fit, it was superhot, which gave me an advantage—hell, it seemed that even the USTA temporarily changed the scoring of the sport to suit me.

For four days I drove to the courts, played my qualifying matches, apparently won, and drove back. Upon reviewing the scores I didn't

---

lose a set in the qualifying. I won twelve straight sets in four days. So obviously I didn't have super long matches and I was feeling great heading into the main draw.

In the first round, I drew an American player named Jack Brasington. Jack was an accomplished player from the University of Texas, a full-time pro, and someone that if I wanted to earn my first ATP point, I would have to beat. Not exactly a great draw, but he was unseeded so not exactly a terrible draw. My college teammate, Nathan, called me immediately when he saw the draw. "Dude, your game is perfect for beating this guy!" Nathan knew Jack well and had trained with him many times. He gave me the lowdown. "Jack has a very weak second serve, you like to attack it and come in. He hates that. I'm telling you, dude, Jack hates that! This works out really well for you!" Nathan screamed at me through the phone. He was so excited for me.

It was really nice to feel his enthusiasm and excitement, but I also still had to play and win the match. I kept repeating that to Nathan. "OK, man, thanks, but I haven't won anything yet."

"I know but believe me, you can beat this guy, I promise!"

I asked a few other players about Jack, and they said the same. Jack had a weak second serve and if you could attack early on, it would bother him. OK, well I guess that's the plan then, and good thing because that was the plan either way.

I remember going to bed the night before the match, lying in bed, looking up at the ceiling fan, thinking, "Tomorrow night at this time, I will either be on the ATP computer or I won't. I will either be preparing for my second round pro tennis match, or I will be out of the tournament." I was nervous, excited, and anxious. I can only imagine what it must feel like to lie in bed the night before a Grand Slam final and think, "Tomorrow night I will either be a Grand Slam champion, or I won't." Does it feel the same as what I was feeling? I'll never know.

I tried to stay calm, remind myself that I was extremely prepared, and it was OK to feel a little nervous and excited, but I couldn't have it become so much that it would affect my play. I can't tell you how many times I've had the same conversation with myself today as a stand-up comic. Before every TV appearance, before taping a special or a show in front of thousands, I try and say the same thing: "Use the nerves, use the excitement, but use just a little bit of it. Instead, heavily rely on your experience, your training, and repetition to get the job done." Tennis is the same.

. . .

The next morning was a little more complicated than I had expected or wanted. My teammate Graydon called and asked me, "Can you take Lindsey's car to the courts?"

"Ah . . . I kind of wanted to take my own car, just because I feel comfortable in it—"

Graydon wasn't having it. "Come on, dude, that's ridiculous, get over here and take Lindsey's car and it will be a big help for us, thank you."

Graydon was a teammate and a guy who had probably lent me his car over a hundred times, driven me over a hundred times, and bought me beer over a hundred times. So that's what I did. I had already agreed to drive my teammate Phil to the courts as well, so we adjusted our plan—not something I recommend before a big match.

Graydon's girlfriend, Lindsey, was the nicest woman around. We all loved her. She lost her mom to a car accident when she was younger. Lindsey survived and she had the energy of someone who knew what was important in life and didn't take people or moments for granted. She was characteristically very gracious and appreciative that I was helping her and she communicated that. It always makes things easier when you hear "thank you." I hopped in her Toyota with Phil and we followed Graydon and Lindsey to I-72 west Decatur.

Graydon, about whom a whole book could be written, was not only very generous, but an all-around great guy and cool cat and also the only guy on a campus of forty thousand people that drove a white Ford Mustang. And to make matters worse, it was automatic. Where I come from—Michigan—it's an embarrassment to drive an American sports car that is automatic. That being said, it was still fast and Graydon still liked to go fast in it, especially when there was a woman sitting next to him.

Phil (six-six) and I (six-four) stuffed ourselves into Lindsey's Toyota Corolla and set off for Decatur, following Graydon, and merged onto I-72 west. Once on the highway, Graydon hit the gas on the "Stang and bang" and he's gone, out of sight, leaving Phil and me puddling along the straightest, most boring highway in America. I am a good ninety minutes away from playing for my first ATP point. Phil, as always, is talking way too much and I am trying my best to stay grounded, calm, and to keep my brain quiet. We were alone on the highway, cruising in the left lane, when I spotted a giant truck roughly a quarter mile in front of us in the right lane, with his right blinker on, pulling over to the side of the road.

Phil said something like, "You want to stop and see if this guy needs help?"

I laughed. "Absolutely not. I'm about to play my first professional main draw match, we are twenty minutes from a city, it looks like a giant truck, I'm sure he has a radio or cell phone, this is not our responsibility."

Phil laughed and we kept going.

We were probably going around 70 mph.When we got to within a hundred feet of the truck, it, out of nowhere, makes a sharp left turn from the right lane crossing over the highway into the median.

"What the fuck!?!?!" I slam on the brakes, whip the wheel to the left trying to avoid it . . . I don't. We smash into this big rig truck in the middle of I-72.

Glass breaks, tires screech, metal crushes. Air bags deploy (Phil's side, not mine). Fucking *SLAM BAM CRUNCH, SHIT!*

A car accident. What a fucking disaster. Thankfully, no one was dead, but everything else was totaled. The other driver, an elderly man who seemed confused and startled, popped out of his truck, apologized, and made sure we were okay. Phil was pretty badly shaken and his airbag messed him up pretty good. I was in shock, totally physically okay, but could not keep my mind from racing. What time was it? Is anyone hurt? Where is Graydon? Lindsey is going to flip. Am I going to have to default my match? Of course this happens to me, goddamn it. I should never have let Graydon talk me into this. If I was in my car this never would have happened (who knows).

I brushed glass and metal off my warm-up jacket as I tried to figure out what the hell I was supposed to do, the noise of the crash still reverberating in my head. I needed to calm down and get to Decatur *stat.*

I worked too hard and was playing too well to let this opportunity slip for my first ATP point. I wasn't going to lose this match because Grandpa over here thought he could make an illegal U turn on I-72.

We needed a cop and we needed a cop *now.* The truck driver knew this, and used his radio to call the police—but he said, "We need a cop here, a young man drove into me . . ."

I immediately corrected him. "Sorry sir, but that is not going to be the statement I give the police officer. You made an illegal left turn/U-turn from the right lane in the middle of the highway and we had no choice but to slam into you."

The crash, thankfully, looked like exactly what happened—our car was crushed into the middle of the left side of his truck. But I knew I needed to be there when the officer arrived in case Old Man Winter tried changing the story. We waited and watched the minutes on the clock tick away.

I remember seeing the cop car from what appeared to be miles away. This is Illinois. It's flat as shit. You can see something coming for a while. This would be the worst state in America to sneak up on someone. When the cop finally did pull up, he moved slowly, taking time to grab his hat, find his pen, go back to his car for his flashlight. He didn't know or care that I was about to play for my first ATP point—for him, it was just another Monday patrolling the middle of Illinois. He probably didn't even know what tennis was.

I gave my statement to the cop and, as kindly as I could, I said to him, "Officer, I know this sounds insane, but I am playing in a pro tennis tournament in Decatur and my match time is at ten a.m. and there is no chance I am going to make it unless I leave *right now*."

He took his glasses off, confused. "What?"

Just then, Graydon's Mustang popped up on the other side of the highway. He had circled back to check on us, which was a smart move. I continued pleading my case to the cop. He wasn't getting it. "You want to leave the scene of a two-totaled–car accident to go play tennis?"

"Yes, Officer, that is correct. This is probably the biggest match of my life and I trust law enforcement to handle this properly."

As I gave him my contact, Graydon pulled over with Lindsey, who, upon seeing her car wrecked and reminded of the tragic accident from her childhood, absolutely lost it. Tears, on her knees, total melt-down. There wasn't a lot we could do other than try to support her. I remember looking over at the Old Man, who was looking at us like, "Who the hell did I run into?" We didn't exactly fit in with most of the other Illinois farming community.

The officer, thankfully, was very understanding and accommodating. He quickly took my statement and said, "If you need to go, I can call you later and wrap up the rest of this. But someone needs to stay at the scene."

Well, I couldn't stay, Lindsey certainly wasn't going to stay, and Graydon needed to drive me (as fast as he could), so it was left to Phil.

Poor Phil. This is what he gets for talking so much. Now you can talk to the cop on our behalf, Phil, thanks.[3]

The trip to Decatur in Graydon's Mustang was no picnic either. I was crammed in the backseat with all my tennis stuff, it was nearly ten a.m., my match start time, and Lindsey was still hyperventilating, having a flashback of her mother's death. All the while I'm as quietly and calmly as possible telling Graydon to *speed up*. I still had the ringing in my ears that accompanies any car accident. Who's ready to play some tennis?

We pull into the courts and, as I kind of expected, it was a shit show as well. I mean, for a player to not show up to his first-round match is extremely uncommon. It also throws off the entire logistics of the tournament and draw. If it's the first round of a tournament, and a player defaults from the first round (as I was close to doing), that players spot is given to a "Lucky Loser," someone who lost last round qualifying. So, most people at the tournament were happy to see me show up, although confused as to why I was so late, but there were also some people that were disappointed to learn I was there—the Lucky Loser himself, his girlfriend, coach, etc. He just went from not in the tournament to in the tournament to back not in the tournament.

I was late, and I was penalized, but I could still play the match. Thank god. The umpire, who was annoyed at me for some reason, informed me that I lost the opportunity to warm up, lost the toss (choice of serving or side), and also went down 2–0 in the first set. Without even hitting a ball. Keep in mind these were short sets, so it was a bad punishment, but still okay considering thirty-five minutes ago I was standing in the middle of a highway picking metal and glass out of my hands and neck.

---

3   I recently reached out to Phil and he reminded me that not only did he stay at the scene of the accident, but he actually stayed there after the Old Man and cop left. He called Craig, our head coach, to come pick him up, but Craig refused, afraid of violating an NCAA rule, transporting an athlete in the off season. He had previously been sanctioned for driving one of his athletes to see his sick father in the hospital and if he got sanctioned again it would be really bad for him and the program. Phil was stuck standing in the middle of I-72, and had to hitchhike back to Champaign.

Gossip around the tournament was spreading, I could hear it: "This guy was *just* in a car accident." I tried my best to calm myself down, shake off the accident, swing my arms a little bit (they were tight, so was my neck and I had a headache.) Upon meeting Jack, my opponent, I said, "Sorry about all this and to keep you waiting."

He was a gentleman and replied, "I'm sorry you had to go through this, but happy you are OK."

I smiled. Despite all this shit I was still excited to execute my game plan against him. I mean, "the show must go on," right?

I ran to my side of the court. The umpire announced the match and then, which was odd, he announced the score, given we hadn't hit a ball yet: "Mr. Brasington leads 2–0."

Jack lined up to serve, missed, and hit a second serve that plopped off his racket so slow and weak I almost fell over laughing. I let my experience take over and I returned his weak shitty serve up the line, and came to net. Jack looked at me like I was an absolute crazy person, like he couldn't believe his eyes. "Is this guy coming to net on the first point after getting into a serious car accident?" He ran to my shot, he was clearly uncomfortable, tried to pass me at net, missed wildly and eighty-five minutes later I had won the match 4–2 4–1 5–3.

"Game. Set. Match, Mr. Kosta."

Holy shit I did it, I just earned my first ATP point. The tournament director came up to me and said, "Congratulations, you are now officially on the ATP computer."

"Thanks," I said and just like Lindsey's car, my life would never be the same.

. . .

Your first ATP point is comparable to your first real TV credit as a comic. Even if you die the next day, your obituary will at least have something in it. The comedy poster will at least have one logo on it

("Michael Kosta from whatever TV show" is comparable to "Michael Kosta #1250"). You didn't die a total loser, at least.

A year later, I was gearing up for my senior year at Illinois. I had 2 ATP points (I can't tell you anything about when I earned my second point; like I said, you remember the first). The US Open had started and a bunch of players were coming over to watch the night matches on TV. As people filed in, I turned on the TV for the men's second round match. Andy Roddick vs Jack Brasington. "Hey, Kosta . . . why aren't you out there right now?" someone said.

"Let's hope his second serve has improved," I said as I cracked open a beer with my friends and watched the match. It had. We then sat and watched Jack lose to Roddick in four sets in a competitive match. Amazing difference a year can make.

• • •

Before I knew it, I had blinked and found myself at my last NCAA championships in College Station, Texas. It was early summer 2002, Illinois was ranked #3 in the country and one of the favorites to win the NCAA team championships. I was playing #4 singles, #3 doubles, and was having a decent year. College tennis was coming to an end, and I was seemingly more focused on the next phase of my life (pros) before the current one (college) was over.

The night before we played USC in the quarterfinals of the NCAA's I stayed up handwriting letters to potential investors in my soon-to-be-pro tennis career. The next day I played a beyond terrible match and finished my college career with a 6–0 6–1 loss. Ouch. Nothing like a painful, debilitating loss to prepare me for the next phase of my life: pro tennis.[4]

---

4   The guy I lost to is now a failed and banned poker player who was accused of running multiple cons in the Las Vegas area. He hasn't been seen since 2011.

Two days later, armed with my 2 ATP points and a world ranking somewhere around #1100, I hopped on a flight to play a $10,000 Future in Mexico. My tennis bag still had my NCAA credential on it, but I was officially a brand-new pro. The days of Illinois paying for everything was over, it was on me now, which leads to the very important question: How did I pay for this?

Tennis is not cheap. You need money. The United States Tennis Association gave me zero dollars. Prince Rackets gave me zero dollars. Nike gave me zero dollars. I paid for my clothes, my travel, my hotel, my food, etc. And when I say "I" I mean, my investors.

My dad was done paying for my tennis. He stopped once I went to college on a scholarship. He paid the bill on junior tennis and that was not a small bill. But what my dad did do—which was so great and wonderful and such a lesson for me and anyone who is or wants to be a dad—is he helped me raise the money that I needed. We set up an LLC and I offered shares of my future prize money earnings for sale. It was $5,000 for one share of Michael Kosta's professional career. We had a ten-year plan of how the money would be paid out (i.e., for the first couple of years I gave them fifty percent of my prize money, and that number lowered as the years advanced).

I contacted everyone I knew that I thought had money and or would also be interested in helping a pro tennis player tackle a seemingly impossible task: making it as a pro tennis player. We were honest about the risks involved but also sold it as an opportunity to help a great tennis player potentially achieve something wonderful. I had friends who were on the tour who certainly weren't household names but had made a decent living over ten years and had done the same thing and paid back the money, and sometimes paid back plus some handsome earnings.

We raised $176,000. That's what I used to play this whole time. Sounds like a lot of money, but consider that a full-time coach would expect $75,000 to $100,000 a year (minimal). That's why I chose not to have a coach. When I was out on tour, I met a lot of kids who had their dad's credit card and they spent it like it was fashionable. Every time I used that investor credit card, I thought about the roughly twenty people who had invested money in me and my career. I thought about them when I didn't want to practice.

I thought about them when I lost a big match and also when I won a big match. Tennis is an individual sport but the only way I was able to do this was through the generosity and help of those investors. We did pay some of the money back, but not all. When I finally decided to stop playing tennis, I even had some investors say "Do you need more money? Do you need more time? We believe in you."

I will never forget that and always appreciate those men and women so much. Thank you from the bottom of my heart. Also, Dad, great call. Great parenting on that one. You didn't give me anything for free, but you helped me get in a position for success, that's all I can ask for.

Thursday June 14

Dear Dad

I think its time for me to get a allowance, I work around the house alot and I don't get money. I also think its time because I'm old enough and I should handle money. If Todd, Kristy, and John want an allowance too I would be happy to buy them things. We could talk about how much it is.

Please think about it

michael Kosta

Chapter 15

Tokyo Hospitality

ELEVEN MONTHS LATER, I had 13 ATP points and a world singles ranking of #864.[1]

This ranking afforded me some new privileges, as I could now enter and usually get directly into the main draw of tournaments, instead of having to play the qualifying. This is a huge advantage. Fewer matches, more important matches for guaranteed money. I could fly somewhere, knowing I was already in the main draw, receive a free hotel room (for the main draw players only), and even if I lost first round, I could make anywhere from $150 to $200. It's not a lot of money but it's still better than having to win three rounds of qualifying just to make it into the main draw, pay for my own hotel room for those nights, and by the time I do qualify (if in fact I do) my shoulder hurts, I have diarrhea, or whatever.

In order to take advantage of my new career high ranking of #864,

---

1   Turns out this would be my career high singles ranking and remains my email signature. I'm very proud of this. Most people laugh when they hear my career high, and I always say, "What was your career high professional athletic ranking?" It is funny, though, I get it. It's not the number most people are expecting to hear. A three-digit number that starts with "8" isn't exactly bragging material, but it's tough to get there, of that I am sure.

I entered as many tournaments as I could. It was the early 2000s, so entering tournaments meant literally faxing an entry form to the International Tennis Federation (ITF) in London with a note about which tournaments you were trying to enter. This was ridiculously time consuming, often expensive, and didn't always work. Several times I had a confirmation from the Kinkos guy who faxed it to London for $12 and then two weeks later when I wouldn't see my name on the list and the deadline passed I would call London for another $12 and they would say in their stupid accent, "Sorry mate, we never got it." There's one week down the drain thanks to a faxing error. I'm not sure Pete Sampras ever had to encounter that in his career.

The only caveat worth noting is that the rules were if you entered a tournament and you got in, you had to go. If you didn't show up, you got fined and your standing with the ITF would be jeopardized.

At this point in my career, I was looking for a hard-court tournament where I would get in the main draw. USA and Canada were long shots with my ranking. Nigeria and Jamaica were pretty likely, but I had heard those were tough places to play (infrastructure, referee issues, travel nightmares, etc.). So, I took my chances with a five-week Japan/Korea run. It wasn't perfect—one of the weeks in Korea would be on clay—but I figured I would enter and see where I got in. It's not like the Koreans were known to be amazing on clay or anything. In the sport of tennis, they weren't really known to be good on anything, to be frank.

I faxed my forms over to London and waited a few weeks to see what happened. To review, there were five weeks of tournaments, four on hard, one on clay, I entered all of them. When the results came back, it was a bit of a mixed bag. I got into three main draw events (this was wonderful) and didn't get into two (which means I would have to play qualifying for those events, not ideal but could be OK considering I got main draw into the other events).

So I planned my trip to Asia. I reached out to a few other tennis buds and we organized a decent group of guys who were also playing tennis at the time, close to the same level as me. One was a guy who played at Notre Dame, let's call him Smith, and the other was a University of Michigan grad, let's call him Hank. I decided to travel with a University of Illinois player and friend named Oli, who was British. Oli was ranked a lot higher than me and was nice enough to agree to play doubles with me during the run (at this point my doubles ranking was in the 500s to 600s).

The plan was to meet Oli in Tokyo and spend five or six days there to get acclimated to the time and culture before heading to our first tournament. We were hosted by this wonderful Canadian guy named Hubert, who was the head pro at a club in Tokyo and had arranged practice and accommodations for us for the days we were there.

My understanding was that we were going to stay at the same place each night, like have a base camp somewhere, but the way Hubert organized it was "Hey, club members, who wants to host a famous American tennis player for a night?" And then five different families jumped up and said "we do, we do," so each day I had to pack up my shit and head to a new house, with new people and stay with them. Kind of like checking in and out of the Motel 6 in Milwaukee.

Oli and I stayed at different houses each night, separate from each other. It was nice for Hubert to arrange it all, but it was cumbersome and annoying—and once you mix in the social etiquette of Japan, it was a pain in the ass. It was not only expected but required that you brought each family a gift, that you had a long dinner with them, breakfast with them, follow the norms of the house, which differ from house to house and also totally hinge on what the father does. You're constantly watching the father to see if it's OK to laugh, OK to taste the food, OK to go to bed. Also did I mention that nobody spoke English?

The first night I stayed in a wonderful house with a wonderful family. The father was American and the wife was Japanese. It got worse from there. The second night Hubert dropped me off at the new house and family right after practice. I was starving. The kind of starving that only athletes get right after a practice, like you could eat a whole horse with your bare hands. I came to this new home, I bowed my ass off to everyone, I gave them a gift (coffee mugs I think), I played with the kid, and then we all waited for the father to come home so we could eat. Apparently in Japan, you can't leave the office until your superior leaves the office. If your boss is there, you are there. And tonight, of all nights, the head of the whole goddamn office decided he was staying late. So everyone was staying late. (And you wonder why they have something called occupational sudden mortality aka Karoshi: people just suddenly die from overworking.)

At around ten p.m., I finally wandered into the kitchen and grabbed a few sesame crackers. The head honcho himself finally walked in around eleven p.m. More bowing and gifts and finally we sat down to eat. By this point, the kid was sound asleep.

The third night really took the cake (I think maybe Hubert was trying to slowly wear us down. So that we would never come back to Japan?). This was a wonderful family with two very young children. Their house was . . . small. Very small. This family was rich in their generosity, rich in their attitude, rich in their desire to help others, but they were poor in their finances. Am I making myself clear here? Look, I prefer poor people to rich people. They are nicer, more fun, they understand what's important in life, but when it comes to whose house I would rather stay at, a poor family or a rich family? I think we all know the answer.

Unlike the night before, when I showed up to this house, dinner was already on the table. It was one of those tiny tables, where you sit on the ground. The family watched me, their six-foot-four American guest, awkwardly try to contort my body into a cross-legged position between the six-inch opening between the table and floor, and politely covered their mouths with their hands as they laughed.

This family was so wonderful, I can't emphasize that enough. They were so generous with the food and hospitality, they made me cake with a tennis racket on it for dessert, they had the smallest salad and they basically gave all of it to me, they sang me a song. They kept asking me if I wanted to go to bed (not in English, they kept doing the international sleeping hands move) and I kept saying "I'm OK" trying not to be rude, but hell yeah, I wanted to go to bed. I wanted to go upstairs, shut the door and read my book and wake up and move on to the next place.

After playing another two hours of basic communication charades, I acted out "bedtime" and as soon as I did, the father picked up the kitchen table, the mom laid a mat down where we were just eating, the daughter ran upstairs and came down with sheets and bedding and within minutes, there was a full bed formed on the kitchen floor. They waved goodnight, went upstairs and I was alone, on the kitchen floor with all the lights out. It was remarkable. It was also like nine-thirty p.m.

That night I lay in "bed" wondering exactly how I should take a piss. I mean the house was impeccably clean, as every Japanese house was. My guess was that they had a one-bedroom apartment and the bedroom, which also had the bathroom, was probably where everyone slept. Four people in a bedroom that also had the bathroom. So I wasn't about to bust into the bedroom which had the bathroom and also four people sleeping and take a piss. I was going to hold it . . . for the next ten hours. And that's what I did.

The next morning the mother and the son came down and quietly woke me up. At that point I had to piss so badly I was almost hallucinating. I had reached a point where in a weird way it started to feel good. You know how people say that when you are dying of hypothermia the last thing you feel is complete and utter warmth? That's kind of where I was. I had to piss so badly that it had crossed over and felt like I was tripping on happy LSD. When I was finally shown to the bathroom, it was, as expected, in the only bedroom, which was smaller than the dorm room I had at University of Illinois. I urinated for about twenty minutes and when I came back downstairs my bed was gone and the kitchen table was filled with breakfast. The Japanese are unbelievably quiet. It's nearly magical. I swear to god I didn't entirely understand how the USA was caught so off guard at Pearl Harbor until I traveled to Japan and realized how quiet they can be.

That morning was a Saturday (not the first or last time I had spent my Friday night sleeping on a kitchen floor), and I was supposed to be at the courts at eight a.m. to help teach a kids tennis class for the club. Hubert had arranged for Oli and me to run a kids clinic as a thank-you for having us at the club all week. We didn't remember saying yes to this idea, but here I was in a car on the way to the courts.

The kids' session was set to start at eight a.m., and when I got to the courts around seven-thirty a.m., I found Oli and we both started bitching about our nights and lack of sleep and cultural shit blah blah blah. It's safe to say we were ready to get into a hotel and start competing and stop doing what felt like a little bit of a USA/England/Japan official state visit. I'm a tennis player not a diplomat, I wanted to get out there and compete.

At seven forty-five a.m., I looked out at the courts and what did I see but thirty kids, under the age of ten, dressed in tennis gear, sitting in a circle, legs crossed, eyes closed, meditating. Completely silent. Read what I just wrote again. There was one instructor slowly walking around the children guiding their meditation. Oli and I were floored. I have coached thousands of hours of tennis for every single age and gender at this point in my life, I had never seen anything like this. Not only were these children fifteen minutes early, they were quiet, ready, and properly dressed. It was remarkable.

Teaching American children goes like this: Half the kids are late, the parents have excuses why they are late. The other half of the kids are wearing jeans and the parents have excuses why they don't have shorts. The kids don't listen to any of the instructions. They talk when you talk. They complain when you tell them what to do, or more typically, they tell their parents that they don't like what you are making them do. As a coach you are constantly repeating the instructions for the drill over and over.

Teaching Japanese kids was completely the opposite. Not only did they do exactly what I asked the first time I asked it, they were receiving my instructions from a translator—they were only nine years old.

When the kids' session ended, we took pictures and shook hands (more bowing). I was truly touched and inspired by their professionalism, kindness, and behavior. Three hours ago, I was lying on a stranger's kitchen floor wondering how I could get out of this obligation, and now I was sticking around chatting with Japanese parents and kids, trying to learn from them. Another experience created through travel that made me a better person, despite the fact that if given the choice I would have one hundred percent said, "No thank you."

Oli and I floated through the rest of the day and had a couple of good practices. We were in good spirits and ready to head to our first tournament in a few days. That feeling of excitement ended when Hubert came into the locker room and told us that our housing fell through for the night but it's OK, he had his assistant go buy three cots and we could sleep in the boardroom upstairs.

Wonderful.

After a completely sleepless night on a cot made for a Japanese child, inside of a half lit Japanese Tennis Club boardroom, Oli and I were ready to get the hell out of Dodge and start competing for real.

In all, the five weeks of this Asian tour have all kind of blended together for me. I can remember strange cultural details, like eating 7-Eleven sushi, which was quite good, but for the most part, I can't remember what city that was in or even who I played or how I did. The internet isn't particularly helpful either in piecing together what cities we were in or our results (it's hard to find details about things that happened before the internet was what it is now). I remember needing to learn the words for "rice" and "water" so I could at least ask for both of those instead of eating something random off a menu I could not decipher. I remember walking into a small video store and then finding two secret little saloon doors in the back that opened into the biggest, most exclusive porn section I have ever seen anywhere. I quickly learned that each video store had these same two secret doors. I remember watching Japanese porn and being totally dumbfounded at what the men must have been turned on by (this was before internet porn was what it is now). I remember noticing that vending machines in train stations sold underwear and hot green tea. I remember giving a hotel clerk my credit card and instead of handing it back to me, she walked all the way around the desk and put it on a silver tray and bowed it over to me. I remember thinking that Japanese culture was completely opposite of American culture. I remember immediately noticing how different South Korea was from Japan. And I remember realizing "Oh these two countries hate each other." That's when I learned about the long history they had and how much Koreans despise Japan mainly for what Japan did to them during WW2 (forced labor, war crimes, google the term "comfort women" for a super messed up Wikipedia page). South Korea, at least to me, definitely had more personality, more grit, less money. Their tennis tournaments were definitely less advanced.

Ultimately, I remember flying home to the US after this trip and realizing that I would never be the same again. I had experienced a part of the world that was so unique and different from my own home that it would be impossible to be the same person afterward. When people ask me about the trip now, I tell them all of this. As for my memories of playing tennis (why I was there), there were highs, and vivid lows.

The first tournament gave Oli and me a good taste of what was ahead. After our sleepless night at the club, Hubert stopped by to give us directions for the ninety-minute bullet train ride to the courts, which somehow was still considered a part of Tokyo, which should give you an indication of the size of the city—a ninety-minute train ride out of Tokyo and we were still in Tokyo.

Hubert wrote the name of our stop down on a piece of paper in Japanese. The train stops were in both Japanese *and* English around the city center of Tokyo, but further out, it was just Japanese—which obviously made it a lot tougher. Around eighty minutes into the train ride, we started to look at the signs and look at the piece of paper Hubert gave us and try to distinguish, within the fifteen seconds the train doors opened, if we should get off or not. It went something like this:

ME: OK, Oli, what does this stop's sign look like? <doors open>
OLI: Two triangles, two slashes, a circle <doors begin to close> and a squiggly.
ME: OK this one is not our stop. We are looking for three slashes, two circles, a smaller triangle, and an oval-looking shape with a dot in the middle.

This happened about five or six times and got progressively more stressful. It reminded me of a board game I used to play as a kid with my mom, where you had to try and match different shapes on cards to other different shapes on cards. It was a test of both memory and card location (I think the TV version was called *Concentration* and it was hosted by a much younger and "hipper" Alex Trebek). It was exactly what Oli and I were doing fifteen years later as grown-ups on the Japanese train. Another life skill I acquired thanks to good parenting.

Oli and I eventually found our stop ("That's it, go! go! go!" I yelled as the doors shut). We were on our way. People kept stopping us and asking for pictures. I guess because we were tall and white and carrying tennis bags? I don't know. I mean it's not like TV hadn't been invented yet, but somewhere in Japan a bunch of people have pictures of us at train stations, coffee shops, and eating lunch.

Upon checking into the hotel, we were immediately surprised at the price—$240 a night. Suddenly, Oli and I missed the free kitchen floor we had just left. We shook it off, then connected with our other Western friends, Hank and Smith, and had dinner. Because Smith had graduated from Notre Dame, he was able to tap into the Global Alumni Association and actually secure himself housing while at this tournament in a nearby Tokyo suburb. When I asked Hank where he was staying, he said, "With you two, I thought."

Oli looked at me and raised his eyebrows. Huh.

I wasn't going to let my fellow American sleep at the train station (which would have been cleaner than ninety-five percent of Americans homes, by the way) so I told him to come up to the room. There were two beds for three grown men, but as we were all on a budget, we decided to split the room three ways and determine who slept on the floor based on who was scheduled to play when. If you had a match the next day, you got a bed. If you had the day off, you take the floor.

The next day was a practice day, so we drew straws, and I got the floor. You would think Hank might opt for the floor considering we made the reservation, put our credit cards down, and checked in, but that's not how it went down. How it went down was I called the front desk and asked for an extra pillow.

The lasting story of the tournament didn't end up being our results. I remember I won a round in singles (that's one ATP point and a few extra hundred bucks).

Oli was in the tournament the longest, which was unsurprising, as he was the best player. Smith lost early (call it Tuesday). On Wednesday morning Hank, Oli, and I were on the court warming up for our matches and we saw a taxicab pull up next to the courts. The driver popped out, opened the trunk, took out a bunch of bags, and Smith waddled out of the taxi and dragged his bags over to our court. What happened to his housing? We were all a little confused, but we had matches to get ready for, so we weren't too worried about Smith; he was a grown man, after all.

I lost. Hank lost. Smith had already lost. It sucks to lose (duh) but this was a good week. I had made some money, I was with some friends, and it was only the first week. When you have only 13 ATP points, earning just one is helpful and it certainly made me glad I had decided to come to Japan where the competition was a little weaker and the hard courts suit my game. I had improved my world ranking by about ten percent. So we were all in pretty good moods.

Hank said to me, "Let's go get lunch with Smith and find out why he has all his bags with him."

Smith smiled sheepishly and we walked over to the clubhouse cafe, which besides having noodles did offer a western breakfast so that's what we went with naturally.

So over runny eggs served with limp bacon and white rice (what? yeah), Smith explained the reason he had his bags with him was because he was kicked out of his housing. How does one get kicked out of their housing when the housing is proud to be a supporter of Notre Dame alumni and also *volunteered* to house you in the first place? Something terrible must have happened. And by terrible I mean terribly funny.

Turns out that Smith wasn't just staying with the mom and dad of the house but also their twenty-year-old Indiana University sophomore daughter, who just happened to be visiting her parents for the summer in Tokyo and, according to Smith, just happened to appreciate the company of a young male professional tennis player, who just happened to be sleeping five feet down the hall. The story was, they had some wine with family dinner, the parents went to sleep, the attractive Kappa Alpha Theta suggested she and Smith take it to the next level, two consenting adults sharing their common love for the state of Indiana through physical touch while in a very foreign land.

Smith says to us as we slurp down sloppy eggs, "I use a condom, I throw it in the guest bathroom trash can, she sneaks down the hall to her room, everyone wins, right?" We are laughing. Cleary something isn't "right." I mean, here is Smith telling us this with his bags next to him.

"So . . . why are your bags here right now?" Hank asks the obvious question.

Smith: "So this morning, I'm having breakfast with the family. The daughter and I share a smile, everything is fine. All of a sudden, we hear the dog start yacking in the other room. He keeps doing it over and over again, it's annoying. The mom brings the dog into the kitchen, the dog is really struggling. The father reaches into the dog's mouth and pulls out . . . the condom. My condom! The only used condom in the house. The fucking dog, rummaged through the trash can in the guest bedroom and found the condom and ate it!"

Hank and I spit out our eggs. Smith follows up "So . . . can I stay with you guys?"

We were floored. I had never heard a story like that and haven't heard one since. Hank and I sat at the restaurant table totally dumbfounded and silent. Eventually Smith said, "Say something, guys," and we looked at each other, tried to speak, and nothing came out.

Meanwhile, Oli won his match. We were happy for him but it certainly made it more difficult for him because he was sharing a room with three other people who were not in the tournament. Could we have probably gotten another hotel room? Most likely. Would I have done that now? Of course. Are there other tennis players reading this that are thinking, "Hey dumbasses, this is your profession, spend the extra $300 on a proper night's sleep." That would have been the right decision. But it isn't what happened.

The next day Oli lost with the three of us cheering him on. Smith, who had settled down a lot since being kicked out of his guest housing, was back to his normal self. Let's be honest, he had a great story for the rest of his life. So did we. I may have even said at one point, "This should be in a book."

Oli came off the court with his typical smooth British smile on his face. He had played well but lost to a better player. "Anyone want to get drunk and go into Tokyo tonight?" he said.

"We were hoping you would say that," I said, and we all walked back to our hotel room together. We had four days until the next tournament.

• • •

Hank had a Japanese friend and it was a huge help. It always helps knowing someone from the area (Sun Tzu in the *Art of War*: "Never underestimate the importance of a local guide"), but it helps the most when you are looking for a fun place to get drunk that has girls. We were twenty-year-old men, girls were important to us. If you are just figuring that out right now, where have you been?

We had a couple beers in the hotel room and then we met up with our local guide, Peter, who lived in Tokyo, spoke perfect Japanese and English, and was very nice and fun and immediately fit right in. We were investing our entire night into Peter and his local knowledge. It was the right thing to do and, really, we had no choice. We knew absolutely nothing about Tokyo nightlife.

I have a wonderful memory of the five of us, Peter, Oli, Smith, Hank, and I sitting outside under streetlights drinking beers and smoking cigarettes waiting for the train. It was one of those moments that comes and goes so quickly but has stayed with me forever. What I wouldn't give to go back to that time right now. To be twenty-something years old, with your buddies, a little drunk, and about to head into a world-renowned city for the first time . . . it felt like we were about to shoot off to the moon or something. As with every night out, the beginning is always the best time. Everyone together, no one too drunk, enjoying each other's company without muddled bar noise or competition of chasing girls.

But we didn't know that then, then we were always in a rush to *get* somewhere. Old people are never in a rush. They know, once they get there, it's not as fun. Getting there is the fun. Young people, slow down, enjoy the journey.

Peter wrote down our train stop in Japanese on four different pieces of paper and handed it to each of us. "Once we get into town, it can get a little nuts, always good to have this on you so you can get home," he said.

"We're not gonna split up or anything man, we'll be fine," someone said.

Peter laughed like he knew something we didn't and just said, "Better just hold on to that."

He was right. We cracked open another beer and Peter said, "Better make this the last one, the train will be here in twenty minutes." I can remember this moment like it was yesterday. Five beers cracked open with that tremendous sound and we sat outside, under the elevated train platform listening to Tokyo from a distance, about to enter a world we knew nothing about.

Chapter 16

An American Bar in Tokyo

PETER WAS NOT only right about it being a little nuts—he was really A-plus, one hundred percent right. We walked out of the train stop and *wham* were hit in the face with Tokyo. Goddamn, Tokyo! I have never in all my life seen such busyness. It was like my brain was on every drug imaginable at once. It's hard to even breathe when you see it all. It's like every color, noise, action, intensity, smell, feeling, all hitting you at the same time. I patted the pocket where I placed the paper from Peter, like gripping a security blanket. It felt like looking back to your home before sailing off into the night.

Some people are good city guides, some people are bad city guides—Peter was an excellent city guide. If he isn't working in the hospitality field right now, it's a shame. This guy took us on a little trip through Tokyo, through shopping malls, restaurants, strip clubs, karaoke bars, and everywhere in between. Years later, when I first saw the Bill Murray movie *Lost in Translation*, I felt like they copied our evening experience for the movie. It's just *nuts*. It's totally out there. It's like this magnetic field of energy and the entire country got sucked into it, everything that had any personality got sucked up into Tokyo nightlife.

The first bar Peter took us to was an American-themed country bar. "Why would you take real Americans to a fake American country bar?" I thought. And then we walked in. There wasn't a jukebox but if there was it would have stopped playing music immediately. Four tall white males walk in (with one medium-sized Japanese guy) and the place just turned and stared at us. Girls literally started giggling. Hordes of people surrounded us, trying to talk to us, take our picture, touch us. The staff from the bar was bowing to us with the prayer hands. It made no sense. This was year 2000ish, clearly they had seen Americans or been visited by Americans before. I didn't get it, but I also didn't give a shit. We were drunk, looking for a good time, and Peter took us to a place that seemed to actually *worship* our kind. I was A-OK with that.

We had stepped maybe three feet into the bar before we were stopped by women wanting to talk to us, touch us (not a joke), take our picture. Oli and I started talking to two girls over very loud country music, they both were wearing, and I am not joking, school-girl outfits. White button down, short skirt. This place was apparently so influenced by American culture that all the girls decide to just dress like Britney Spears from the 1999 *Rolling Stone* cover. When one of the girls finally listened to Oli speak and realized he had an English accent. Her face got flush, and she collapsed, not a joke. Her friend picked her up and fanned her off and they were giggling and giggling together.

Smith and Hank were gone and I didn't see them until the next day.

So there we were, Peter, Oli, and I talking to these two attractive women dressed as my literal porn fantasy and behind them was a line of other women waiting to talk to us. It was like a celebrity line, wait here to take a picture or touch the tall white round-eye guys. Peter was acting more like our handler, moving us around, making sure the whole bar saw us, ordering us drinks, translating. Clearly he knew what we had walked into, and thank god because we did not. I've had a few (emphasis on few) celebrity moments in my day, nothing, nothing even comes close to the reaction the #864 (me) and #641 (Oli) ranked tennis players in the world in year 200whatever received when walking into this Tokyo American country bar.

One of the girls (cute? I hope? I think? Let's say yes) grabbed my arm and pulled me away from everyone. I waved goodbye to Oli and Peter and that was the last I saw of them. Just like that, in a matter of thirty minutes, we were split up.

Now, many years later, the part of the night that I value the most was just the guys and our time together under the train tracks, drinking, smoking, telling stories about our lives and where we came from. Those people were and still are important to me. I still see those men and we reminisce about that time. We're all married, some have kids and real jobs, life continued quickly after this night, but what we wouldn't give to go back to that evening and relish that moment more. Maybe instead of saying "Hurry up, the train will be here in twenty minutes" we would say "Let's get the next train, or the one after that." But that's life, right? You can't do that. You can't go back. You can only hope you learned from that time and apply it to the present time or a future time. There is also the argument that the reason we value that time together so much was *because* we got on the train twenty minutes later. The time was so valuable because it was short. OK, enough mushy stuff, all that wonderful friendship stuff is great but what happened next at the bar isn't exactly a terrible memory either.

As I watched Peter and Oli fade off into the Tokyo American country bar night, I let myself be led into the unknown by a Japanese woman I had met three minutes earlier. She didn't speak English; I didn't speak Japanese. My friends were gone; her friends were gone. We were in a crowded bar, where it was difficult to hear each other, but we didn't really have anything to say. What was I going to say? "So you enjoying living in Tokyo? Do you live in Tokyo? Who are you? What is going on?"

Fortunately, I was overthinking it. It turned out she wasn't too concerned about talking. She took my hand and led me to one of those secret side bathrooms that every bar has, that only locals know about. I remember the door was all wooden and there were American sports pennants hanging up on the wall all around. But not real ones, not "Cubs" and "Seahawks" but ones that literally said "Sports," "Happy," "Fun Times." Just random basic American English words. I mean, does it matter? If you went to a Japanese bar in America and saw a poster of a sumo wrestler and it had Japanese words written beneath it, would you know that it really said "Happy" or "Beer time" on it? This bar was smart, they got to post baseball pennants up without having to ask the MLB for permission.

This bar was a wonderful stereotype of America. I remember there was a framed picture of George W. Bush on the wall (duh, every American bar has that). I was in a strange hormonal dream state; as I held hands with my new friend, I was vaguely noticing all these oddities surrounding me: they poured Japanese beer but into a Budweiser Cup, oh wait that's not the Bud Logo just a cheap knock-off, is this girl cute I can't even—holy shit a poster from the movie *Goonies*.

She closed the bathroom door and I remember a bartender looking at us and not doing anything or not caring at all (maybe he'd seen this before?). And she pulled me into the single bathroom and slid the lock into position, *click*. There was a sink facing the door with a mirror above it, the toilet was to our left and signatures and graffiti were all over the bathroom walls (you know, how they are in every American bar). I was beginning to see that this woman wasn't too concerned about chatting over the music either, or that there was a language barrier, or that you don't have sex on the first date or that her friends are looking for her or that—she faced the mirror, got on tiptoes, and lifted her skirt up. I was behind her looking at her in the mirror. She put her left hand around me to move me closer to her and put her right hand flat on the mirror. It happened so fast that (1) I was certain this was all too good to be true, and (2) I wasn't even close to having an erection. I mean, sex? Yes, of course, but even I need a few moments to get in the mood and despite how sexual I may have been at this point in my life, I just saw a poster of George Walker Bush, so I'm not exactly rock hard right now.

We kissed for a little, I put my hands on her body, everything felt good. Her skin was really soft and Japanese. I'm not sure what that means but I'm sticking to it. Probably two minutes of heavy petting passed and then we were ready to go. What I'm trying to say is this was not an Amsterdam forty percent boner situation. She went back to her original position and I unbuttoned my jeans and we started the process that is called copulation. We couldn't communicate but eighty percent of a message is nonverbal and we were definitely expressing ourselves nonverbally.

This lasted thirty to sixty seconds? But I would also say that these thirty to sixty seconds has been the most replayed thirty to sixty seconds of my life. Look, I'm a skeptic. That's why I'm a comic. I question what other people don't, I don't trust what other people do, my job and my skill is that I usually realize something isn't as good as it was meant to be or is said to be. However, sometimes the stars align. Sometimes you win easily against a tough opponent. It's important to cherish those moments and take those wins. That was my mindset in this bathroom.

I remember she kept acting like I was punishing her so badly. Like I was this giant Tyrannosaurus rex or something and she was being sooo submissive and naughty. Dominance and submission are a big part of this culture, I take it. Watch some Japanese porn and you tell me what the fuck is going on. It's really different stuff, man.

Anyways, I came inside the schoolgirl-dressed Japanese woman that I had just met six and a half minutes ago in a Tokyo American-themed country bar side-stall bathroom. She got off her tippy toes, landed on her heels, pulled her skirt down, and kissed me on the lips and said something in Japanese (to this day I wonder what exactly did she tell me?). We haphazardly washed up in the sink, heard a knocking on the door and walked out.

I remember passing a bunch of people on the way out that were waiting for the bathroom. There was a line. A couple dudes were looking at me like I was an asshole and the girls were all pissed because they had to wait. I tried to act cool but it was pretty obvious what had happened. Everyone hates waiting in line for a bathroom that is being occupied for something other than using the toilet, although because of this moment I can't exactly fault someone when I'm the one waiting in line now. It's happened a few times where I am standing there trying not to piss myself and I finally see a man and a woman pop out of the restroom and I can't *not* look at them and think, "Well, I deserve this, that was me twenty years ago in Tokyo. I wonder what she is doing now?"

That's the last I saw of her . . . I looked around for my friends, they were gone. The girl was gone. I was drunk, in Tokyo, I just had sex.

What a difference thirty minutes makes. Half an hour ago I had friends, a guide, confidence. Now, I was alone, in what appeared to be the biggest city in the world, and I had absolutely no clue what to do. I assumed my friends got caught up in the moment just like I did, and they were somewhere else right now figuring out what to do next or having sex in a bathroom or dancing with strangers or getting arrested by Japanese police. Whatever the case was, they were gone, no cell phones, no way to connect, the only thing I had in my pocket was the name of my hotel and train stop.

I was on too much of a high to go home. Certainly if we just walked into a bar and were that well received, I could walk into a different bar and be equally well received, right? Wrong. I entered another bar, saw people look at me and then look away as if "yikes, what is *he* doing here?" I tried another place. And another place. I went to a lounge and sat in a plush couch, a server came over and started yelling at me.

Normally when an evening is starting to become crappy I follow this simple rule, which usually helps: Have more to drink.

I downed three more beers. I sat and watched. Wonderful people watching. From the outside looking in, Tokyo is like the most intense video game you've ever seen, and I was right there on the sideline. I remember looking up at all the light and electronic billboards and I started to notice that the boards were beginning to turn off. The sun was slowly creeping up. Wow that went fast.

I walked to a train station, found the train, and started the process of getting home to my stop and my hotel. It took about an hour (thank god for that piece of paper, thanks Peter). I had to walk past the tennis courts to get to the hotel. Two days ago, I was *in that* tournament, now the players were warming up for the final. I hadn't gone to bed yet and was still definitely drunk. I walked past those courts quickly with my head down trying not to see the tournament director, coaches, and other players. When I walked into the lobby of the hotel, it was busy with check-outs, breakfast, business.

When I walked into the hotel room it was probably seven a.m. Oli was asleep in one of the beds. Hank and Smith were not. I crawled into bed. An hour later I heard the door open and two drunk asses walked in talking way too loud. We said hi briefly and laughed, and then we all went to sleep for nine hours.

• • •

Did this level of partying affect our tennis? Yes, yes it probably did. But there are a few things to remember:

We were in the best shape of our lives, our bodies recovered pretty

quickly from this type of behavior. Now, it takes me five days to recover from a night out. Back then, a long nap usually did it.

We felt a lot of stress and pressure. This was the easiest way that
we knew how to disperse that pressure. We were all high achievers,
accomplished tennis players, we all were the best in our region growing up and most likely the best in our region *ever*. We were used to
winning and expected to win and had people in our lives who expected us to win. So . . . when you lose over and over again in the pros
(which is inevitable unless you're the top one percent of the top one
percent) then you *had* to do *something* to get your mind off it. Meditation, journaling, calling home, going for a walk—that all helped.
But we were also traveling the world as pro tennis players. Every once
in a while you needed to feel like a superstar and act like a superstar
and let yourself get sucked into the nightlife and the moment of what
we were doing.

Even so, staying up until sunrise wasn't the norm on tour.

But every once in a while, after all the practicing and pressure and
winning and losing and putting up with it all, you had to blow the
top off and that's what we did that night in Tokyo. But Michael, are
the best players in the world doing this as well? Well, I don't personally know Roger Federer or Pete Sampras or Rafa Nadal, but I know
a lot of guys that played in the Grand Slams their whole career and
I know a lot of guys who were top fifty, who have made millions of
dollars playing tennis and I'll answer as succinctly as possible: yes,
yes they are.

I'm now forty-five and I have never been back to Tokyo.

• • •

The next week in Japan was a real mess. It rained the whole week; we
were staying in a weird hotel next to the side of a highway.

Because of the weather, they had to move to an indoor location, which was this peculiar university/temple. A really beautiful and serene place but they had only two courts, and they were on a different surface. A strange indoor carpet with sand on top of it. Something I, or anyone in North America, had never seen or played on. Also, there was absolutely no food anywhere. It was like playing inside a museum, they had artifacts surrounding the courts underneath these beautiful giant windows that showed out to a garden. It was all too much for me to handle and I lost first round qualies. I remember at one point I was so angry about my play, the match, the surface change, the one shuttle, the no food, the porn, the rain, that I was losing, that I smacked a ball out of the courts and it hit one of the giant windows, making an enormous *clang* and then the ball bounced around upstairs barely missing a bunch of the old artifacts that were balancing on pedestals. It felt very good to hit the ball that hard, I was super pissed and frustrated at the tournament for switching the surface like that . . . it did not feel good watching my ball narrowly miss what was probably a priceless Japanese artifact from the Kamakura period. I was given a point penalty and fined $150.

After the match when they presented me with the fine, besides the tournament director scolding me, they brought in this Japanese man, maybe he was the museum curator, and he looked at me and waved his finger and said, "Very bad, very bad."

The next week was in Kumamoto City, on the south island. Oli and I made the doubles final and lost to a couple of Japanese players. We were considerably better than them and our rankings were way higher than them, but we couldn't beat them. They were playing for country and pride and we were playing for . . . well, I guess the same thing but they just did it better. They gave us sake and chopsticks during the trophy ceremony and brought in a translator. We gave short speeches and that was the first time I realized how jokes do not translate well. I said something along the lines of "Thank you for the sake, because we lost I will finish the bottle tonight." Then the translator said what I said and no one laughed at all. Huh. Then a man came over to me after the ceremony and said in bad English, "No drink all sake, will make you sick." Today that bottle of sake is sitting in my parent's bar, unopened.

Maybe it was losing the doubles final, maybe it was the stress of being in such a foreign land together, whatever it was, Oli and I were starting to get really annoyed with each other. We didn't have the money to get our own hotel rooms (looking back, we should have) so we were *really* spending a lot of time together. I was feeling lonely and isolated and, as anyone who has been to the other side of the world, was really craving some kind of connection to my home, my country, my people. I started calling my sister, my brother, my ex-girlfriend,[1] my parents. Oli would not leave the room for this, he'd just stay watching TV, volume up, on the bed. It seemed pretty standard to me, that when someone makes a call you would pop out for a little. I did that for him. One time it erupted and I said, "Hey, man, can you go down to the lobby for thirty minutes while I chat with my family," and he said, "I paid for this room, I'm not going anywhere." Just petty shit that probably bothered us both more because we were spending so much time together. One hotel had a phone in the bathroom, so I would lie in the empty bathtub, fully dressed, and make calls, just to have some alone time.

---

1   Was she my "ex"? Did she want to be my ex? Well, we had some stuff to figure out. That's another book.

Chapter 17

White Guys in South Korea

SOUTH KOREA WAS a rude awakening to how much different Korea was from Japan. We landed in Seoul and it immediately felt rougher, more aggressive, more in your face. Lots of people spitting on the streets, lots of smoking. Definitely a far cry from a Japanese hotel clerk running my credit card over to me and bowing to me every few minutes.

The tournament was being played on red "clay." I put clay in quotations because it was different from the clay used around the world, the clay we played on in the Netherlands. The best word for this clay was . . . dirt? Dust? Brown air? Whatever it was holy shit it was slippery, impossible to get your footing. This was going to be a terrible tournament for both of us. Meanwhile, we look around the courts and these Koreans are just dancing across the stuff. They look like flying dragons with delicate feet bouncing from ball to ball, perfect slides, starts/stops. We were beginning to understand why the Korean Tennis Association put this tournament on this surface. It practically guaranteed a Korean would win.

Also: no one was smiling. I can honestly say that for the two weeks I was in Korea I saw roughly three people smiling: me, Oli, and a coach we met from South Africa. I don't know if it was the weather (it was cold and rainy), if it was the economy (rough), or if they are still pissed about the Japanese; whatever it was, these guys were pissed.

It was very uncomfortable. That's a good way to describe my time in South Korea: uncomfortable. Whereas the Japanese were welcoming, excited to have you, taking pictures of you for their scrapbook, the Koreans did not want you there.

Oli and I tried to find a court to hit on. I remember standing on the side of the court looking at the courts, like actually studying them. There weren't any lines. I turned to Oli and said, "Oli, where are the lines?" The lines on a tennis court are pretty important. How do you know if a ball is in or out? How do you know where to stand to serve? Literally the entire basis for all sports relies on lines. Was that a three-pointer or a two-pointer? Was that a touchdown? Did that ball cross the goal line? All these very important questions are answered thanks to lines.[1]

Take a moment and be thankful for lines. I can say with utmost certainty that no other book about sports and/or tennis and/or comedy has ever written that sentence.[2]

As I scrolled through the draw, it wasn't difficult finding our names

---

1   In South Korea, apparently, the tennis lines are a soft, easily movable in the lightest wind, powdered chalk.

2   I once played a Future in Mexico and upon arriving to the courts the day before the matches started, I saw twenty men bent over hand-painting the lines on the courts with paintbrushes. No one could practice because the lines weren't dry. Do you think this happens at the US Open?

among all the Korean names. There were two names that sounded liked white-guy names. Those were us. Between Qi and Wang and Qu, I couldn't distinguish any one name from another, and I also couldn't differentiate the players from one another. That might sound stereotypical, but I encourage you to enter a Korean tennis tournament and be the only white guys in the tournament among a hundred Korean tennis players, who are all wearing the same brands, using the same rackets, and see if you can make out who is who. I had absolutely no clue who anyone was.

It also made me think about all the tournaments I played back home where there would be a few Koreans or Japanese players, and how they must have felt exactly like we did when they showed up to the courts in St. Joe, Missouri, or Sunnyvale, California. What I am trying to say is, traveling out of my comfort zone made me empathize with how difficult a situation and how difficult a feeling it is to be the only one there. You feel alone, you feel singled out, you feel unwelcome. Probably because you are alone, you are singled out, and you aren't welcome. I decided next time I played an American tournament and saw a few foreigners, I would be nice and smile and be helpful.

But what really mattered was that we were there to try and win and win as much as we could. Looking at the draw I noticed that I was playing a Qi, Oli was playing a Qe, that's all we knew. All *they* knew was that they were playing the tall pale guys who hadn't practiced yet. As I found myself saying many times in Korea, I would rather have been in their position than ours.

That night Oli and I shared a room that had one twin-sized bed. This was not good for us. We needed our own rooms at this point, and I don't know why we didn't just go for it. Both of us would have seriously benefited from some quality alone time and sleep, but we didn't, probably because we were too cheap. I remember taking a taxi to what appeared to be a "happening" part of town for dinner. We took one look at all the restaurants, all the signs in Korean, all the foods we had no clue about, and we both quickly opted for the one thing that would maybe bring us some comfort, some sign of home: Pizza Hut. Goddamn wonderful Pizza Hut. The most unauthentic "Italian" pizza out there.

When I opened the four-page strongly laminated menu, a sense of calm coursed through my body. In this land of unknowns—unknown names, unknown surface, unknown language, unknown lines—there was one thing that I could rely on: shitty, delicious American "Italian" pizza. Pizza Hut reminded us of home. Huge glasses of ice water with tons of ice (nothing is more American than wasting lots of ice), an absurd amount of napkins (like they are begging us to make a mess), sports on all the TVs, giant wood booths to fit our giant American bodies, pictures of all the food on the menus. Oli and I ordered a large pizza (we argued about what toppings), ate tons of salad and breadsticks and drank shitloads of water. I didn't want to go back to our hotel: back to reality, back to facing off against a Korean kid tomorrow who dreamed his whole life of defeating a loud, proud American.

As we taxied back, I noticed what appeared to be a street festival happening at the bottom of our street. Maybe a hundred yards from our hotel, at the bottom of a hill, there was a few carnival games, lights flashing, etc. It looked very budget and very Korean. I was fed up with Oli (he was fed up with me), so I told the driver to let me out and I told Oli I would see him back in the room. He looked at me like I was crazy but in the decision between sitting in the room on a twin-sized bed with him arguing about who knows what or going to an authentic Korean street festival where I might get robbed, stabbed, or worse, I felt the street festival seemed like a better and more fun option.

Chapter 18

A Korean Street Festival, I Think

WHILE I'M GLAD I went to the festival, I also did fear for my life a few times. It was a strange place. For all I knew, this was a street gathering of some sort. "Gathering" is probably a better word than "festival." "Festival" is too cherry, optimistic for what this was. This looked like a gang, and their plus ones, bought some lights and arcade games and put it out on the street.

Despite it feeling like I walked into the wrong party at the wrong time, the time alone did feel nice. I was simply there to observe, walk around, take in some "culture" (if possible), and just let my mind wander and be a traveler, not a tennis player, for a moment.

Traveling with someone is no easy task. You spend loads of time together and loads of time together in compact locations: cars, buses, trains, bedrooms. Also on this trip they were Asian cars, Asian buses, Asian trains, Asian bedrooms. Just like all those things are bigger in Scandinavian countries where every man is over six feet, all those things are smaller in Japan and Korea. You talk a lot, eat together, smell each other, hear each other, pay for stuff, all of life's activities, stresses, emotions, all happen to you when you are traveling. Oli and I were friends, then we traveled together and our friendship significantly cooled. Now, thanks to time and maturity we are back to being buds again, but this shows you how powerful traveling together can be. It can literally break up two men who are just friends.[1]

As I walked around the gang gathering, feeling different eyes staring at me, getting bumped into quite a bit, hearing noises and smelling smells I had never heard or smelled before, I noticed what appeared to be one of those stuffed animal crane games. You know the one. Put in a quarter, move the crane, drop the crane, pick up a stuffed animal, and try and dump it into the hole and take it home. I'd love to know what a good percentage of success is on these games (maybe thirty percent? Less?), but I tend to think I am better than most people at these games and my bedrooms and closets tend to agree (lots of useless stuffed animals, mini basketballs, and what-not, stored on the shelves from my successes). Being a competitive person, I have been known to spend well over $10 "earning" a fifty-cent prize (still better than getting defeated by a machine).

The game was off in the corner, away from the action, and seemed like a good place for me to hide out and lose a couple Korean whatever the currency was.

As I walked over, hands in my pockets feeling for change, I had a

---

1   Think you like that girl a lot that you're dating? Take her on a road trip and you might have a different answer after the weekend. The best relationship test (romantic or otherwise) is to take a road trip together. As a comic, I'm often given the opportunity to bring an opening act with me, and it always astonishes me that someone who I think I like, once I take a road trip with them, will be absolutely the worst.

weird feeling. Something about this game was a little different from the games I was used to playing back at Pinball Pete's in Ann Arbor, or every Denny's I had ever visited. Now that I think about it, something was different about this entire place, first Korea but also this actual location, this street, this part of the street. It just felt odd. I approached the device and looked in to check out what exactly I would be moving my crane toward, that's when it became quite clear what was different. Inside the locked, airtight device, under dim lights were probably fifty live, living, baby chickens. Chicks I believe is what they are called. We would be craning for chicks, in this game.

It took my breath away, to be honest. I was expecting some stuffed animals with some fun Korean eyes (you know what I mean), maybe a key chain with the city name on it, you know a *normal prize*. But this blew me away. Are they alive? Yes, very much so. I looked around, as if I was being pranked, but nope, no one seemed to be paying attention to me (for once). What I did next still confuses me . . . I played the game. I don't know exactly why I did this, what was I going to do with a chick? Take it back to the hotel? Take it home to the US? Give it to a child at the "festival"? Surely that would get me killed.

I found the correct change somehow and pushed it into the machine. It started right up. The lights brightened a little more, a Korean song started to play, I had control of the crane. There wasn't a thirty-second countdown like I was used to in the US, but I figured I didn't have much time to make a selection. Also there wasn't much choosing in the first place, a chick is a chick is a chick. I don't think I could have deciphered one from the other at all, to keep with the Korea theme that I was experiencing. One thing that I certainly didn't expect was once I started moving the crane, the chicks, got very very excited. Peeping and peeping!! *Peep! Peep! Peep!* As I moved the crane, they would follow its path, as if they knew that their only way out of this Korean baby chicken killing machine was to somehow get picked up by the robotic arm that the pale-faced round eye was in control of. It was then and still is as I write this, very sad. Just the idea that these living creatures were trapped in a box with a heat lamp on them and for the price of twenty-five cents (maybe? No clue what I paid) I could release this living breathing baby who up until a few days ago was probably safe and sound with its mother, from a feeble, silly game for humans.

Time ran out. The music stopped. The lights turned off. The crane returned to its original position. The peeps quieted down and the baby chickens returned to the corner where they were huddled together to keep warm. I had lost. The Korean machine had defeated me. Despite all my previously mentioned concerns (animal cruelty being the foremost) the fact that I lost pissed me off. Losing sucks, even when it's at the hand of a crane machine picking up baby animals. So in went another foreign coin and back up again it started. This thought did cross my mind: What am I doing playing this "game"? Keep in mind I am not great at touching living things. Cats, OK, dogs, yes. A chick? I don't even think I would be able to or would want to touch a chick. I mean what do I do then? Pet it? This device shows the weakness of being a competitive person. I was so pissed that I lost that I continued to play the game, even though in reality *I did not want to win*. I did not want the spoils of this victory (in this case a living being that I would have to care for).

The crane moved again, I had a little better feel for it this time, the music started, the chicks ran toward the crane, *PEEP! PEEP! PEEP!* I was a little less taken aback by the whole thing this time. I gripped the handle like my racket, loosened the tips of my fingers a little. Shook my neck back and forth. It would have looked like I was about to return a serve. I had already played this game once and the animal cruelty wasn't as bothersome this time. I got the crane to what I thought was the best location and pressed the button, the crane dropped . . . the ratchety toothed mouth opened. Upon seeing the jaws widen, the peeps grew even louder. *PEEP! PEEP! PEEP!* They knew that once the mouth opened one of them had a chance at survival. The mouth delicately closed around a peeping chick, it landed safely inside the contraption and just like that he/she/it was in the mouth of the device. Time moved fast for this chick, no time to say goodbye to its friends and family. No time to get its affairs in order. It was escape time. I suspect that's how it feels to escape anything. It happens fast, but it happens.

The crane picked up the peeping chick. The others continued their array of noises and jumps and as I sit here and write this now it absolutely breaks my heart how hard these chicks were trying to get out of there. What kind of messed-up festival was this, man? The crane was returning to its original position with a chick safely in its grasp. The feeling of satisfaction and accomplishment waved over me. You think I can't win at your stupid crane game? I'm one of the best tennis players in the world. The other chicks started huddling back together for warmth and comfort. In slow motion the crane's mouth opened. In a matter of seconds this chick, would be safely in a secluded shoebox-sized compartment where I could pick him/her/it up and do what, I don't know.

As the mouth opened, the chick inside of it, in all its excitement decided to jump. Why? I don't know. Why does a living animal do anything? Why was I still playing this insane game? The universe is a cruel place. The chick, trying to jump, maybe trying to secure its escape, actually sabotaged it. If this chick would have just let the universe take care of what was supposed to happen, it would have landed in my arms in a matter of seconds. But instead it pushed, it tried too hard, it, just like me on a break point, attempted to secure a result instead of focusing on the process and, by doing so, ruined what was set to happen. The chick eagerly leapt toward the window, toward me, and by doing so ricocheted off the ledge and landed back into the main compartment. It paused for a moment, somberly, maybe recognizing the floor, the feeling on its feet, the air possibly, and then, just like that, just like a child being separated from its parents or family, it noticed what was up and bolted back toward the pack, who quickly surrounded it, and it was gone in a sea of birds.

I stood there astonished. I just picked up a baby chicken with a crane and almost would have had it, in my hands, if it hadn't jumped toward me, but now it was back with its friends, with its peep.[2]

I took a deep breath, thought about playing again, and was smart enough to realize that probably the best thing that could have happened, did. I felt someone looking at me so I turned my head to the right and there was an old Korean man standing there smiling. My estimation is that he had six to seven teeth. He repeated something in Korean to me many times, laughing while he said it. Was he laughing with me? Was he laughing at me? What was he saying? Pretty clear he was laughing at me. I smiled and waved (sticks and stones) took a last look at those chicks huddled there, now in the darker light. I felt bad for them. They were not in a winning situation. They were doomed for the worst possible outcome. The feeling felt familiar. But I convinced myself that at least they had each other. Maybe that chick wasn't jumping toward me, maybe it was jumping back toward the others, that loved it.

I walked back to the hotel feeling as if I had visited the moon and back. I wasn't sure if I should tell Oli, tell anyone, or if I should just let this moment be a moment for me. Maybe I could tell my son someday or something. Maybe not. I didn't need to decide right now. It was bedtime and I had a match tomorrow. I quietly walked into the room, Oli was asleep in the bed. The only bed. He was nice enough to leave a pillow on the chair. I grabbed it and huddled in the corner, like the chicks, and fell asleep.

---

2 A group of chicks is a peep. Take a moment and read through the names of groups of animals, it is time well spent. Just as a taste here's one, a group of lemurs is called a conspiracy.

Ann Arbor, Christmas, 1984 The best gift I have ever received came from my brother John on Christmas day, 1984. This Roddy Racket changed my life forever.

Here's every member of my family embracing me as a baby, truly disgusting stuff.

Ann Arbor, 1984
I asked my mom to help me train for the upcoming Big Wheel race.

The Big Wheel race. Those are my siblings John and Kristy running alongside me, I love how excited they are. How could I possibly lose with that support?

I won it.

1980
A Kosta family picture taken on one of our mandatory Kosta Family Adventures. I'm the little one. I guess we were sponsored by a . . . vest company?

Siblings John, Kristy, and Todd, taken before I was born. Notice how miserable they look.

Ann Arbor, 1990
Grandpa Burt was a true gentleman and always impeccably dressed.

1989
The Ann Arbor
Junior Open Boys'
10 & Under final,
Racquet Club of
Ann Arbor, Court
10. Taken before
the match. It never
crossed my mind
that my opponent,
Bradley Adams,
might be a good
player and could
beat me.

My brother
John consoling
me as I cried
on court during
the final—which
was incredibly
sad and
embarrassing
then and still
today.

When you lose in
tennis you lose
alone. (Now, as
a parent myself,
I wonder . . . why
did my parents
take this picture?
WTF.)

Old fc
team t
to win

City tennis tou
nearing comp

By JIM CNOCKAERT
NEWS SPORTS REPORTER

☐ Junior winners crowned, D1

Robbie Risdon and Ruby Olegario, veterans of Women's A Doubles in the Ann Arbor City Tennis Tournament.

But until this summer, they were on opposite sides of the net.

"This tournament was the first time we'd even played a set of doubles together," Risdon said following their 6-4, 6-4 quarterfinal win against Hinkes and Lisa Davies Thursday night at the Pioneer High courts.

"We'd only played two or three games together before this," Olegario said.

But they've quickly discovered in the tournament that their styles complement each other well.

"Robbie's a good net player," said Olegario. "And Ruby a good baseline player," added Risdon.

They needed to be at their best a shivers.

"It was a roller-coaster match. They had a few points and got even, then let us off the hook. But we won that needed to be won."

Risdon and Olegario, the flight's take an second-seeded Sheila Itai Vanvick in one semifinal at 3:45 Burns Park.

In the other semifinal at 2:30 p. seeded Kriste Miner and Anna Sc No. 3 Carol Miller and Emily Bower

"The semifinals are going to be Risdon said. "All four seeds are b are going true to form. I think the teams could pull it out."

Men's A Doubles – Top seeds Ju Ihlman have yet to lose a game i fact that Morris attributes to the tv

I also won a fair amount. Pictured here in the late 80s in *The Ann Arbor News*, with the caption: "Michael Kosta returns a shot in the Boys' 12 Final, which he won in straight sets. Kosta finished the tournament a triple-winner."

(Credit: The Ann Arbor News / Nat Ehrlich / News Photo)

NEWS PHOTO/+ NAT EHRLICH

Michael Kosta returns a shot in the Boys' 12 final, which he won in straight sets. Kosta finished the tournament a triple-winner.

Pair vault into U.S. Olympic Trial spotli

FROM THE ASSOCIATED PRESS

INDIANAPOLIS — Kory Tarpenning was pole vaulting with all seriousness. Tim Bright was doing it just for fun.

Together, they put on a dramatic show as the U.S. Olympic Track and Field Trials Thursday night.

Tarpenning became the second-best American outdoor pole vaulter, clearing 19 feet, 3¼ inches and overshadowing a courageous performance by versatile Tim Bright.

But while Tarpenning won with the best

effort by an American this year and moved into ninth place on the all-time list, Bright captivated the crowd of 10,768 with his determination.

After finishing second in the decathlon, taking 13 vaults during the competition, he came back in the open vault and finished fourth at 18-4, where he made nine attempts before going out with three misses at 18-0.

Earl Bell, the co-bronze medalist in the 1984 Olympics, finished second in the vault

See TRIALS, D3

Athletes to get cash from USOC

FROM THE ASSOCIATED PRESS

COLORADO SPRINGS, Colo. — The U.S. Olympic Committee said Thursday that for the first time ever it plans to make direct cash payments to top American athletes to help offset training costs.

"It is simply no longer possible for a world class athlete to compete success-

fully and at the same time in a full-time job," Robert Helmick said.

"Our ultimate goal is top-level athletes with part for living and train that they may spend sary to train and comp

I love this picture of my dad and me. He was always so proud and supportive of his kids, no matter the endeavor.

Ann Arbor, 1993
As I got older I started to win a lot, which only led to more winning and more trophies.

Ann Arbor, 1993
The comedian in me was always right there also.

Ann Arbor, prom night, 1997/1998 Todd "helping" me get ready amidst the trophies and chaos of being a walking competitive teenage hormone.

Ann Arbor, graduation from Huron High School, 1998 That yellow sash was really important (to my mom and grandma).

Ann Arbor, 2000s As the youngest in my family, I was frequently the punchline, which might explain why I do comedy now.

Athens, GA, NCAA's year 2000
My backhand was my strength and never let me down.
(Credit: University of Illinois Athletics)

Athens, GA, NCAA's year 2000
There's a saying in tennis that you're
only as good as your second serve.
(Credit: University of Illinois Athletics)

Athens, GA, NCAA's year 2000
After beating VCU my sophomore
year.
(Credit: University of Illinois Athletics)

Columbus, OH, Big Ten championships, senior year, 2002 University of Illinois Big Ten champs. Over my four years at Illinois our combined Big Ten team record was 51-1.

Columbus, OH, Big Ten championships, senior year, 2002 Mom and Dad were big fans of Craig and Bruce and Illinois tennis and they made it to almost all the matches.

Champaign, IL, 2000s Here's how good Illinois tennis was: at one point my doubles partner, Nathan Zeder, and I were ranked #6 in the *country* and we played #3 doubles on our *team*, the last position.

Columbus, OH, Big Ten championships, senior year, 2002 With Craig and Bruce. I had just won my match and these were their "we are happy" faces.

Champaign,IL, 2000s Craig demanded a lot from us and expected success, which I am thankful for now, but at the time could be tough.

The Netherlands,
summer 2000
A small break to look at
a windmill in between
slipping and losing on
the red clay circuit of the
Netherlands.

The Netherlands, summer 2000
Jeff won the French money tournament by
beating me in the finals. I would have won
if it hadn't rained. We pooled the money
and split it between ourselves because
we didn't want to play each other for
thousands of dollars.

France, summer 2000
Me, Illinois teammates Jeff, Alex, and Arnaud doing the Europe thing.

Kumamoto City, Japan, 2003
Oli and I lost in the doubles final of this Japanese 10k Future and I guess we played under a cell phone tower?

apan, 2003
t a Japanese
Ok Future, can
ou spot the
merican?

Korea, 2003
A very tough, very unfriendly tournament in Korea. Notice the lines or whatever is left of them.

Ann Arbor, 2004
On court coaching
Michigan players
Steve Peretz and Vinny
Gossain. In that black
folder were probably
a bunch of jokes about
butts.

(Credit: Michigan Athletics)

Ann Arbor, 2004
Coaching under Bruce
Berque was hard work
and I learned a lot.
Mostly I learned that
what I really wanted to
be, was a comedian.

(Credit: Michigan Athletics)

Western Canada,
Yuk Yuks tour,
2006
A pretty typical
comedy audience
for me at that
point in my career.

Western Canada,
Yuk Yuks tour, 2006
Early on in comedy,
you barely get paid,
so your compensation
was attention from the
opposite sex, which I
was fine with.

Appleton, WI, Skyline Comedy Club, mid 2000s
Onstage.
(credit: Kristina Kosta)

2008
Moving to LA to be a star, which I thought would take roughly six to eight weeks.

West Hollywood, CA, 2008
Days after moving to LA. I shared this bedroom with cockroaches and other rodents.

Detroit, Mark Ridley's Comedy Castle, 2006ish
My first agent, Dave Moroz, was pivotal in getting some money in my pocket, getting me to think about my comedy more seriously, and most importantly, securing tons of stage time.

Hermosa Beach, CA, Comedy & Magic Club,
late 2000s
Jordan Tilzer, far left, has been my manager for
nearly fifteen years. He picks up the phone every
time I call, which says a lot.

Hollywood
Improv,
late 2000s
Onstage.

Hermosa Beach, CA, Comedy & Magic Club,
late 2000s
Comedy & Magic Club was the first LA club to use
me consistently, which gave me a lot of confidence
and helped me make some friends. Shown here
Kevin Nealon, Russell Peters, and Paul Morrissey.

Burbank, CA, *The Tonight Show*, April 8, 2010
My green room consisted of a lot of tennis players. (Left to right) Todd Kosta, Evan Zeder, Ken Lovell. All of whom wiped out *The Tonight Show*'s Heineken supply pretty quickly.

Burbank, CA, *The Tonight Show*, April 8, 2010
Jay Leno loves comedy and made sure to always spend time with the comics on his show, which I loved.

Burbank, CA, *The Tonight Show*, April 8, 2010
Showing actress Mary McCormack my trophy, naturally.

Burbank, CA, *The Tonight Show*, April 8, 2010
Onstage, feeling comfortable because I had practiced that set hundreds of times.

(Stacie McChesney/ ©NBCUniversal/Getty Images)

• • •

Any animosity we had felt the day before at the courts was small compared to what we walked into the next day. Straight up anger toward us. I put my bag down and a Korean player would put his bag down on top of it, or move his chair into it aggressively. It was wild.

The gist of that day was, I lost. Oli lost, too. My match was a hard fought three-setter where the only memorable moment came when I was forced, while the umpire wasn't looking, to body check my opponent on a changeover, knocking him to the ground. I hit him because three games earlier, he checked me, into the umpire chair. My point is he started it. It was ugly and not fun and felt like I was in the tennis version of the 1988 film *Bloodsport* starring Jean-Claude Van Damme. In all, the tournament got what they wanted. The two tall white boys got their asses handed to them. It sucked. Losing always sucks. Even now, I look back on this moment and it makes me mad. I wish so badly Oli and I would have met in the finals and made those Koreans watch us play. But that's not what happened, and lots of times in life, what you want to happen, isn't what happens. In fact, it's usually pretty unusual when it does. Those are the moments you celebrate. I remember leaving the tennis courts happy that I would never be back.

Oli and I, still annoyed at each other but more annoyed at the tournament and its competition, bonded a little bit. We ate at Pizza Hut again, packed our bags and the next day headed to JeJu Island, a small fishing island where the last tournament was being played. Thankfully, this one was on hard courts.

Chapter 19

JeJu Island

ANY GOOD GRACES Oli and I had for each other dissolved on the flight. We were not getting along. I was on a fishing island off South Korea. And islands always make you feel alone. You are alone, you're floating in the middle of the ocean.

I remember looking outside of the JeJu airport as we hopped in a taxi in the rain and headed to our hotel. Oli hadn't loaded my tennis rackets into the trunk like I thought he would, so they sat on the curb in the rain while I negotiated our taxi cost with the driver. I finally get in and see my racket bag soaked, sitting alone, out the window. I yell "STOP" and I run out and throw it on Oli's lap as aggressively as I could. I was over it.

We checked into our hotel and thank god, it was decent. We had two beds. There was a lobby, and a place to get away from each other. That was needed tremendously. I remember there being a Popeyes chicken across the street from the hotel. Of all the American chains to have on a small island in Korea, the one they have is a Popeyes? Is this what Koreans think Americans like to eat? I never saw anyone in that Popeyes chicken the whole time I was there.

Traveling the world playing professional tennis had always been a dream, it always seemed like the best life. Monte Carlo, Paris, London, Moscow, New York. Eating at the best restaurants, beautiful celebrities watching me play, I think it abruptly hit me in Korea that I wasn't playing those cities and I probably wasn't ever going to have that life. (I mean for one, how could I get out of these shit tournaments if I couldn't even win a few rounds in them?)

I should have been focused on one thing and one thing only, the tennis. I was back on a hard court, I was still extremely fit, and I was in the main draw of yet another pro tournament. These are positives and I should have been feeling excited about the opportunity to finish this trip with a wonderful tournament. Instead, I felt as dreary as the weather outside. I was ready to go home, ready to eat a turkey sandwich, ready to take a shit without some contraption shooting water up my ass, ready for the adventure to turn into a familiar path. I should have been tougher, given myself a little pep talk about the opportunity I had in front of me, felt grateful that there were talented players around the world who would never have the chance I had the next day: to play in a pro tournament main draw. But I only felt depressed, and that somehow I was the victim.

Call it the road, call it being a bitch, call it being a rich kid, call it not having a coach, I don't know, I just know how I felt.

Having a good night's sleep changes a lot of things, doesn't it? As I read my own words now, it's possible I wasn't depressed at all, it's possible I was just tired! Sharing beds, dealing with Oli, losing a lot—it's all stressful. I wonder how different the whole thing would have been if I had my own hotel room, slept nine to ten hours of good sleep a night, and had three decent meals a day instead of Pizza Hut and Popeyes. Maybe I would have won each week and qualified for Wimbledon. Yes, let's go with that.

The next day I remember waking up to the rain, ordering breakfast in the rain, taking a cab to the courts in the rain. Once I got to the tournament, though, the sun came out. Also, this was a nice

tournament. There was a nice players lounge to hang. They had am-
ple bathrooms and the staff was friendly and accommodating. There
were ball kids. Maybe it wasn't Koreans that were assholes maybe it
was just the Koreans who lived in that last city. It would be like if your
first visit to the US was staying in midtown New York. "Holy shit,
what's wrong with Americans? All these people are assholes." Then
you fly down to Charleston for your next stop and you're like, "Holy
shit, these are the nicest people I have ever met."

· · ·

I remember winning the first set pretty easily. It was clear my opponent was overmatched. He moved awkwardly and couldn't return my
serve. I started to gain some confidence. I was dropping heat, using
all the spins, serving and volleying, taking his serve and coming to
net. I felt like a hard-court master and he looked like I did last week:
spinning his wheels but not going anywhere. The first set finished
quickly and I felt completely in control. All that self-doubt and pity
was gone. Crazy that all it took was winning one set and my fear was
gone.

    Then all of a sudden the second set got closer. He started to move
better, started to pass me at net easier. My confidence shifted, "Is
this guy good?" I thought. The first set was so easy, what changed?
Self-doubt started to creep in. At 4–4 he broke me and served the set
out, winning the second set. I was going to have to play a third set to
finish this guy.

    As I sat down on the changeover I started to feel all sad again.
"Why does this always happen to me? Why can't I just win easily in
straight sets like so many other people can?" My life is so difficult,
ya know? Never once did it cross my mind that maybe my opponent
was a good tennis player. Or that he deserved the right to be there
also (we were ranked close to each other in the world rankings). Or

that he needed a set to figure out this surface for himself. I never once thought about giving my opponent any credit, instead I thought about how hard my life was and how unfair it was that I lost the second set. I needed my dad to grab my shoulder and snap me out of my "I'm a victim" monologue.

I probably had another forty-five seconds left on the changeover. I closed my eyes, put the towel over my head. Tried to quiet my mind. "Just relax man," I thought. I tried to remove any thoughts about the result, about "winning" or "losing." Tried to remind myself that I enjoyed tennis and I enjoyed figuring out different opponents. Usually it was fun. That challenge was fun, like a puzzle. They seem so hard at first but then you slowly figure it out and all of a sudden you look at the end result and it's like "Did I just do all that?"

Well, whatever I told myself worked. I shot out of the gate. The Kosta pity party was over and I was a new man. I started the third set pretending to be confident and slowly and surely the "fake it till you make it" plan worked. I went up 3–0. *Boom*. Feet were moving like I was on fire. I could hear my own feet and shoes squeaking as I ran around the court, getting everything, pressing my opponent. With every shot I gained more confidence and my opponent gained less. He started to get pissed.

At 4–1 me, he got a point penalty for hitting a ball out of the court. I told myself to stay focused, keep on him, the end was near.

I went up 5–1 . . . There was a coach watching my match now, a guy I respected from South Africa. He was coaching some of the other players. Having a coach must be nice. When the umpire turned the scorecard to 5–1, I saw the coach look at the score and look at me. He was impressed. Good, yeah, I'm a great player. I bet he'll want to coach me after this. I wonder where he trains out of? Will I move there or will he move to the States? I wonder who I play next round?

I'm up 5–1 serving in the third. My opponent just got a code violation and I'm one hundred percent in the driver's seat. I've played enough tennis to know that this one isn't over, but let's be honest, it's over. I tell myself the adage that has comforted me many times throughout my tennis life: "I'd rather be in my position than his." I serve, 15-Love. I serve again, decent rally, he eventually makes an error. 30-Love. I wonder where I'll go to dinner tonight? Popeyes chicken? Nah, maybe the tournament director knows a good place. I look over to my opponent and he's furious. Ranting and raving, huffing and puffing.

I serve, up 30-Love, and he, in a fit of anger and reluctance just *smacks* the ball as hard as he can. It zooms past me for a winner: 30–15. What was that? He just gave up on the point and yet somehow won it. Alright, who cares. I serve again, this time he re-created the last shot. Closes his eyes and swings as hard as he can, he rips a forehand winner past me *again*. Jesus Christ. 30–30. He has given up, these weren't swings for the fences because he thought he might win, these were swings for the fences because he lost. It was over to him. 30–30. I double faulted. I missed my first serve, a little intimidated that he might try this lucky shit again and then somehow the tiniest seed of worry crept into my brain and that one little tiny doubt caused my elbow to get a little bit tighter and I pushed the serve long. Break point.

Wow, how did this happen? At 30–40 I made a first serve and he took a huge rip at the ball. I lined up for a forehand and took a tentative, scared swing, I heard the ball flop onto my racket frame (not the strings) and next thing I knew the ball was flying out of the court and the game was his. Shit.

I sat down on the changeover up 5–2 but it didn't feel right. I can't tell you how it happened, but I just slowly lost. I don't have any interesting reflection on exactly what happened. It just went up in the air, the match. Like holding a dandelion outside. One second it's there, it's beautiful, and the next second you're holding an empty stem. I couldn't stop the snowball of losing. And with every point he won, with every point I lost, he got better, I got worse. I can still remember the emotions of it all: 5–2, 5–3, 5–4. At 5–4 I had a couple match points, holy shit, that would have changed everything, right? I must have been doing something well to put myself in position to win. But . . . being up 5–1 in the third set and losing is one hundred percent a choke, no matter how you look at it. No matter how many years pass. No matter how hard it is to admit or relive, I *choked*. I honestly believe that if I won one of those match points I wouldn't have written this book.

I skipped the shuttle home. I needed to be alone, plus I remember my opponent being in the car as well. He was the last person I wanted to see. Would it kill the tournament to have an extra shuttle around, just in case one of the players blows a 5–1 lead in the third and doesn't want to ride home with the guy he just lost to? So I walked. How long? I don't know. Where was I? I don't know. Where was I going? I don't know. Like Forrest Gump after his mom dies, I just walked. On my way back to the hotel, I remember walking through this fishing market and seeing fish there I had never seen in my life. Huge fish with tiny mouths, tiny fish with huge mouths, fish that looked like frogs, frogs that looked like fish, how these living creatures would ever be eaten I do not know. None of them looked appetizing. They were dead or dying. I could empathize. From 5–1 up to losing is as close to getting hooked and dragged to your death as you could get in tennis.

I remember staring at this half eel half fish half frog half whatever the fuck it was and I was thinking the reason I played tennis was because I loved being around my family. I loved riding my bike down to the Racquet Club for Family Tennis. The six of us playing on two courts, while the evening light went down. We couldn't even see the ball anymore but we were having so much fun out there playing together.

I loved the idea that I got to spend an hour with my dad on the court. I loved that my mom and I would play doubles together and she never cared what the score was, never knew what the score was, just liked being on the same side of the court as me. I loved that. Tennis to me was family. It was my happy place. It was time with people that I loved and who loved me. It was pulling that Roddy racket out of the bag, a Christmas gift from my brother, and anticipating the excitement and love that I was about to experience.

And now, tennis was being stuck in this South Korean fishing village alone after blowing one of the biggest leads you can have. I was staring at this disgusting blowfish and I let my brain wander to the happy days of tennis, when it was the safety of home, the comfort of family, the protection and innocence of childhood. It was an odd experience to be staring at a Korean fish while contemplating my childhood and family.

Most people can understand how alone you can feel on a tennis court, but as a tennis player there are moments when you feel just as isolated *off* the court. That moment is one I'll never forget. Today, I appreciate being around people who love me because of that crappy match. I never want to experience that feeling of loneliness again.

Chapter 20

Inventory

LOSING THAT MATCH crushed me. It was and still is the biggest lead I had ever blown playing competitive tennis. I still can't believe it and I'm a professional comedian now. "How did you lose that match?" I asked myself that today waiting for the C train—I can't shake it. This match was worth $200 and one ATP point. Now, twenty years later, I will have a wonderful, full day. A day of comedy, friendship, great meals, exercise, dogs, family, celebrations, and I will go to bed with a smile on my face and dream about this fucking match. It's not like I wake up crying, sweating in the corner, unable to love again. It wasn't the Vietnam War, but it still lingers. Crazy, right? Maybe this is just what life is, sometimes regrets pop into your mind. Probably the same way it pops in your mind that one time the jerk in middle school made fun of your nose or you witnessed a car crash or whatever. If we are alive and consuming life, some memories are going to linger. I'm pretty happy that the memory that haunts me is a silly tennis match, and I hope it remains that way. Still, though, it does haunt me.

The morning after that horrific match, back in JeJu Island, Korea, I woke up at five a.m., left the hotel room with Oli sleeping (that was the last time I ever saw him), and hopped on the first of three flights back to the US. I had some serious thinking to do. The best place to do that was at home. What was home? Where was home? At this point I had personal belongings scattered across four locations. The majority was stored at my parents' house in Ann Arbor. But much like an astronaut who has to leave equipment at the international space station on the way to Mars, I had shit everywhere.

CHAMPAIGN, ILLINOIS

NOTABLE ITEMS: Lots and lots of U of Illinois clothes, a framed quote from Theodore Roosevelt ("The credit belongs to the man who is actually in the arena . . ."), and 5 boxes of racket string.
ITEMS LAST SEEN: June 2002

I had a teammate at Illinois named Alex who was local, born and raised in Champaign. Wonderful kid, really smart, hard worker. He was a non-scholarship player and the more accomplished players—the scholarship players—took advantage of Alex. He was constantly doing the dirty work that no one else on the team wanted to do. When we asked Alex for a favor, he said yes. I can't remember a time when he said no. Because Alex's family lived in town, we'd store our stuff in his garage when we left for the summer. It never crossed our minds that this garage was his family's garage. The world and its places were there to support and facilitate *us*.

One summer before I left to go back to Ann Arbor, I rolled over to Alex's house with a car full of stuff. I had to move out of my apartment, and it never crossed my mind that I should get a storage facility, or move in early or . . . manage the situation like a mature adult. "Store it at Alex's house," everyone said. So I drove over, probably unannounced, and started unloading my stuff into his family's garage. This was awfully ballsy of me, given that six months prior I had asked Alex to get me his dad's elite faculty parking pass (Alex's dad is a world-class musician who was teaching at the school). He had one of those parking passes that you could just park anywhere, all the time, and no one would ever ticket you. I think it was officially called the "Presidents Pass." I was a sophomore in college, didn't have any money, and these parking tickets were adding up. The natural solution wasn't to take the bus, or walk, or look for parking, or carpool with someone, or ride my bike, but to ask my teammate—a friend and roommate—to steal his dad's prestigious parking pass for a couple of hours so I could color copy it at Kinkos, laminate it, cut it to the perfect shape (with razor blades I bought at a supply store), and use it. I don't know what is crazier, that I even asked my friend to do that, or that he said "Yes."

Looking back, I definitely took advantage of that friendship; based on the power dynamic that existed with our "winner take all" attitude of Illinois tennis, Alex felt obliged to help a more "prominent," scholarship player. What I did wasn't cool, and to Alex and his dad: I am sorry.

Like all cheating and deceit, the Presidents Parking Pass worked brilliantly until it didn't. By the time *my* phone rang, Alex's dad, Craig the head coach, Sally the academic advisor, plus multiple security and parking officers were aware of what was going on. I tried to say I stole the pass from Alex, against his knowledge, but he also told the truth so that didn't work. I met with the head of the university police in his office. He was wearing all his "police" stuff, the radio kept going off, he was stern and mean and scared the shit out of me. I apologized profusely, I told him I understood that this could have been a security risk (could it, though?), but most of all I was embarrassed and felt like a dipshit for taking advantage of Alex and our friendship. This was particularly shitty because a year prior, Mr. Hobson and his wife had invited the entire tennis team over to his house for dinner, and we all sat around and watched him play piano. I'll never forget him jamming away on "The Flight of the Bumblebee."

The chief of police asked me how I forged the pass so well. I explained it to him step by step and for a brief second he seemed impressed. The next year, the *new* parking passes had holograms on them.

I'm thankful that Illinois is a relatively small community and they believe in second chances. (Maybe I wouldn't have been so lucky in a bigger city, or if I wasn't on the tennis team, or if my skin was a darker color. That's something I think a lot about now.)

When I went back to get my stuff from the Hobson family garage the next fall, all of it was gone. I'm OK with that.

HILLSBOROUGH COMMUNITY COLLEGE, TAMPA, FLORIDA

NOTABLE ITEMS: 4 rackets, 3 pairs of shoes, some journals, some books (*The Art of War* by Sun Tzu, *Alexander: Child of a Dream* by Valerio Massimo Manfredi), some letters from my college GF
ITEMS LAST SEEN: December 2003

After leaving college, I was a full-time pro tennis player, but I lacked something that the best players in the world travel with: a coach. Coaches were extremely expensive and I had a limited amount of money, so the less I paid for a coach, the longer I could travel and use the valuable time to learn how to be successful on tour. Of course, the argument could also be made that I would have had *more* success if I was traveling with a coach, a qualified expert to help me work on my weaknesses, keep me motivated and injury free, create match strategies so I win more often, etc. It was a constant balance of me both trying to save money so I could last longer on tour but also spend my money on good coaching and support so I could potentially have more success. One of my solutions was to occasionally pull out the pocketbook and pay a coach in Tampa, let's call him Sam. Sam was an extremely hard worker, knew the game very well, and had about forty courts, both hard courts and clay courts, available to him at all times. Plus, Tampa was the perfect climate for tennis training and there were loads of other pros in the area so finding practice partners was never difficult.

However, the thought of going there from Korea, in my tender emotional state, made me shudder. Sam was . . . challenging. Knowledgeable, bright, and a total dick. My former doubles partner, Raven Klassen, who also utilized Coach Sam in Tampa, said it best: "He's all information, no presentation." This guy Mansplained before that was even a word (He . . . Samsplained?). As his player, you would practice for four hours in the morning in the Tampa heat, take an hour for lunch at CiCi's pizza (gross), four more hours in the hotter Tampa afternoon heat, do some footwork drills on the grass field, then I'd get assigned to his kids court for a couple of hours, which was really just free babysitting for him (they were excellent tennis players, but hated the sport), and then sit in his office for a tennis lecture. Tennis was already my life but after eight hours of practicing tennis, I didn't need nor did I want to then sit down and listen to more tennis.

I couldn't go back to Tampa. I couldn't sit in his classroom chairs and listen to his lengthy oration about how a crosscourt shot has six and a half more feet of court to work with than a down-the-line shot, how a one-degree change in the racket face angle upon contact is equivalent to eight feet of distance that the ball travels. Listening to Sam teach tennis reminded me of reading a comedy special review in the *New Yorker*. There was a lot of deconstruction, a lot of "theory," a lot of analyzing, very little laughing. Sometimes smart comedy critics forget that slipping on a banana makes us laugh, and sometimes Sam forgot that the best tennis players were quite dumb.

I was watching a match with Sam one time and he said to me, "Michael, look at this player's racket face upon contact in relation to the lower body torque, focus on the stillness of his head and the location of the nondominant hand . . ."

I replied, "Sam, he hit it in the net."

He hated when I said stuff like that, but I was so sick of his *theory* of tennis, his *theory* of competition, his *theory* of success. I was out there day after day losing over and over again and his cute theories weren't getting me into the second round.

I left those belongings in Tampa and never saw them again.

A decade later, I was living in New York City and had just finished a Saturday night of comedy (multiple sets, at multiple clubs, in front of entirely different audiences). I was a bit drunk and not ready to go to sleep, so I turned on ESPN and the 2014 Australian Open doubles final was on. I almost spit out my beer upon seeing my friend and former Sam disciple, Raven Klassen, playing in the finals, the finals of a Grand Slam. Ten years ago, we were grinding on the clay and hard courts of a Tampa community college while Sam drove us to exhaustion (Raven sitting in his desk chair taking notes like the teacher's pet), and now Raven was playing for one of the most important trophies in the game and I was watching him, mostly drunk, wiping burrito sauce off my shirt, at three a.m. So, obviously, Sam *did* know what he was talking about.

For a very brief moment it dawned on me that I might have made a mistake. That if I had just stuck with tennis, not been sidetracked by my comedy delusions, it would be me in the Grand Slam final right now and someone else would be watching *me* on TV compete for one of the biggest trophies in the sport. But thankfully that thought immediately evaporated when I remembered that Raven, for the past ten years—four thousand days—had been training, traveling, bank rolling, struggling, sleeping two maybe three to a bed, rushing to make connecting flights, booking practice courts, stringing rackets, dealing with injuries and the mental challenges of competing; it all sounded so terrible. If I can be really honest, I felt sorry for Raven. To work that hard (he was an extremely hard worker), for that long, and to still be fighting for every point in a high-status match that he lost pretty handily—that's tough. Yes, there might have been chipotle sauce dripping onto my drunk bare chest as I thought that, but it was a genuine thought and maybe it helped that the last time I played Raven (in doubles), at a $10,000 Future in Godfrey, Illinois, I won (knuckle crack).

Tokyo, Japan

NOTABLE ITEMS: 2 pairs of black dress shoes
ITEMS LAST SEEN: May 2003

When I finally arrived "home," in Ann Arbor, with more or less what I owned, I had some decisions to make about what to do next. I was twenty-four, I was very good at tennis, but my results weren't convincing me that I was going to play Wimbledon anytime soon. I was running out of money. Maybe professional tennis wasn't in the cards, but I did have to do *something*. And up until this point, tennis was the only thing I did.

I had a college degree but it was in speech communication, which I still don't even know what that does for me (I mean, we all speak and communicate so how exactly did this degree set me apart from anyone other than a baby?). My résumé pretty much said one thing: Michael plays tennis.

I thought it would be helpful to do an honest, potentially brutally honest, inventory of what I had and where I stood so I could see what the next steps should be. So I made a list. It was the end of May 2003. Or, for the past twenty years, I *thought* it was the end of May 2003. Before we go any further here, I have a confession.

Upon sitting down to write this book and rehash my tennis exploits, I explicitly remember losing in JeJu Island, coming home to Ann Arbor, and making this list. In fact, in the first two drafts of this book, that's how it was written because that's what I thought was true. Then, one night as I lay awake poking around in the bowels of the low-level pro tennis internet sites, I found a list of my pro tournaments and results. All of them. And as it turns out, after my match in JeJu Island, the one that I still think about while waiting for the C train, the one that can dig its way into my dreams as I sleep, the one that, as my memory convinced me, basically made me quit tennis, I actually played pro tennis for another fourteen months after this match. *Fourteen* months. I had no idea. I had no recollection of those tournaments and of those results. Upon reviewing them, I was even more surprised to find that I actually had some good results—I won some big matches, I made a few decent runs into real pro tennis tournaments, there were some decent checks. It blew me away. The emotional turmoil of that JeJu Island loss was so powerful (remember: we only remember things that make us *feel* something) that I had forgotten everything that happened after it. It's like for the next fourteen months I was a tennis zombie, my body was playing (and oddly winning) but my brain and heart were dead. Previously, I thought that JeJu Island loss was the *physical* ending to my career, but now, knowing that I played for fourteen more months and don't even remember it, I realize that that match was the emotional ending of my career. My brain didn't record the matches that followed because they didn't make me feel anything.

So . . . here's the list that I made in July 2004—not May 2003.

What I Have
- **ATP RANKING #864.** That's a good ranking, but one had to be ranked Top 200 in the world to actually make a decent living in pro tennis.
- **$9,000.** This was what I had left for travel, coaching, equipment, food, etc. If I wanted to continue playing pro tennis, I needed more money. The only option was to ask the people that had given to me from the start for more. Some of those generous

people had even reached out proactively, asking if I needed it. I can't communicate how supported that made me feel. I was slow to respond to them because I was unsure—unsure of my remaining balance of the most important asset a pro athlete needs to be successful: belief.

• **BELIEF.** Belief is harder to measure than a ranking or number in a bank account but it's definitely the most important. Without the belief to pursue, to compete, to work, to wake up and train, there was no point.

I *believed* I was good at tennis. I believed I was a hard worker. I believed I had made sacrifices. I believed I was very fit and I believed that if I served well, I could beat anybody on any given day. But did I really believe, deep down, that I could qualify for the Slams consistently? Did I believe that I could get to be Top 200? And even if I believed—did I *want* it?

The answer was no. The belief was waning. And now, having peeled the curtain back, seeing the reality of pro tennis, it was safe to say that even if I did have the belief, I didn't *want* to go through with it in the first place. If you would have told me that in one month I would be playing the US Open, I would have stuck it out, but I knew better than that. I saw players like me struggle for six, seven, even ten years before a breakthrough (it took Raven ten years to make a Grand Slam final, his only one). Older college players that I idolized were still buried deep in the trenches of pro tennis. Slowly moving their rankings up year after year—700, 660, 600, 585—and honestly, it looked miserable. It looked deflating and exhausting and when I saw them at the tournament sign-ins, I didn't envy them, I pitied them. Their tennis bags were faded, they had been wearing the same match shirts for seven years now, their eyes didn't have the hunger, or the spark or the belief. I didn't want to be thirty-three years old, staying in a Holiday Inn Express, stringing my own rackets, making oatmeal in the hotel lobby. I didn't want to have those "far away eyes" (to borrow a Rolling Stones song title) that I was seeing on these players. And I was twenty-four, young enough still that I could avoid it.

If pro tennis is a marathon with thousands of competitors, I was doing pretty good. I was in the top middle of the pack, there were thousands and thousands of runners behind me, runners who would gladly exchange places with me if given the opportunity. But I wasn't focused on what was behind me, I was looking at the runners in *front* of me, who were extremely fast, and from my vantage point, moving further and further away. I was breathing heavy, my legs were feeling like stone, and, here's probably the biggest kiss of death, I was satisfied with what I had accomplished and the rankings that I had. Put all that in the pot and stir it around for a little bit and you end up with a dish called retirement. Or, when you are ranked #864 in the world in tennis, you don't say "I am retiring" you say "I am quitting."

...

As happens often in life, once that seed was planted in my mind, the universe pushed me in that direction as well. Within days of mostly deciding pro tennis was over, two distinct options presented themselves to me, practically fell in my lap, and they would change the course of my life.

The first was the firing of the University of Michigan men's tennis coach. The second was spotting a chalkboard sign on the sidewalk in front of a bar I happened to walk by in downtown Ann Arbor. It read: "Tuesday night comedy open mic."

Michigan has one of the best athletic departments in the country, but their tennis team had been struggling for a while, and the coach was let go. This was a huge opportunity in the tennis world—getting that job meant taking over an enormously prestigious program with a huge budget. At that point in college tennis, University of Illinois was a national powerhouse (having won all Big Ten championships and some national championships as well) and a natural pick for that Michigan head coach position was the U of Illinois assistant coach Bruce Berque. Michigan hadn't beaten Illinois in over ten years (*I* had never lost to Michigan ever, singles or doubles or team event—sorry I had to write that), so why try to beat Illinois when it might just be easier to steal one of their coaches?

Bruce (currently the head coach at University of Texas) was the best coach I ever had. Committed, smart, honest, competitive—you name it. He is exactly who you want your kid to be coached by. He might not have the polish or the diplomatic sensibilities of a Coach Craig, but he knew how to win, and he was the perfect guy to take a Michigan program and whip it into shape. Also, Bruce had coached me, and liked me. And I, an Ann Arbor native, who was about to wrap up my pro playing career, was the perfect candidate to be his assistant at Michigan.

Despite me sending a six-page proposal to the Michigan athletic director ("Why you should hire Michael Kosta as the new men's tennis coach"—they never responded), they made the right decision and hired Bruce as the head coach. This left an open position for the assistant job at University of Illinois, my alma mater, the school I had helped win four Big Ten titles and achieve a #1 NCAA ranking. *Supposedly* (emphasis on supposedly), Craig was also "interested" in hiring me as his new assistant.

Nine days ago, I was a failed pro tennis player, staying at my parents' house with what little belongings I owned, wondering what to do with my life, and today I appeared to have two potential job offers at both University of Michigan and University of Illinois. The tides were turning.

Bruce did what Bruce always does—he called me and communicated clearly and directly. I trusted him and I trusted that what he said was what he meant. Bruce hadn't offered me the job yet, but

I was confident that he would if I told him that's what I wanted to do. I told Bruce I needed to call Craig and find out his interest in hiring me. This was not an easy decision. I loved the University of Illinois, and I felt I owed a lot to Craig and the program. But Michigan had more upside (at the time, Illinois was ranked #6 in the country and Michigan was #54—the opportunity to make a dramatic improvement at Michigan was greater) and working with Bruce, in my opinion, might be more hours, might require some managing of his personality, but would overall be simpler. He would be a boss that was easier to understand and move on a clear path with. Bruce was a cannon. Able to create huge amounts of force, when all the mechanisms are lined up properly. Hard to move, hard to adjust, not soft or sentimental but if you followed directions, you could kill a lot of stuff. Craig, on the other hand, was a cannon . . . and a machine gun and a fighter jet, and a politician and a salesman and a diplomat and a sword and a killer mosquito and a father figure and an obsessive worker and . . . I think you get the point.

That second sign from the universe was also in the back of my head: "Tuesday night comedy open mic." Ann Arbor is an arts town, I knew that if I settled down there I could, potentially, dive into the arts—or, at the very least, comedy on Tuesday nights. Also, I thought, Detroit is thirty-five minutes from Ann Arbor. There are comedy clubs in Detroit, there must be even more open mics. I had yet to even step on a stage, but the draw, the desire to perform comedy was an undeniable influence. Here's the real mental fuckery of it all: years prior, when I was grinding out tennis losses, working into the dark in Tampa, listening to a Sam lecture about the proper way to drink water (real), Craig left me a voicemail that went something like this:

Michael, it's Craig, I was watching a comedian on TV today and he was terrible. You are so much funnier than him and I'm just calling to tell you that if you ever decide to go for it in comedy, I think you'll be tremendously successful. You are extremely funny. Just do it. Bye.

This is the kind of shit that Craig would do all the time—and it really messes with you. The other week, actually, I was at Kevin Anderson's (former world #4, and U of Illinois player) charity event and I got talking to the event photographer, Kenny Kim. I asked him why he became a photographer and he said, "Well, I liked taking pictures when I was in college and one day Craig pulled me aside and said, 'You have a great eye, you should start your own photography business, you would be really successful.' That was twenty years ago and now I can thankfully call myself a professional photographer." Those who knew Craig well didn't hear his words as just light advice, we respected him so much and his ability to get results, that when he spoke it was scripture to us. He was like a cult leader without all the sex and tax evasion. So he was . . . a leader and a powerful one.

But, like a lot of powerful leaders, Craig was complicated. I called him and asked him point-blank: "Are you considering me for the assistant position at University of Illinois?" I learned from Bruce to not mince words. Craig, however, was not Bruce. He did what powerful people do when they don't want to answer the question (something I now know from interviewing so many politicians for *The Daily Show*): he talked. And talked. He talked about his vision and South Africa's Davis Cup history, and the success he's had, and what he ate for lunch, and why the electoral college was a silly idea. I asked him again, "Are you considering me for the assistant position at University of Illinois?" This time he was more concise, and he said that he was considering me along with many others, and he rattled off a bunch of names, some of whom had Grand Slam titles, most of whom I had watched play tennis on TV, and all of whom were considerably more qualified and successful than I was. I slept on it for twenty-four hours then called Bruce and he offered me the job on the spot.

As a courtesy, I called Craig and told him I had accepted the University of Michigan job. I was on a cordless phone in my parents' driveway, the same place where my dad told my mom that her father was dead inside. Craig was silent for about five seconds and then he yelled at me for five minutes. Told me I was never a real Illinois supporter, that I always loved Michigan more, that I was always more loyal to Bruce, that I was making the wrong decision, and then he hung up. It was seven years before we spoke again.

One of the first things I did after verbally accepting the Michigan job was drive down to the music store and buy a microphone and mic stand. I was planning on going to the open mic show that night as a spectator and was curious how the performers used and worked the mic and stand. That's pretty telling, isn't it? I was offered a new coaching job, a job that was sought after by hundreds of other qualified coaches/players, and the first thing I did was go buy comedy equipment. I didn't draw out plans for Michigan tennis, strategize with Bruce, learn the players' names, or tour the facility, no, I started to plant seeds for a career in comedy. It was hard to pinpoint, but there was a feeling in the air that was exciting, optimistic, and a bit dangerous. Now I know—that's the feeling you get when you take the first steps toward a dream.

...

Johnny Carson left *The Tonight Show* in May 1992, when was I was twelve. I wanted to see his last episode so badly that my parents let me bring a small color TV into my room and watch it in bed. The V-shaped antennas were sticking out of the covers as I watched from under them. I barely remember it, but I remember the feeling it gave me. A single person, in front of a curtain, trying to (and usually) making me laugh. It seemed so simple and so complicated at the same time.

My family loved tennis, but comedy was definitely my family's love language. Yes, you had to step over cans of tennis balls in the living room, and someone frequently knocked over the rackets leaned up against the walls, but, in my opinion, the foundational core of my family was comedy. Here are some examples:

- My mom would cut out funny cartoons from the paper and put them on the fridge. One in particular comes to mind of a wife washing her hair in the sink and says to her husband, "Darling, can you pass me the hair dryer?" The image depicts the husband handing her a handgun. This was on our fridge in the center of our house.

- My parents were going to a Halloween costume party competition, where you had to dress as a well-known couple. Couples dressed as Bonnie and Clyde, Ronald and Nancy Reagan, etc. My parents dressed as tennis great Monica Seles and the German man who stabbed her. My dad wore stereotypical German clothing and my mom wore a tennis outfit with a knife in her back. They won the contest.

- My uncles (who, let's be honest, were really the reason we made Polish jokes—blame everything on the uncles) were very funny. One of my favorite bits they did was the "Cry at the restaurant bill" bit. Whenever we would go out to eat, one of them would generously and kindly offer to pick up the tab. Then when the bill came, whoever had picked up the tab would slowly and systematically study the bill (making sure everyone at the table was paying attention) and then would slowly and very publicly start to cry. The bill was just that big that he couldn't hold back the tears. The joke climaxed when the payer would grab a dirty napkin and pretend to wipe away the tears. It's a beautiful joke that encompasses the real pain behind wanting to do a good deed. I love it and have one hundred percent stolen it from them, and every time I do, I know my dad is proud of me for honoring his uncles' legacy.

- The first stand-up I ever saw live was Bill Cosby (cancel sound), but the comic that really inspired me and got me excited about stand-up comedy was Dennis Miller. When I was twelve, my mom took me to see him at the Power Center in Ann Arbor. Dennis covered politics and has an out-of-this-world vocabulary (I wish I had a better word to describe this). I barely even knew who the president was, so there's no way I really knew what he was talking about (I still don't understand half the shit he says), but I loved his persona, his arrogance, and his performative style. I loved the idea that he was the smartest person in the room and he knew it and he acted like it. Other kids my age wanted to go to the Monster Truck show and here I was laughing at a Dennis Miller rant about Mikhail Gorbachev's Leninistic rule of the Soviet people. OK, babe.

- When my mom tucked us in at night, she always asked us a few questions to get us to reflect on our day and our world. She would share her answers, too. It was a great way to wind down and connect with my mom, and now I realize it taught us the foundation of good conversation. It helped us feel safe and loved and next thing you knew you were asleep. The questions were as follows: What's something that you did today that you liked? What's something nice you did for someone else (this was hardest for me to answer)? What's something you're looking forward to tomorrow? After a few years of this, I asked her if we could add the question "What's something I laughed at today?" We talked about the different things that made us laugh each night. Not only did I look back to find the comedy in my day, but I was also preparing to look for it the next day.

This is literally how one trains their mind to observe and find comedy everywhere. When I got a little older and started daily journaling, I finished each day with "something that I laughed at." Over the course of many years, I had a long list of things that made me laugh, or that I found funny. This helped me understand not only my sense of humor but also the possibilities of comedy everywhere. You know how depressed people always see the sad stuff? Negative people always see the negative side of things? I was learning and teaching myself to see the funny. Funny people see the funny.

Comedy is a part of my critical makeup as a person and as part of my family unit. So when I finally stepped on stage to do stand-up, it didn't feel like a departure from my playing and coaching tennis, it felt like I was coming back to my original state, like I was sitting around the dinner table trying to make my family laugh.

People ask me all the time "How did you go from tennis into comedy?!" but the more astute observation is that I went from comedy to tennis . . . and then back to comedy. Comedy was there from day one; tennis was an alternate path that took me down a totally different avenue—probably because I was good at it and had success with it and when you grow up in Michigan and you don't know anyone in show business, it never crosses your mind that you can be a comedian. I'm still not sure how I pulled it off. (This book is helping me unpack it all, so thanks for joining me on this journey.)

BYE BRUCE

1ST TIME HEADLINING $75

I'm Happy

 BYE MANAGER

PART 4
Comedy,
Seriously...
2004–2010

 YUK YUKS

MOVE TO LA I'M A STAR

CROTCH KARATE

Not as Funny

COMEDY STORE OPEN MIC "EDDIE?"

HOW COMEDIANS CARRY THEMSELVES

 MOOSE LODGE

 LA ACTING CLASS

LOCKED BIKE LOCKED

PERFORMING FOR A COLUM

CAR SOBBING

MY-KID-NEEDS-MEDS CON

 CONAN SHOWCASE

 US HEALTH CARE

COCKROACH APARTMENT

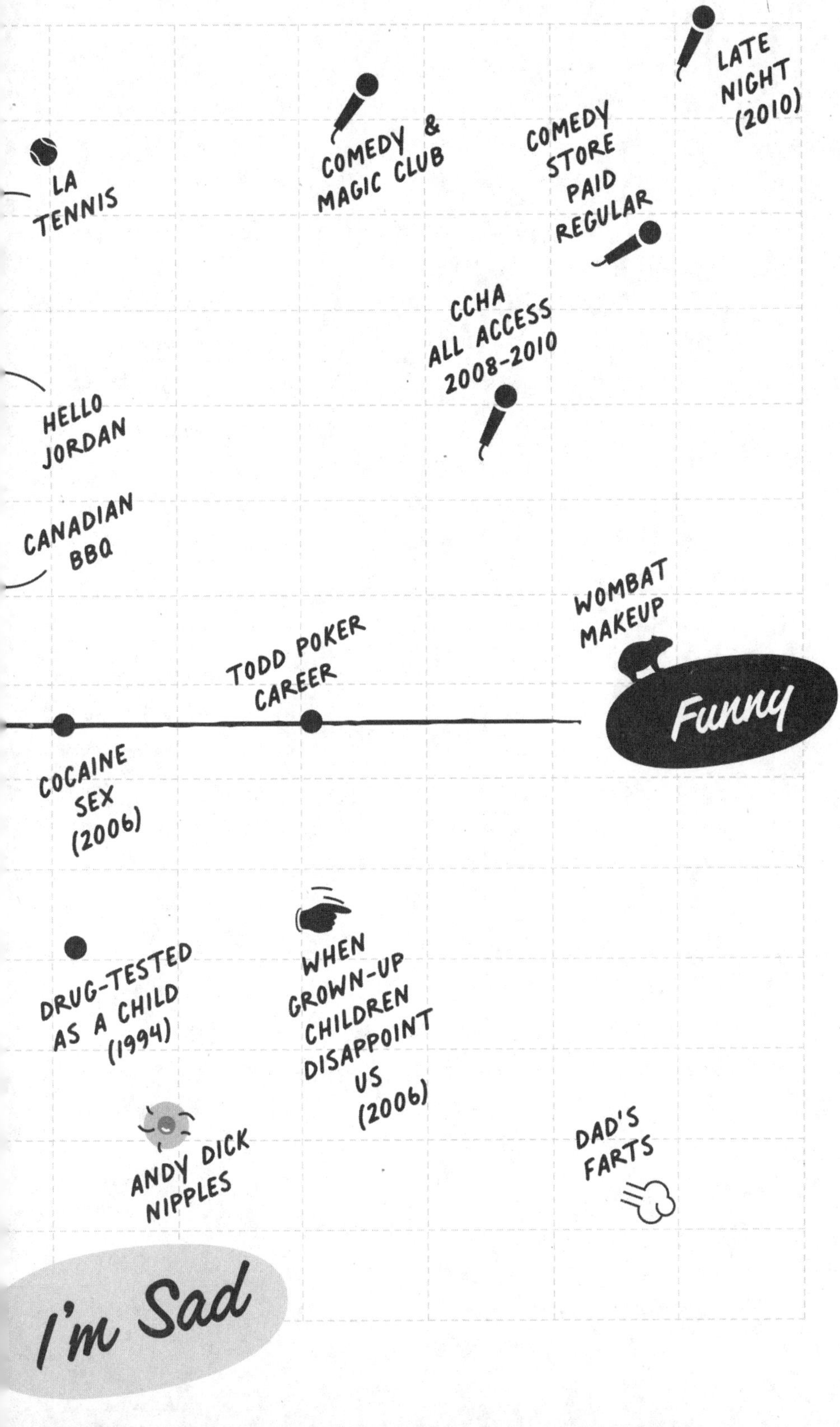

LATE
NIGHT
(2010)

LA
TENNIS

COMEDY &
MAGIC CLUB

COMEDY
STORE
PAID
REGULAR

CCHA
ALL ACCESS
2008-2010

HELLO
JORDAN

CANADIAN
BBQ

WOMBAT
MAKEUP

TODD POKER
CAREER

Funny

COCAINE
SEX
(2006)

DRUG-TESTED
AS A CHILD
(1994)

WHEN
GROWN-UP
CHILDREN
DISAPPOINT
US
(2006)

DAD'S
FARTS

ANDY DICK
NIPPLES

I'm Sad

Chapter 21

Game Set Match, Comedy

LOADED WITH A purchased mic stand and microphone stashed in the basement of my parents' house, a copy of Richard Belzer's 1988 book: *How to Be a Stand-Up Comic* from the Ann Arbor Public library, and a new job as the University of Michigan men's tennis assistant coach, I was ready to, at the very least, start seriously researching stand-up comedy.

It was early summer, and the Michigan tennis season was going to start in a matter of weeks. And even with this amazing coaching opportunity, a job that hundreds of other qualified coaches applied for, the part that I was most excited about was that I was finally going to be stationary for a while and I could dig into and try my hand at stand-up. A strange priority, especially for someone who had never even stepped foot on stage.

I read somewhere that Paul Reiser, stand-up comic and actor, said that you don't get inspired by watching genius, you get inspired by watching mediocrity and thinking "I can at least do that." (Years later I worked with Reiser a few times at the Comedy and Magic Club in Hermosa Beach, California, and I asked him where he said that and he told me, "I don't think I ever said that.") Either way, it sums up what I thought while watching the Open Mic at the Heidelberg Bar on Main Street downtown Ann Arbor that Tuesday Night.

How do I say this nicely, let's just say I was very . . . inspired. After going to a few more of the open mics and watching the local comedians, I had a gist of what I was about to dive into. And what I was about to dive into was a very loose, very unorganized, very amateur comedy situation. There were some funny jokes and a few funny people, but for the most part I was completely taken aback by how unprofessional everyone was. Keep in mind, I was still seeing the world from the frame of a high-level tennis player/college coach. I was seeing all this as someone who was told to tuck in his shirt, shave his face, shake hands with strength, don't do drugs, look people in the eye, project confidence. Some observations I wrote down at the time:

- Comedians are dressed very poorly, filthy
- Many are noticeably drunk
- Half are not speaking clearly or are mumbling into the microphone
- They aren't making eye contact with audience
- Mic stand is causing visual interference (comic standing behind mic stand)
- Comics are incredibly socially awkward
- Lots of jokes about drugs

There were usually about ten comics on the lineup. Half made me laugh, half made me cringe. I loved how different each person was. When done right, stand-up comedy gives you an inside look into that person's unique brain, point of view, and experiences. If you asked ten quality comics to write a joke with the word "pirate" in it, they would all write something different that only their mind could think of (the opposite of that—jokes that most everyone can think of—are generally referred to as "hacky" or easy and common).

I observed two different open mic nights at the Heidelberg Bar in Ann Arbor. Both times there were small but supportive audiences, mostly girlfriends and buddies, but still an audience. I noticed that a good joke would get laughs and a bad joke or bad performance would not. Bombing was very much an option. And what I wanted to do, on my first time performing, was not bomb. This room would be a fair litmus test to determine if something was funny or, more specifically, if *I* was funny.

Another thing that surprised me with this comedy community was how friendly everyone was. By my second time as an audience member, I knew almost all the performers and felt like they knew and at least were pretending to like me. We hung out, had beers, and I absolutely loved hearing the comics talk to each other about their jokes, ways to improve their setups, tag something, tighten something. It was like peeling back the curtain and listening to two hired assassins talk about the best bullet caliber or something murder-y like that. Comedy was the complete opposite of the tense, competitive feeling around a tennis tournament, where everyone is sizing everyone else up, not giving away too much information, puffing their chests out. I even wrote down in my journal: "They really seem to be rooting for each other and trying to help each other." For better or worse, I was seeing them as competitors (which is particularly arrogant because I had zero stage time at this point). This is a mindset I still work on silencing because as I have climbed up the ladder of showbiz, I find it's not helpful, and if anything it drives you mad. Ironically, that competitive mindset was quite helpful in tennis, but in comedy I've had to learn over the last twenty years to stop worrying about *them* and just focus on *you*. I hear athletes say that all the time now, but for me, I didn't really learn that until I switched out of sports and into stand-up.

Motivated from watching some of the mediocre comedians, and knowing that I was in a transition period of my life, I said "screw it," and I signed up for a seven-minute slot the next Tuesday night at the open mic. It was sudden, it came a little bit out of nowhere, but it felt right. It felt like I had finally honored (succumbed to?) my secret desire to be a stand-up comedian. Remembering what my dad told me at Warmdaddy's blues bar years earlier, I wasn't about to talk myself out of something that I dreamed of doing. What's the worst that could happen? I bomb in front of a bunch of overweight, self-conscious, mustard-stained-shirt-wearing barely comics? Shit, I had lost tennis matches crying my eyes out with my entire family watching in the stands, I had lost 6–0 6–1 in my last collegiate match for Illinois—nothing could hurt that bad.[1] I had a loose set list of jokes, I had been practicing holding and moving the mic in and out of the mic stand for about a week (this reminded me of the years of tennis swingwork I did in front of the mirror over and over again, trying to beat the perfect technique into my brain), and thanks to years of having to speak at trophy ceremonies, tennis camps, and award banquets I was confident in my ability to publicly speak. I figured that alone already put me somewhere in the middle of this amateur comedy pack. I mean, some of these performers were whispering on stage holding the mic three feet away from their face. The same way someone might sign up for a Tough Mudder without truly knowing what to expect, I signed up and thought, "OK, let's do this shit and find out what you are made of."

I had a sense of urgency because I knew once the Michigan tennis

---

1   Reminder: the guy I lost to is now a failed and banned poker player who was accused of running multiple scams in the Las Vegas area ☺

season started in a few weeks, Bruce was going to smother me with work. Part of the reason why Bruce is a brilliant coach is that he doesn't just dot the i's and cross the t's—he double-checks that the dots are perfect on the i's and the crosses are the correct length on the t's. Then he double-checks that. Really annoying shit, but the shit that separates good coaches from great. It's the reason he had won NCAA championships *before* taking the Michigan job, and won again *after* taking this job. His attention to detail created an odd dichotomy for me because in my comedy life, a life I soon developed over the course of the next few months, the phrase "attention to detail" was nowhere to be found. Comedians (at the level that I was entering), frequently slept past the show time, or forgot they even had a show. Once I even saw a comic wearing two different shoes while on stage, and it didn't appear to be on purpose (real show, Joey's Comedy Club, 2006). If it sounds like I am being judgmental here, I was. The coaching world is incredibly regimented and structured, with rights and wrongs, expectations are either met or they aren't. Take that mindset into the comedy world and my mind could not let go of how much stuff these other comics were doing wrong. It took me a long time to let go of some of that judgment and learn that in the arts things are not as linear and black-and-white as they are in sports.

My first performance was on a Tuesday in June 2004, at the Heidelberg Bar on Main Street. Since signing up seven days earlier, the anticipation and butterflies I felt had grown larger each day. It was a warm night and I was tense and nervous, but even just saying I was going to do an open mic felt like an accomplishment. Like I was already halfway there.

At this point in my life, I was trained like an animal to prepare and tackle challenges with extreme confidence. That was the athlete way. You don't see an Olympic gymnast, prior to competing, gingerly approach the high beam with prayer hands mouthing "Please don't fall, please don't ruin your life, please don't embarrass yourself." No, they approach with confidence, swagger, and disciplined focus. Even if they don't believe it, they *look* like they believe it. Because I didn't know any other way, because for the last eighteen years I had learned to act, was coached to act that way when challenged, that's how I approached my first comedy set.

Don't get me wrong, I was definitely nervous, but it was a competition nerve, it was result-oriented. I knew how to handle that. It wasn't a "Holy shit you could completely humiliate yourself and your family." It was more "*Win*, don't lose." My comedy now, I hope, has a lot more humility, awareness, less bravado, but my comedy then, especially the first time I performed, was a direct reflection of who I *was* then. And who I was, was a cocky, talented, likable douchebag. If you don't believe me, wait till you hear the two jokes I attempted. Also, to help tame the nerves I had four Labatt Blues beforehand, which didn't tame them, just made me feel them less. God, I had so much to learn.

It was important to me that I attempt a "physical" joke or an "act out" joke. I thought physical comedy was really funny (i.e., Steve Martin arrow through the head) and I figured why ease into it, go for it right away. This was supposed to be a leap, not a stroll, so I leapt. After my name was announced by the MC, I confidently strolled past him on stage, grabbed the microphone, and moved the stand to the back of the stage like I practiced in my parents' basement. It was a high stage, and with my height, I felt like I was towering over everyone. There were maybe thirty to forty people there, and most people sat at two tops with bottles of beer on the table. There was a side bar, and a grumpy bartender who everyone hated—it was hard to make him laugh people told me. I grabbed the mic, avoided direct eye contact with anyone in the audience, and launched into my first joke, determined to bulldoze any butterflies that existed with energy, beer, machismo, and volume.

Armed with the confidence of a state and Big Ten tennis champion, I cockily strutted through my first joke ever. "Good evening, ladies and gentlemen, I have a black belt, black belt in karate . . . crotch karate." And then I ran around the stage pretending to karate chop audience members with my crotch. Are you laughing? Is it funny? Is it funny because it's funny or is it funny because it isn't funny? At the time, I thought it was funny because it was funny, but now I think it's funny because it isn't funny. I don't, however, think it isn't funny. Two things were for certain: (1) it broke the ice and (2) no one else, on this show at least, was trying this type of comedy. So, at a minimum, I was memorable.

The joke didn't bomb, but it didn't exactly kill either. I remember hearing one big chuckle, which was my sister Kristy, god bless her soul (to this day, she is a wonderful supporter and sometimes the only one laughing, love ya TT), and maybe a few other whispers of a laugh but that could have been more "wtf is going on here" than "omg this is so funny." It hadn't crossed my mind that I wouldn't be in the free and clear for my second joke. How do I keep that energy, bravado, and confidence going if the first joke doesn't do well? If I was a bobsledder, it was like I had spent all my time preparing for the first turn but never thought about or realized I had six more turns to go. Well shit, I'm about to die. What an idiot!

I watch newer comics today and this is a common problem, and a trap that I fell directly into. Whatever psychosis us comics are stricken by, we always think our brain and our idea is just so funny everyone will like it. I mean, who won't think karate chopping my dick around the stage, yelling "Hiya! Hiya!" wouldn't be the funniest joke ever told? Well, guess what? It wasn't. And in this line of work, the only way you learn what is truly funny to the audience, to other people, is through the pain of performing in front of them—and at this moment I was learning that exact lesson live and in person.

I credit tennis one hundred percent for, in this brief time between my first joke and second joke, my ability to regroup, stay composed, and stay on track. I had a comedy set, it was seven minutes long, I just did a joke that lasted fifteen seconds and it didn't tear the roof off the place like I had hoped. If I was boxing, it was like I got punched in the face right away, and it hurt, but thanks to my thousands of hours of competing, I wasn't knocked out and I still had a few punches left. The fight was still happening; I had to get my shit together so I didn't get knocked out. Is this too many sports metaphors? As a reader, are you feeling like a hockey goalie and I'm slapshotting metaphor pucks at your face? (Last one.)

But for a few seconds, which felt like minutes, I couldn't think of my next joke. I couldn't think of anything. I just stood there, bright lights on my face, microphone in hand, I remember looking to my left and there was a woman sitting with her friend and they were just staring at me, and for a brief, brief flutter I felt my heart stop, the sweat ducts on my right palm became activated, my six-foot-four-inch spine shrunk to two feet, I saw my sister shuffle in her seat. If there was music, it stopped, and then, just like that, just like the sun rising, like a ball bouncing, like a clock moving, my heart started, my spine elongated, my sweat ducts shriveled up, I got my breath back and the set list I had rehearsed and written down over and over came to the front of my mind. "It's time to do your second joke," I thought, and we were back on track. I nervously shook out my shoulders, told myself I was a successful tennis player and none of these people mattered to me (false bravado but I needed something) and delivered the next one. I remember thinking, "I'm really gonna know what they think of me after this."

The problem, of course, and I bet you are thinking it, is that my second joke wasn't any better . . . but it was *so* ridiculous that it actually got real laughs. If crotch karate got chuckles out of "holy shit what is wrong with this kid," my next joke just made people laugh, viscerally, and it was a tremendous feeling. Maybe the audience was more willing to go with me because of how stupid the opening joke was; maybe I'm a comedy genius, you can decide for yourself. The joke went something like "I have a girlfriend and she's a virgin . . . well, she *was* a virgin" and then, in keeping with a theme, I went around the stage pretending to high-five audience members. *Wham.* Real laughs. Actual laughs, not pity laughs. I even saw the grumpy bartender crack a smile. Hey, this wasn't exactly Shakespeare, but I wasn't going for Shakespeare, I was going for laughs at a bar in front of drunk people, and I got it. It was pure and perfect and exhilarating and marvelous. *Wow.* I've been chasing that feeling ever since.

The rest of my set? I don't remember. Everything was a blur by this point. It was like the fourteen months of tennis I played after my JeJu Island loss. I had gotten a couple of laughs, some sympathy laughs, some real actual laughs, and that was all I needed. I was hooked. I had thought of something in my mind, written it down, performed it into a microphone and watched people laugh, in real time, right in front of me. I changed their face from a resting face to a laughing face—it felt like I had a superpower. This wasn't theory, this was as simple as: I told a joke; people laughed.

That night, so many things clicked, so many of my feelings, emotions, personality traits made sense. Constantly getting in trouble for acting out in class, the incessant report cards that read "Michael is wonderful but he always demands the most attention," my parents always telling me to just sit quietly and stop cracking jokes, every girlfriend I ever had at some point said to me "Are you *always* trying to be funny?" . . . there was such a sense of *ease* in my brain after that first performance. It was like I was a speed junkie my whole life and I finally flew a fighter jet. I honestly remember my brain, the RPMs of my mind, slowing *down* after the performance. I was in a more regulated space. I wrote in my journal that night: "I wonder if this whole time, I was playing tennis because I liked the attention of being good, not because I really loved the sport." That was the first time I questioned my passion for tennis, but it was a valid question. I had officially five minutes of stage time under my belt.

It should be noted that after my first time on stage, I got drunk. I was so relieved that it went well(ish) and I felt accomplished and wanted to celebrate. The way I knew to celebrate, the way that high-level collegiate athletes and many pro athletes celebrated, was they got drunk. The reality of what it took to train at that level, compete with those pressures was high, so when something went well, you blew off steam, usually with alcohol.[2] That night, I got drunk with my sister, the other comedians, whoever else was around. It reminded me of drinking with the Illinois tennis team after a big win, I had a built-in group of friends—albeit they didn't exactly look like championship athletes—they were fun, nice, and it was refreshing to interact with a totally different community. Looking back, it's clear I was also setting up a habit, a ritual, of getting drunk after the show, after the stress of performing, the anxiety associated with "will it or won't it go well?" I had established that, after all that, I would have a few beers. I don't recommend starting a new segment of your life this way. I was creating a pretty strong bond between the relationship of performing comedy and also getting drunk afterward. They became a couple: perform, get drunk. Next night: perform, get drunk. Sometimes, depending on the stress associated with the show, or the number of people in the audience, they were a power couple. And within the comedy community, getting drunk is hardly seen as problematic. Unlike athletes, comedians would never say, "Hey, slow down, Kosta, you have a big show tomorrow." Usually it was more like "Let's get messed up and celebrate how we just survived this insane thing."

One of the things I remember most about taking that giant leap

---

2   Athletes are commonly drug tested. They are tested during competitions and randomly throughout the year for performance enhancing drugs, but many street drugs are also banned and if caught will jeopardize your ability to compete and make money. The first time I was ever drug tested was at the Boys 14 National Clay Court Championships in Nashville, Tennessee. I was twelve. My opponent—who I had just lost to 6–1 6–1—was not selected to be tested. I remember looking at the official and immediately said, "Don't you think I might have done better if I was taking illegal performance-enhancing drugs?"

into comedy is the support of my sister Kristy. She was there for my first night and showed up as one of my biggest comedy fans for many more nights of comedy (still is always laughing and always support-ive). When I remember that first performance, after the crotch karate joke, I still hear one laugh in my memory. One person laughed at that joke. It was my sister. That's really, really nice and hard to describe how helpful it made me feel then and still now. Knowing Kristy was in the audience was also a wonderful safety net—no matter what happens here tonight I know my sister loves me and will still be my sister. I have experienced some terrible sets of comedy, I have bombed so hard that my ass sweat through my jeans, I have bombed so hard that you can hear the automatic paper towel dispenser dispensing paper towels in the bathroom in the restaurant attached to the building—not even in the comedy club. I have bombed so hard that a man threw a beer bottle at me and the security guard told him he had "good aim," but I have never bombed so hard that my own family filled out all the paperwork required to un-family me. Knowing my sister was there was beautiful. Also, Kristy, like all of us in our family, liked to drink alcohol.

It has taken a lot of struggle, a lot of willpower and discipline to *break* the habit of getting drunk after each set. If I could go back now to that first night, I would just perform, hang out, have some water, and go home. My one regret from that night is forming that habit. As my comedy life progressed, so did the alcohol portion. They had to; they were in a relationship after all. Now, my relationship with alcohol is hard to label and best described as complicated, but at the moment I can say I have a much healthier grip on it. My sister Kristy has been sober for seventeen years. My point, kids, is if you are about to start a new, challenging, scary adventure of your life, just keep in mind that the habits you set up in the beginning will stick with you, good and bad. Sorry, I know this sounds like coach-speak, but at this point in my life, I was also a collegiate coach, so deal with it.

Chapter 22

Collision

OVER THE NEXT few months, while Bruce and I were also launching a drastically new and improved Michigan men's tennis program, the local Ann Arbor comedians, the funny ones, quickly became my friends and comedy peers. It's not that the unfunny ones weren't my friends, it's just the funny ones got booked together more often, and thankfully I was seen as one of the funny ones. This group was kind to me, the tall, cocky tennis coach who infiltrated their comedy circle; they treated me as a friend and peer. These comics were John F. O'Donnell, Brent Sullivan, Jesse Popp, Vince Averill, and Vince Paparelli, to name a few. Some of them I keep in touch with, some moved to LA after I did and we stayed friends, some are gone and I don't know where they are. They are all funny comics and their jokes still float around in my head from time to time, because when I started this portion of my life, they were the jokes I knew and heard.

One thing that became really obvious quickly is that comics really liked to talk shit about other comics. At first, I found it funny and amusing, but as it continued it started to make me uncomfortable and wasn't something I wanted to be around. Comedy is hard enough as it is—it's literally handling a panic attack almost every single night (in front of strangers)—why would I also want to deal with the guy I carpooled with to the show talking shit about me behind my back?

It also struck me that the tennis world, oddly, didn't really have this. You might talk a little shit in sports but at the end of the day, the scoreboard does an excellent job at clearing up any beef. You think I suck at tennis? I just beat you 6–2 6–2. It doesn't matter what you think. I decided this was how I had to approach comedy as well. It would be easy to get wrapped in the shit talking, in the gossip, in the other people, but as I told my players all the time, "Focus on you, you can control you." That's how I moved forward. And like a Formula 1 driver given the go-ahead by his team principal, or in my case, a newly hired tennis coach who had found his true calling (and it wasn't tennis), I moved forward pretty quickly.

• • •

I knew I needed stage time, so goddamn it that's what I did. The Michigan coaching job was full steam ahead and if I thought Bruce was going to run me ragged, I had underestimated it, "ragged" would have been wonderful; he was running me to the point of complete exhaustion. But I remembered a passage from *How to Be a Stand-Up Comic*: "You are always a stand-up comic. If you are working as a car mechanic, you are a stand-up comic. If you are a waitress, you are a stand-up comic. Those jobs are only so you can afford to be a stand-up comic." I took that to heart.

I had recently moved out of my parents' place and closed on a small two-bedroom house within walking distance from downtown Ann Arbor. It afforded me the ability to come and go as I pleased without my mom saying something to me the next morning like "Well, you were out late last night . . ." and then me staring blankly out the window. With new house keys and a new excitement for my life, I performed comedy wherever and whenever. Just like a tennis player needs to get "match tough," I needed to get good at comedy, and the only way I knew how to do that was to perform at bowling alleys, restaurants, wedding showers, above bars, below bars, white comedy clubs, black comedy clubs, Arab comedy clubs, Canadian comedy clubs, tennis clubs, golf clubs, barns, haunted hotels, hotel rooms, personal apartments, improv stages, drive-ins, outdoor malls, kids camps, weddings. You name it, I was there, and I gave it my all.

My goal was to get good at comedy so I could quit tennis. I was coaching tennis to earn money ($31,000 a year) so I could afford comedy (I think I just described an addiction?). I started this whole thing as a tennis player, who occasionally would write down jokes in between matches, and now I was a comedian who in my free moments would teach forehands and backhands so I could go back to writing and performing jokes full-time.

Comedy was all I could think about, which is good if you are a comedian but bad if you are the assistant tennis coach at a very prominent national university. I wrote down three rules that I needed to hold myself to in order to make it as a comedian, and I taped the paper to the mirror in my bedroom. The rules were:

- Write every day
- No drugs
- No babies[1]

I slowly got better. Emphasis on slowly. I kept a pile of index cards next to my bed and before I fell asleep I would write down one joke. I had been doing this since I was a kid, in my journal, so now I was just more official about it. A bedtime routine instilled in me by my mom at age six was now an integral part of my comedy life: looking for humor throughout my day. I watched the documentary *Comedian* over and over again. I thought it was so cool how Jerry Seinfeld would just pop into the Gotham Comedy Club in New York City and do a

---

1   Today, I have two kids, don't write every day, and have certainly done drugs (shrug).

set in front of surprised audiences (now I'm lucky enough to know that for every superstar who pops in, there are five less famous comics in the back who just got bumped off the show).

I tried to tackle comedy the way an athlete would tackle his sport. Through hard work and diligence. Resilience came up a lot. I remember an older local Michigan comic said to me, "How are you able to go up every night like you do, don't you need time to recover after your bad sets?"

I thought he was joking. "Time to recover from my bad sets?" Dude, there is no time, you just keep going. In tennis, after you lose, you go practice so you feel better. I once lost so bad at a small pro event in Joplin, Missouri, that I kept my court shoes on and ran two and a half miles on the track next door afterward. My opponent was still packing up his car and looked over and I was puking on the track. Bad set in comedy? Let's drive an hour to that other open mic and see if we can get another set in before the show is over. I'm so thankful that tennis toughened me up emotionally to handle and understand what losing and failure were all about. It gave me the armor and resilience I needed to build a comedy career without worrying about each crappy joke I told. And holy shit did I tell a lot of terrible jokes.[2]

Eventually, after three to four months of this, some of the local comedy club owners and high-level comics in town started to notice my resilience. One guy pulled me aside and said, "Hey dude, you're funny, you want to come do my show at Joey's Comedy Club, it has a wood stage floor." Holy shit a wood stage floor!? Hell yeah, I want to! Still no pay, but I bet my jokes will land a lot harder knowing I am standing on real wood as opposed to the stained carpet I usually perform on.

That same club, with the wood floor—Joey's Comedy Club in

---

2   Some bad joke subjects I remember: rocketship exhaust; fish relaxation; plus-sized models; a critique; baby carrots vs baby corn. I still stand by the fish relaxation joke.

Livonia, Michigan—started to use me more and more. Maybe it's because I was funny, maybe it's because I kept bringing Pam, the booker, flowers every time she used me. (A trick I learned from my tennis days—I kept bribing the tournament director in Mexico with Marlboro Red cartons so he would schedule me at night, when it was much cooler). Giving the comedy booker flowers so she kept using me? Yeah, a bit icky, a bit forward, but I wanted stage time. To me, the stage time was more valuable than real money. Besides, my UM paycheck was giving me roughly $1,700 a month, so I didn't care.[3]

Roughly six months into the Michigan job, at the start of winter 2004, I was proud to say I had perfected the balance of coaching tennis all day and doing comedy at night. Because the Michigan job was so prominent, because people pointed you out at cafes and restaurants as a member of the UofM coaching staff, because parents would introduce themselves to you all over town, I kept my comedy a secret as best I could. I had so much respect for Bruce and for college coaches, I didn't want to lose a potential recruit or tarnish Michigan's reputation by promoting my comedy shows, where, at the time, I was running around the stage high-fiving people because my girlfriend was no longer a virgin.

I led a double life and a normal daily schedule looked like this:

6:00 a.m.—Be with the men's tennis team in the Michigan weight room (I wasn't working out, just there as support for our players, even though there were three full-time strength

---

3   Eighteen years later I was sitting at the comics table at the Comedy Cellar in New York. The booker was there, holding court, taking visitors, like royalty. One by one, I watched comedians come by and present her with gifts, cards, flowers, even a gift card to get her hair done. I started to mock these desperate comics in my mind, then I remembered how I used to bring Pam flowers after each set at Joey's Comedy Club, which then reminded me of how I used to bring that tournament director cigarettes in Mexico. I guess we all do what we feel we have to do at the time.

coaches already doing that, another one of Bruce's annoying requirements, but also the reason he got results).

8:00–11:00 a.m.—On court private lessons with my players at the tennis facility.

12:00 p.m.–2:00 p.m.—Have lunch hiding from Bruce (sometimes in my car, which I parked far from his parking spot just in case he saw me) so I could write jokes or try and review my audio recording from the show the night before.

2:00–5:30 p.m.—Team practice.

5:35 p.m.—In the car, changing out of my very official, Nike-appointed team clothes into my very unofficial comedy clothes. I would often drive over an hour to maybe do a three- to five-minute set anywhere in the central/southeast Michigan area. In the car, I would talk to Bruce on the phone about the upcoming recruits, strategize logistics for the team, and listen to him brainstorm practice plans (emphasis on listen).

8:00–11:00 p.m.—Usually one show, sometimes two if I could organize it, always an open mic, no pay, in front of twenty people tops. I remember noticing how all the comics looked sleepy and groggy. "I just woke up" one would say or "I didn't do anything today" another might.

MIDNIGHT—Try to write one more joke and go to sleep. Tomorrow we were doing it all over again.

I kept this up for a little over a year. It was fairly manageable because I wasn't well known as a comic and people in Ann Arbor think so highly of Michigan coaches, no one ever thought one of us wanted to be anything other than a Michigan coach (Michigan fans/alum are righteously self-absorbed).

But in my second year at Michigan—one year into stand-up comedy—the worlds collided, and it became tougher to manage both. I took an inventory after 12 months: I had performed comedy roughly 260 times (approximately 52 weeks x 5 times a week: I estimated I had performed around 1,600 minutes). I was moving up the comedy ladder and getting more stage time, all while the Michigan tennis team was getting better and playing more matches in locations that were farther away.

As stated, I was living two lives: one as a respectable, highly re-garded tennis coach of a major Big Ten school, and the other as a hustling, hungry, sometimes funny stand-up comic. It was exhaust-ing, and much like a man keeping two families, I often got caught in a few strange predicaments.

Among these instances, three collisions still stick out in my mind. The first was on one of my first recruiting trips, in my first year at Michigan, to Mobile, Alabama. It was the fall of 2004, and Bruce had sent me there to recruit a bunch of high school kids playing in a national tournament (head coaches recruit in Los Angeles, New York, and Miami; assistant coaches get Mobile). As a college coach, you weren't allowed to talk to the players while they were in high school, just observe their matches, and possibly say hi to the parents, but you weren't allowed to converse with them until they made a declaration to officially visit your school. It's a stupid rule but one the NCAA took seriously, so as a coach, the strategy was to make sure you wore loud obnoxious clothing with your team logo on it and sat front and center in front of the kid's parents so they saw that you were watch-ing their kid and knew that you were considering them as a recruit. Essentially planting your school's flag without speaking to anyone.

Bruce really wanted me to watch this one specific player, and of course he played at eight a.m., and of course I was a little hungover and of course I was annoyed that I was a tennis coach when I wanted to be a comedian. But duty calls, so I woke up early, put on my ten pieces of bright yellow clothing with the block Michigan *M* on it, put on my Nike sunglasses to hide my bloodshot eyes, pulled my car out of the Motor Inn or whatever the bad motel was, and proceeded to "watch" this player. It was an awful match, and of course he was playing on the only outdoor court that didn't have any shade. I can't even remember if the kid was any good. I made sure his parents saw me, gave them the old nod, and then sat down to watch and take notes.

About ten minutes in, I realized the parents had no idea what I was actually writing in my notebook, all that really mattered was that they *thought* I was writing important college coach notes about their kid. I might have been a college coach, but by then, I was emotionally, spiritually a comic. I couldn't get jokes and comedy out of my mind. My comic friend had told me of a writing exercise where you write ten different jokes with the same punch line as a way to expand your writing and creativity in how you think about the same topic in different ways. The goal wasn't necessarily to write ten amazing jokes but just write ten *different* ones. So, in my official University of Michigan black leather recruiting portfolio, I started writing jokes where each joke finished (the punch line) with "ashtray."

I was down to joke eight when I look up and the mom of the kid I am supposed to be recruiting, is sitting right behind me, reading my "tennis notes" over my shoulder. She says, "My dad's farts smell like an ashtray, what?—"

I slammed the book closed and said, "We aren't allowed to talk to each other, it's against NCAA rules . . ." and I stumbled out of there.

Later Bruce asked me what I thought of the player, and I made something up, "Ahh, I don't think he's Michigan material."

I avoided a mess there, but around nine months later, the worlds collided again, and this time, there was no escaping it.

One of the things I enjoyed about leaving pro tennis, and being a coach in Ann Arbor, was that I could actually settle into a real way of life. I could have a regular coffee shop, my own house, I could enjoy the benefits of staying in one place for more than five days. For the first time in my adult life, I could explore the city of Ann Arbor— and in particular the local comedy scene. Ann Arbor even had its own comedy club, the Ann Arbor Comedy Showcase. This was a real comedy club, unlike the Heidelberg Bar where I did my first stand-up spot. They had an open mic and I signed up, earning a spot on a Thursday. They were also kind enough to let comics drink as much draft beer as they wanted, so that was a huge bonus and probably the reason I had diarrhea every time I performed there.

One Thursday, the host brings me up, "Ladies and gentleman, Michael Kosta," and I hear someone yell out "Kosta— What are you doing up there, man?" I looked over and it was the entire Michigan women's water polo team, the head coach recognized me from one of our athletic department coaching obligations that we had to do. I had been coaching at Michigan for about a year at this point and knew a lot more people. This is not an advantage when you are trying to lead a secret life.

"Ah, hi Mark, I'm a comic, so I'm . . . ah, gonna do comedy" and then I stumbled my way through a very mediocre set in front of Mark, and the entire water polo team he had brought with him as part of a team-building exercise. Until this point, I had successfully kept my comedy a secret from Bruce, but there was absolutely no way I could keep that up.

Sure enough, the next day in the office he said, "I heard you did comedy last night, that's cool," and walked away. He didn't make it seem like a big deal at all, but I sensed that things were heating up.

The third and last example of the impossibility of keeping my two lives separate is essentially what did my tennis coaching career in. It's hard to stress how seriously this affected me at the time. Now, I know everything is going to be OK, but back then, this situation really stressed me out and I wondered if I would ever be able to do what I truly wanted—which was to be a stand-up comic.

In the spring of the 2006 season, my life as a double agent—an operation I had been maintaining for nearly two years at that point—wasn't working anymore. The reason was that I got decent at comedy. Not excellent, not great, but decent. I had a solid ten to fifteen minutes of material that did well in a variety of rooms, and was a unique comedic perspective from the other comics. My goal was to play the arrogant handsome guy, because I knew no one else could/would, and I figured it would set me apart from the others, which was good intuition. In my opinion, the person you are on stage can be whoever you want to be. I was myself *all the time*, so why not pick a personality, for the stage, that was a bit of a fantasy? And for me, the enormous confidence, the hilariously arrogant, Andre Agassi "Image Is Everything" persona was just so silly and funny. It probably connected with me because my mom had trained us so well to be polite, be kind, send thank-you cards, that I loved the idea of, even if just for five minutes at a time, I got to be the guy who bulldozed his way into and out of everything and expected you to thank him. What's funnier than a guy who thinks he's never going to die? We're all gonna die!

I still love the idea of that type of comedy character on stage, but today it's harder for me to pull off, because growing up has humbled some of the arrogance and also . . . ahem, I'm not as handsome as I was at twenty-four. Ironically, the longer I've been doing stand-up, the closer my stage persona has become to, well, actually me.

At this point, I am as close to me on stage as I've ever been. There's a comfort in that. I'm OK with me, I think me is funny enough and I believe you'll think so, too. The stage gives me permission to exaggerate, use language I normally wouldn't use, dive deeper into topics that normally aren't appropriate, but in all, it is me. I watch old videos of my performances as the cocky dude and I think, "Holy shit, who *is that guy!*"

So, when I started, I was playing a pretty silly character, but I was naturally comfortable on stage, something I attribute to twenty years of playing high-level tennis and being very used to people watching me and expecting something. I was decent and a few people started to notice.

I started booking sets at a great comedy club in Detroit called Mark Ridley's Comedy Castle. The legendary club owner, Mark Ridley himself, who was also a talent manager at the time, approached me one night after a set of and said, "Hey, I want to introduce you to someone."

He pulled me over to the bar and I met a jovial, round-faced, warm, local talent agent named Dave. It was fun to meet an agent; I didn't even know Michigan had agents. "Agent" is one of those words you hear growing up in the Midwest but you think only exists in LA or New York. Here I was talking to a real agent in Detroit—it did surprise me that he drove a Toyota Camry, but who cares, he's an agent.

Dave and I hit it off. He was very familiar with my act and seemed to really care about comedy in general, and he was close friends with Mark Ridley, which was all the vouch I needed. Mark is a tremendous guy and a trustworthy figure in a business that seems to have few. Eventually Dave asked if he could record my set and potentially use it to help me get some lucrative work. Lucrative was his word. There was no YouTube at this point, no worry about the wrong people seeing my set or being bullied online because they hated my jokes, so I was all for it. You want to try to get me comedy work? Go for it.

A few months later Dave revealed that he had done a very agenty thing and submitted me to a comedy festival without my knowledge. Not that I would have told him not to, I loved the idea of doing a comedy festival, and also loved that anyone in the comedy world even thought I was funny enough to represent me, but I knew the reality of my working life at Michigan meant it would be tough for me to get away and do a comedy festival, not only logistically but also optically. It's one thing to be a coach representing a university who occasionally does comedy as a hobby, it's another to be representing the university and have your name and face plastered all over a comedy festival on the other side of the country (also, it's worth noting one of my "best" jokes at the time was telling people to check out my website 17InchPenis.com). Submitting to a comedy festival wasn't an easy feat back then, Dave had to videotape my set, send a hard copy of that tape to the submission office, etc. Now you send a link, and can even track if someone clicked it, back then you sent a videotape and just hoped someone watched it, or that it didn't arrive damaged, or that it even arrived. One day Dave called me and said, "I have some very exciting news."

"OK?" I had no idea what he could be talking about.

"You have been hand selected to perform at the Washington, DC, Comedy Festival, one of the most prestigious comedy festivals in the world."

I didn't know that he had even submitted me, I didn't even know what a comedy festival is, but a "festival"—that sounds cool, right? I wasn't going to any festivals as a tennis coach, that's for sure. "Wow, that's awesome, does this world-class, prestigious comedy festival, that *hand* selected me . . . pay by any chance?"

"No," he replied. "But it's great exposure." This would officially mark the first time in my comedy career that I heard the phrase "No, but it's great exposure." Twenty years later I have heard that phrase close to a million times. All it means is "You will work for free."

The Washington, DC, comedy festival was not a prestigious festival, and certainly nobody handpicked me, but it was *something* and it was certainly a step up for me, an unknown, hustling comedian who was picking up tennis balls for a living. So I can't say I wasn't excited, I was—I just knew it was gonna be a problem with Bruce. The festival fell on the same weekend that Michigan was scheduled to play Indiana, one of our Big Ten rivals. I still had the audacity to call a meeting with Bruce and ask him if I could skip the Indiana match so I could pursue a comedy festival in Washington, DC.

Bruce's facial expression was worth more than anything he could have said. "What? No, of course not, don't be ridiculous," he grumbled, and it was clear that the meeting was over.

I called Dave, the agent, and told him the news and he was beside himself. "But I submitted you and taped you and pushed for you," he declared.

"Yeah, I know, Dave, but sometimes I think we forget that I am a full-time collegiate coach," I said, more of a reminder to myself than him.

So the first comedy festival I ever got in, I had to pass on. I was disappointed but certainly understood the reality: until I quit the coaching job, I would have to prioritize tennis above comedy every time there was a conflict. That Sunday, the last day of the comedy festival, Michigan Men's tennis barely beat Indiana, 4–3. The final match came down to a freshman, one of my own recruits. I coached him through his match as he clinched the victory not only for himself, but for the entire team. It was pivotal that I was there. Ten years later, that same player brought his parents to see me perform at the Palm Beach Improv. We hugged and talked about this match.

Bruce wasn't going to let me drop my coaching responsibilities (and when you worked for Bruce, there were a lot of them)[4] for a comedy show—but he was still my friend and he cared about me. That spring break, a few days before our match against Pepperdine, as we

---

4 Real email I received from Bruce while we both sat in our adjacent offices, November 17, 2005. The email only had a subject. *Subject: Any way you can go to the fridge, and get me the sandwich in the tin foil?*

walked along the promenade in Santa Monica, he kindly said to me, "You know, if you want to leave this job so you can pursue comedy, that's OK, you just need to let me know—"

Before he finished the sentence, I said, "I want to, I want this to be my last season with the team."

He wasn't surprised at my decision, maybe just surprised at how quickly I said it. But I was ready, and he gave me an opening, so I took it. I don't even remember making that decision prior to him telling me, it just came out—which is a sign that it was the right move.

It was March 2006 and I had said out loud to the world (Bruce, really) that I made the decision to leave my coaching job, to pursue comedy full-time. I had been doing stand-up for twenty-three months. I use baby month language because that's how I felt as a comedian, like a baby. I could smile, I could crawl, but I still shit my pants quite a bit and probably shouldn't be left alone for long periods of time. And thanks to an aggressive agent who wouldn't stop hustling for me, long periods of time alone is what I was about to get.

Chapter 23

Canadian Comedian

THIS IS AN email from Dave, the agent, that showed up in my inbox in March 2006, nearly two weeks after telling Bruce I wanted out. To this day, I wish my current agents would be this honest. (I also must say, a quick search through my inbox and I had forgotten how many gigs he had gotten me. Good stuff, Dave.)

Subject: Comedy Offer Canada

Hello Michael

You will be opening 4 shows for Mitch Fatel in Calgary AB Canada on June 9 and 10. The pay will be minimal. In fact, I'm pretty sure it will end up costing you money.

This booking, however, will be part of a 5–6 week Canadian tour where you will either MC or feature at Yuk Yuks clubs from one end of Canada to the other. You will drive forever, receive very little pay, and curse me along the way. You will, however, gain invaluable experience, and probably learn more in 6 weeks than you would in 6 years. Think of it as your Graduate Degree program in Comedy; you pay to do all the work in order to improve yourself.

Hope you're having fun this weekend doing that "tennis thing." We'll talk soon.

Dave

One of my favorite agent moves here is how Dave starts the email with "You will be . . ." this tells you a little about where I was in the comedy world. He wasn't asking me what I wanted to do, he was telling me. And, like an eager boy hungry to please daddy (that didn't sound right), I was doing it. This was such a great opportunity for me to get exactly what I needed, tons of stage time in front of people I would never see again. Hence my response:

Subject: Re: Comedy Offer Canada

Wow!

Sounds exciting. Can't write much because I am on the road but count me in. Hopefully it will lead to a lot more bookings.

Comedy career here we come!

Michael

I might have been joking, but in reality my actual comedy career was just about to start.

If the scariest day of my life was doing my first open mic, the second scariest was actually leaving my tennis job, leaving the security of the paycheck, free clothes, travel, the title, and notoriety that came from being a coach at Michigan living in Ann Arbor and jumping all the way into comedy with both feet. Before quitting the Michigan job, comedy was a fun bar trick, a hobby, that I took seriously, but I still had good health care and an office and could fill up the gas tank without wincing. Now I was leaving a highly sought-after work position and betting my time, money, and worth on becoming a full-time comic.

• • •

Coincidentally, I wasn't the only Kosta going through a few changes at this time. Here's an aerial view of what all four Kosta kids were managing as I was boarding a flight to Vancouver; it might offer some perspective. This would be roughly spring 2006.

#1 OLDEST, JOHN: Hurricane Katrina had sent John and his wife into a tailspin, losing their condo in New Orleans (despite having hurricane insurance) and losing touch with a lot of the Kosta family. Despite our best efforts no one really knew what was going on. It was sad and scary.

#2 SISTER KRISTY: Kristy had just fled a terrible nursing position in Florida (at a psych ward, where she was treated less than ideally) and was back in Ann Arbor trying to pick up the pieces. She was a few weeks away from becoming sober (aka she hadn't hit bottom yet).

#3 TODD: Todd always landed on his feet but at this point in his life he was playing professional poker, driving to the Detroit casinos day and night trying his luck at Texas Hold 'Em ("It's not luck"—Todd).

#4 YOUNGEST, MICHAEL: Just left a secure and well-respected Michigan coaching job to pursue a comedy career. That first year he made about $9,700 as a comic.

We were all at these critical junctures in our lives—some more self-inflicted than others. The one person wasn't entirely on board with all this? Mom. This whole "I'm gonna walk the earth and see what passions sing out to me" Kosta kid philosophy didn't fall into her Catholic, extremely concerned-that-she-had-raised-quality-children-who-positively-contributed-to-society mindset.

One night, I went over to my parents' house for dinner, and Mom and Dad didn't seem to be anywhere. I called for them but no answer, they must have stepped out, most of the lights were off except for the light above the kitchen table, which was glowing like a spotlight, showcasing an item in the middle of the table. It looked like that holy grail in the *Indiana Jones* scene. I went over to it and picked it up; it was a book titled *When Our Grown Kids Disappoint Us*. I thumbed through it. Just then the garage door opened and in walked Mom and Dad. Mom saw what I was holding and quickly grabbed it out of my hands and put it on the shelf. She never mentioned it again, but it was clear to me that I had better start making progress in comedy, and soon.

• • •

The Canadian tour was exactly how Dave described it. Lots of driving, lots of cursing him, lots of stage time, and lots of fun. Also, very little money. At this point in my life, no one ever had any money. I didn't, the other comics didn't, the comedy clubs didn't, the bookers of course never had any money. No one ever had any goddamn money.[1]

During my first weekend on the road with the Yuk Yuks in Van-

---

1   In the tennis world I had just come from, *everyone* had money. At one of the tournaments I played in Mexico, one of the other players put his dad's credit card down at the local strip club and bought anyone as many lap dances as they wanted. Umpires included.

couver, a local Canadian comedian showed me a picture of his son, who was sick, and asked me for $50 so I could help him get his medication. I gave it to him. The next weekend I was in Alberta and another comic asked who I worked with last weekend and I told him and he immediately said, "Did he give you the whole I-can't-afford-my-kid's-medication bit?" Yeah, I even saw a picture of the kid, he looked sick. "He's using a picture now? Wow, he's improved the con."

"Tour" was a generous name for the adventure I was about to go on. A more appropriate term might have been "A bunch of gigs in the middle of nowhere spaced out all over the fucking place." Tour sounds nice though, so they went with tour. Over the next six weeks I would perform in about fifteen different western Canadian cities, pretty much every night. Sometimes driving ten to twelve hours a day. To regular people "Western" Canada means British Columbia, to the Yuk Yuks booking department "Western" Canada means British Columbia, Alberta, and Saskatchewan. Take a look at a map, that's a lot of land to cover. Thankfully I didn't have to pay for the rental car, but I did have to drive or share the driving with the comics I was opening for. I would get paid weekly, with a check at the Yuk Yuks office in Calgary. Calgary was the home base. Even if you did a gig that was a twelve-hour drive, you would come back to Calgary eventually to get paid.

On this Yuk Yuks "tour," I kept a meticulous journal of my expenses, much to the chagrin of the more experienced Canadian comedians. Of course, I can't find that expense journal now, but I do remember these numbers: I got paid $1,500 and I spent $1,459 (flights, food, beer). So, after six weeks, roughly forty shows, I had flown home and walked away with $41 profit. I couldn't wait to share those numbers with my mom.

Fortunately for me, I was more concerned with stage time, the most valuable currency, and I had figured out that I got about 850 minutes of stage time (38 shows where I was doing 20-minute sets and 2 shows where I headlined and did an hour both times). Eight hundred fifty minutes is a lot of comedy. In Michigan, it would have taken me roughly eighteen months. So I crammed a year and half of stage time into six weeks in Canada. Plus, I got laid a few times.

Here are some Canada highlights, let's start with the sex one because I know that's all you really care about, you dirty bitch.

Sex

One night after a show in Edmonton, I went back to the hotel and was enjoying the fact that this wasn't going to be a late night. Canadians like to drink and stay up late and I was fresh off twenty years of discipline, of going to bed early, eating the right things, checking in with Bruce before doing anything—so I felt like the last soldier to return home from the war. I was having a *lot* of fun, and for once in my life it was totally OK to do it.

Digital video was barely happening at this point, my camera had a memory card that could hold something like seven minutes of video, but nonetheless I was bringing a small tripod and camera to my shows to record part of my set. This night when I got back to the hotel room, I put the tripod on the desk facing the bed, not really thinking about it. Then the phone rang, not my cell phone, the actual hotel phone.[2]

I cautiously picked it up, "Hello?"

"Hello, is this you, the comedian?" A woman's voice came through the line. "We are downstairs and wanted to keep partying, can we come up?"

---

2   When it came to cell phones, I had a Sprint phone with four hundred minutes, and when you were in Canada if you wanted to use it you had to sign a contract saying Sprint was allowed to physically and emotionally torture you and your loved ones. I love for-profit American media conglomerates.

Huh. This was certainly something I hadn't experienced before. Usually when the hotel phone rang, it was the team bus driver calling Bruce and my room to tell us that we needed to get the team down to the lobby. Or it was the front desk telling me I had to check out soon. It was never—and I mean *never* a girl from the show I just performed on asking if "we?" could come up and "party"?

"Who is 'we'?" I said, envisioning her and her three boyfriends coming up and robbing me or beating me up—not that she would tell the truth at this point, but it was worth a shot.

"Me and my girlfriends," she said. "What's your room number?" Well, huh, I thought. You wanted to be a comedian, so be a comedian.

A few minutes later, there was a knock on the hotel door and three woman I vaguely remembered from the show walk in. They had tattoos, streaks of black in their hair, a few tongue rings—they kind of looked like how you think they would look for the type of girls that call a comedian and invite themselves up to his hotel room. These ladies weren't exactly the kind of women I envisioned bringing home to my mother, but they were definitely attractive, and I had to keep reminding myself that I wasn't bringing them home to my mother, I was "hosting" them at my hotel "party" that they both created and invited themselves to.

When they walked in, the more talkative of the three noticed the tripod, and pointed at the bed. "Oh, is that for us?" she said, in between tongue ring clicks. They all laughed. I was a bit embarrassed and a bit unsure of how to navigate this whole situation. The last time I had anyone in my hotel room it was a Michigan tennis player crying about his position in the lineup. Thankfully, these ladies were happy to take control. *Canadian people are a great people,* I thought.

"Let's do this," one of them said, and the other one took a bag of cocaine (I think? White? Small bag? Maybe meth?) out of her bra and started chopping up lines on the hotel desk.

"You wanna do coke with us?" the chattier one (let's call her Ski Bunny) said.

I guess it was cocaine. Quickly every single DARE commercial I was ever forced to watch flashed before my eyes, all the memories of my junior tennis drug testing—"You have been selected to be drug tested, put your bag down, do not approach anybody else, and walk with this official to the bathroom where we will collect your urine." Nancy Reagan's Just Say No, the whole thing. "No thanks, but you go ahead," I said in a very uncomfortable voice, trying to pretend like this whole thing was normal and I totally knew how to handle it.

Anyone that has any experience with cocaine knows what happens next: ten minutes later my hotel room was a complete shit show. Everyone talking at once, someone put on really loud, bad music, one of the girls called the front desk asking for beers only to have me hang up the phone and tell her not to do that. It was quickly becoming irritating. I was a few beers in, but these girls were lots of beers in, and a few lines of drugs. We were at different levels.

I was about to pull the plug on the whole thing when Ski Bunny grabbed my hand and pulled me into my hotel bathroom (what is it with this book and bathroom sex?). She looked at her friends and mouthed "I'll be in here" and they rolled their eyes.

We started kissing in the bathroom and I remember the metallic taste of her mouth, it didn't seem like tongue ring metal, like something harsher, more synthetic (coke mouth?).

Just as things were starting to heat up, she stopped and said, "Do you want to grab your camera?"

Wow. Ah yes, yes I do. So I popped back out, nodded hello to her friends who were doing what people who do coke do—more coke—grabbed the camera and tripod, and went back to the bathroom. When I got there, I turned on the camera and my memory card was full. "Let's not worry about the camera," I said, and we got back to very clumsy, very unexpected, one-person-high-on-coke-clicking-her-tongue-ring, bathroom sex.

OK there, I had sex, get over it, OK?

I remember waking up the next morning and thinking "Wow, that was fun." What a strange, funny, entertaining experience. I lay there thinking about it, excited to tell that story to my friends back home in Michigan. But they were in Michigan right now, I was alone in a hotel room in Edmonton. Normally, when I stayed in a hotel, we had a team breakfast in the morning or I had a bunch of friends staying down the hall. Comedy was different, you were alone so often. That was something I had to get used to. Turns out, the drugs and sex adventure that I had just gone on was a lot more fun when you could tell someone about it the next day. I just packed my bags and called a cab. I would be alone for the next twenty hours. I would share the story with my friends a few months later back home, but by then it had lost a lot of the luster and I wasn't as excited about telling it. This was a different loneliness than what I felt as a pro tennis player. That was I was alone and losing. Comedy loneliness, I was beginning to learn, was more like "Oh this is fun . . . but I'm alone and don't have anyone to share it with." Oddly, the comedy loneliness felt worse.

Lethbridge

Doing about forty shows in six weeks is a *lot* of comedy. I had some great sets in some great rooms and some terrible sets in some terrible rooms. The sheer number of gigs meant they all blurred together and ultimately balanced each other out. It was kind of like the Yuk Yuks tour was a class in college, and the teacher (me) was giving the student (also me) a test every day. With so many chances to score by the end of the term, bombing one night didn't mean failing the whole course. I was also learning a lot—it wasn't entirely linear, but my confidence and overall performance was trending upwards as the weeks went on.

But much like an athlete can tell you every detail about every single loss and not much about the wins, the terrible sets still to this day seep into my existence when I least expect it. Here's one that crashed into my head while I was patiently waiting for the C train yesterday— the same non-highlight reel that includes the JeJu Island match I blew and my brother wiping the tears off my face while I lost to that Bradley Adams fucker back in 1989.

One of the venues we played was at a bar in Lethbridge, a mid-size southern central city in Alberta. For whatever reason (probably integrity of the building structure) there was a giant foundational pillar smack dab in front of the stage. Not *on* the stage, *in front* of the stage, so you couldn't avoid looking at it. A big one, maybe five feet wide, and it ran all the way up to the ceiling. As the opening comedian, this meant I started the show cold (no opener for me), I was handed a microphone and walked out on stage, even though no one could see me because I was standing behind a giant pole. I went on to tell twenty minutes of jokes to the "audience" that was really just a big concrete column. Good news: I couldn't see the faces of the audience that hated me. Bad news: they hated me. At one point I even said, "Are you guys even paying attention?" and all I heard was billiard balls knocking and the sound of hockey on TV. Then, to make it worse, I brought up the more experienced headliner who told thirty minutes of jokes about the giant pole obstacle, everyone was on the floor laughing (the audience was so engaged with him, you could hear a pin drop between laughs). The headliner drove me back to the hotel after the show and before dropping me off said, "Don't worry about Lethbridge, you'll never have to perform in front of a support beam again." It's been twenty years, and he was right.

Moose Lodge

The Canadian comedians who had been on this tour and done these rooms before (some many, many times) were really savvy. They adjusted their material for each location, and overall had great jokes and were very funny. I, on the other hand, had twenty minutes of material, and kept having to learn the same lessons over and over like a big dumb idiot. This came to a peak during one show at a Moose Hunting Lodge. The audience were people who, you guessed it, hunted moose (meece? mice?).

The lodge was in the middle of the forest, tucked away next to a stream. The log cabin where I was supposedly sleeping was attached to the lodge/kitchen/cafeteria/animal cleaning area and for tonight, comedy club.

I took the stage—as the opener again—wearing tight jeans, a white ironed button down, my hair perfectly tousled, and told my first joke about playing pro tennis. Silence. I tell a joke about the American stock market. Silence. I decide to switch it up and tell a joke about space travel. Silence. At this show, I actually wished there was a giant pole in front of me. Please someone put on a hockey game so I can at least hear something. That was the worst kind of bombing—the audience was not only quiet and paying attention, they wanted to laugh and were really looking for me to help them get there. But I was in over my head. I was a moose and they were hunters and I was shot dead before I even knew it.

Similar to Lethbridge, the headliner then came out and absolutely ripped the place to shreds, telling stories about hunting with his dad, the differences between a moose and an elk and a deer, jokes about ammunition and caliber size. He finished with a story about when his friend got so drunk hunting he almost shot his dick off—the audience fell over laughing. After the show, he took pictures with everyone and

I sat in the corner alone, nursing a Kokanee. One audience member tried to console me: "Your jeans are too tight," she said as she walked away.

The good news was that thanks to tennis and the mindset that an athlete is trained with, I never sulked too long and I always tried to learn something from each bad performance. Also there wasn't time to sulk; thanks to the tour, I had another show in twenty-one hours. "Always change a losing game," my dad told us over and over again. "Champions adjust," tennis great Billy Jean King is credited with saying. So I tried to change and adjust.

Oil Country

A few days after I bombed at the moose lodge, an opportunity fell in my lap—one that I certainly wasn't ready for but was forced to do (maybe the best kind of opportunity?).

I got the good news from Dave, in an email that said something like:

Get your hour ready, you are going up to oil country tomorrow to HEADLINE (for $75).

The biggest issue wasn't the money. It was the time. I still only had twenty minutes of material. And that was when the audience was laughing. If they weren't, that shrunk down to seven minutes real quick. I just did twenty minutes in front of a moose lodge and the most memorable part of my performance was my jeans. I didn't know how the hell I was going to do an hour . . . in oil country. Where am I going, Saudi Arabia?

Turns out Canada has a little bit of oil. Yes, it's buried deep under the sand fields and requires lots of water and pressure and whatever the shit to get it out, and who knows what it's doing to our precious planet, but my point is, Canada has it. And at the time of this performance, the province of Alberta was making so much money from said oil that they actually gave some of the profits back to the citizens of Alberta.

Americans, read that again. The government of Alberta was so profitable they gave each citizen $800. Not tax-paying citizen, just citizen, so babies, kids, elderly in hospice, they all got $800 as a thank-you for being an Albertan or some shit. Families were getting checks for thousands of dollars from the government on top of their normal work wages. GET YOUR GOVERNMENT OUT OF MY LIFE . . . oh wait. These people, in particular the oil workers, were very happy, very rich, and ready to laugh.

After an eleven-hour solo drive north of Calgary, I checked into the hotel, which was attached to the curling club (of course), and quickly pieced together a badly butchered list of every joke I had ever performed, written, or thought of. I even wrote a few brand-new jokes in the passenger seated notebook while driving just so I could at least get to, hopefully, sixty minutes.

After doing my hair and ironing my shirt, I walked into the venue and said to the very tattooed, very gruff bartender, "Hi, I'm Michael Kosta, tonight's headliner." It felt good to say that. Inside the bar, as I ducked so as not to hit the bras and five-dollar bills hanging down from the ceiling, I reminded myself that in tennis, some of my best wins had come after some really heartbreaking losses. I was looking for anything just to give me a little bit of confidence/hope that I could pull off this sixty-minute show after barely pulling off twenty minutes the night before.

It worked. The next sixty minutes, inside of a very cramped, very damp, low-ceilinged bar hosting a comedy night, I bobbed, I weaved, I told a joke about the curling club across the street (did well), I did a joke about how my tennis joke wasn't going to do well (did well),

Lucky Loser

I even made fun of how tight my jeans were (big laugh). Last night I couldn't break an egg doing twenty minutes in a forest and tonight I was crushing doing sixty minutes in an oil field. It was a tremendous feeling. Not only did I just headline, but I headlined *well*. People wanted to take pictures with *me*. I shook so many hands after the show that night, that when I pulled the door handle on my car, I noticed oil all over the door. My audience had transferred the oil from their oil field hard-ass working hands to me, in appreciation (this doesn't happen at the Hermosa Beach Comedy and Magic Club). It felt like we had made a blood bond but in this case the blood is the oil or whatever (go with it).

I happily went back to the hotel room attached to the curling club and couldn't sleep; I was too excited. It felt like I had made another step forward in this totally insane, totally humbling, but occasionally incredibly rewarding new profession. *Go to sleep* I told myself. I had to be up in six hours if I wanted to make it to my next show, tomorrow night.

Canadian BBQ (Honorable Mention)

Eventually, the driving, the expense note-taking, the bombing and succeeding came to an end. I was done, my flight was tomorrow and I actually had a night off. I was in Calgary, and one of the local comics invited me over for a BBQ with a bunch of other comics. It was really great. To be in a home, eating home cooking, conversing, meeting someone's wife and kids; it was heartwarming. I was reminded that I was a human again, not just a traveling clown. It reminded me of going over to Arnaud's house in France when he threw the bread into the trash can. (Still funny.)

Before the tour, all I knew was the local Michigan comedy scene. Yes, we were friends, but there was also a competitive tension that

250

was always there, people trying to get ahead of you, talking shit about you or other comics, trying to sit closer to the booker or not laugh too hard at other comics' material, just in case it showed someone important that you thought they were funny. In Calgary as I sat outside with roughly ten Canadian comedians, sharing food and beer and stories, I was so impressed by the vibe, the camaraderie, I didn't sense any jealousy or bitterness, just community. I even mentioned it to the host, Kerry. I said, "I think it's really nice how you all are here, some headliners, some openers, having fun, not talking about comedy or the business."

Kerry looked surprised. "This isn't the US," he said. "There is only so high you can go in Canada, so we stick together, we don't cut each other down."

Later on, as I started progressing through the US comedy ranks, I sometimes longed for that Canadian BBQ feeling. I still do. Doing comedy in the US *is* cutthroat, it *is* competitive, your friends *are* using you to gain access to new clubs, bookers, TV execs, etc. I love show business and love what it's given me, but authentic friendship is not one of the rewards, unfortunately. Maybe it's the fame or the money that can be won in the US, but there are times when I drive by billboards of comedians or see my peers at awards shows, peers who have clearly worked the system and their Rolodex through mastery of networking and calculated showbiz decisions, and I miss that BBQ in Canada, with a bunch of really funny, really nice comics, whose only motivation was to have a fun hang and get a little drunk. It reminded me of my defeated opponent at the French money tournament who came back to the courts the next day to track me down and have a beer with me. It was lovely.[3]

---

3 These were men, making real human connections with other men, something American men are tremendously terrible at, which, ultimately, I believe, creates serious emotional and societal problems.

...

When I flew to Canada, I was a tennis coach who was trying to be a comic; six weeks later when I flew home to Michigan I was a full-time, professional stand-up comic. I saw my tennis bag in the entryway when I walked into my house, and it made me feel sick. I didn't want to play tennis, I didn't want to teach tennis, I wanted to do comedy and that was it.

The night I got home, I had an open mic in Detroit. It was a seven-minute spot and I remember looking through my notes thinking *which seven minutes should I do*. I had so much more material, so much more confidence. After my set, a comedy buddy came up to me and said, "How is it you get better each time you go on stage?"

He was right, I was in that part of learning where I got better each time; I hadn't plateaued yet. The trip to Canada made me so much sharper, and more importantly, it gave me a small taste of headlining. I wanted to be the headlining comic, the last guy the audience saw. I wanted the pressure of knowing the success or failure of your night, as an audience member, fell on my shoulders. In some screwed-up way, that seemed fun. Little did I know I wouldn't perform sixty minutes on stage for roughly another two years. But being back on American soil, it wasn't lost on me how far I had come since screaming crotch karate into a microphone and pretending to "karate chop" the audience with my dick.

Chapter 24

The Move

THREE MONTHS LATER, the fall of 2006, I turned twenty-seven, and for the first time, I was living in Ann Arbor as a full-time comic, not tennis coach. That meant I did comedy every single night, anywhere within a hundred-mile drive. And I was not only funnier, often times I was the funn-*iest*. Shows where I used to be lucky to get a few laughs, I was now crushing, often closing the show, making some local headliners uncomfortable because they didn't want to follow me. It didn't take long. Maybe three or four months, before I felt antsy. I wanted more. I wanted better.

The problem was this pesky little thing called money. I didn't have any. A normal week of stand-up might be filled with six shows, four that paid nothing (and required gas, car, etc.) and two might pay me $35. In order to survive, to pay the bills, and to develop some type of savings so I could move eventually, I was teaching tennis, naturally. Everyone who worked at the University of Michigan tennis center was still my friend, so they would kindly let me book indoor courts for free, let me teach for free, let me use the showers and balls for free. This was probably some kind of NCAA violation, but man, did it help me and allow me to maximize my time on court and save as much money as possible. I would teach roughly four hours a day, charge around $100 a lesson, and walk out with $400 profit.

This was huge. It allowed me to spend my afternoons writing comedy, trying to get booked on more shows, and ultimately saving up for a move out of the Midwest to somewhere a TV executive could actually see what a comedy genius I was. Michigan was the perfect place to start comedy, lots of stage time with almost no real "stakes." Meaning if you bombed, it wasn't like the booker for HBO was in the room—but I wanted to elevate myself. Much like I had seen the pro tennis players ten years ahead of me and I wanted to avoid becoming them with all my heart, I had witnessed the local Detroit headliners, who were roughly ten to fifteen years ahead of me, and let's just say they looked less than inspiring. Now was the time to move somewhere that might help my career, or even see if I could create one. I became certain that if I really wanted to elevate my comedy game, I had to get out of Michigan.

. . .

Moving to LA was potentially life changing and, because of that, scary. But it was a decision I had researched diligently so I could try and make the most logical and unemotional decision. I had weighed the LA move against the other obvious city to move to if I wanted to make it as a comic—New York City.

I visited and did comedy in both cities, to get a feel for what it would be like. Both trips made it very clear it was not going to be an easy move, and regardless of where I ended up, it was going to be a big adjustment. Ultimately I picked LA for two reasons.

1. It's where TV happens. I wanted to be on TV. That was my passion. When I was ten, I didn't stay up late to watch Richard Pryor's

stand-up special (though I liked him and it), I begged my parents to let me stay up late and watch Johnny Carson. I loved David Letterman, even though his show shot in New York he was a regular at the Comedy Store in LA and an LA comic/performer. When I went to LA, I met people who worked in casting, writing, production, performing; when I visited New York I met people who were artists, store owners, professors, financial analysts. As Michael J. Fox said about moving to LA, "If you want to be a lumberjack, go to the goddamn forest."

2. Tennis. LA has sun and courts and lots and lots of great tennis players. I knew that it was going to take me time to get situated into the LA comedy scene, so I was going to need some friends, some exercise, and an easy way to make money (why wait tables when you can feed tennis balls to a fifty-year-old rich lady in a short tennis skirt on her private tennis court?). Also, for this Michigander, the idea of being outside all year round and ditching my three-quarter-length down feather winter coat was exciting.

My girlfriend at the time, Nadine, was enormously supportive of my move and a big reason I felt confident enough to pursue this dream. We were a good couple, but I personally was not ready to be in a relationship, especially with so much upcoming transition. I communicated that to Nadine (quite frequently if I recall), but somehow, together in the summer of 2007, we packed up my 2000 Honda Civic EX (moon roof #humblebrag), and off we went to LA. In two weeks' time, she would fly back to Michigan from LA, what could go wrong?

I had $13,000 in savings thanks to teaching tennis and a probably criminal relationship with the Michigan tennis center, and a few small bookings back in the Midwest in the coming months. My plan was to get situated in LA while traveling back to the Midwest frequently, where I still understood the people and business and could maybe make a few bucks. The idea of jumping right into LA was a little intimidating for me, so I kept a few irons in the fire back in the home state where I could see my family, do a familiar open mic, etc. Also, thanks to Super Dave the Michigan agent, I had a new TV gig working for Fox Sports Detroit. It hadn't started yet, but it was going to require a lot of travel (no surprise) back to the Midwest, where I would be an on-camera host for a hockey show. I got paid $1,000 an episode for eight episodes. Basically, it was the Yuk Yuks tour all over again, but instead of stand-up it was hosting a TV show about college hockey (albeit with a little better money). Eight thousand isn't a lot of money but it helped to have it on my calendar as guaranteed income. I loved doing the show. More of those stories in the next book.

I had rented a room on Formosa Avenue in the heart of West Hollywood in LA for $800 a month (Craigslist), my roommate was an angry, gay Israeli. I say that because that's how he introduced himself to me when I first looked at the apartment in a test run of LA, a month prior. "Hi, I am Avishay, I am angry, gay, Israeli." At that point in my life, I had never met an Israeli or a gay person, so it's safe to say I was going to be out of my comfort zone. What I didn't comprehend was how far out of my comfort zone I would be with my everything in LA.

After driving the roughly 2,200 miles, we pulled up to my new apartment. We were a little early and Avishay wasn't home, so we decided to walk down to a nearby bar, Jones Cafe, for a bite. Not wanting to leave my bike attached to my car, parked on the street all alone in this new giant big dangerous city, I locked my bike on a railing in front of my new apartment. I would be back in thirty minutes to meet Avishay, get a key, and properly move in. I was a world traveler, I knew how to handle myself and most situations. Parking car, locking bike, going to bar—this was not a difficult scenario. Or so I thought.

I opened the door to Jones Cafe and took about three steps when a man rolled up to me and said, "Well, aren't you cute," and then grabbed both my nipples and twisted them. I had literally been in Los Angeles for three minutes. Nadine hadn't even made it into the bar yet. By the time she walked through the door I was yelling at this man who had just either comedically or sexually aggressively, I couldn't tell, groped me. The bartender yelled, "Andy, leave him alone!" and Nadine grabbed my arm and dragged me to a booth.

I was shocked. I was flustered. My nipples hurt. "Why did that just happen?" I said to Nadine.

"I don't know, but do you know who that is?"

I looked again. All I saw was a very drunk, very sloppy, poorly dressed man, wearing a big black ankle monitor over his white sock. "No, I don't." I said, still pissed off.

"That's Andy Dick," Nadine said, "that weird guy from MTV."

I looked again and holy shit she was right. There was Andy Dick, leaning on the wall, struggling to keep his balance. I learned ten years later that everyone who has ever been to West Hollywood leaves with an Andy Dick story, but for me this was a very odd and very unwelcome welcoming. The Midwest part of me wanted to call the cops and press charges, which thankfully I didn't do. One thing was very clear: I was not in Kansas anymore. (I'm from Michigan but most of you who live on the coasts don't know the difference anyways.)

We left the bar out the side entrance, avoiding Andy Dick, and walked up to the apartment. When I got to the building, I immediately noticed that my bike was exactly where I left it, but there was another lock on it, as in, someone had put another kryptonite lock over my kryptonite lock, one that I didn't have a key to.

"What is this?" I said to Nadine.

Before she had a chance to respond, a giant, wide, angry, wide woman burst out of her garden-level apartment door, which sat directly under my new apartment, screaming at me. We were standing in the courtyard in the center of the apartment complex that all those

1970s-built LA apartment complexes had. I think her screams were in Russian, but it could have been anything. It wasn't English, and it was angry.

"Calm down, calm down," I said to her, which only made her scream louder at me. (Also, why was I saying calm down, I was the one who just found out my bike was kind of stolen?) She was furious. I could see her dead-eyed-looking husband (?) inside their apartment, sitting on a lounger in a white tank top, not even looking at her. I could only imagine what he has to go through each day. I tried to get his attention to see if he could help me, but he was in la la land, a term I was starting to learn the origin of.

A lot of yelling and her pointing at my bike and I started to figure out that she was mad that I had locked my bike to *her* railing and in return for making such a stupid dumb, idiotic decision, she would be in control of my bike until she saw fit, which is why she put her lock over my lock. This was certainly the most secure bike in all of Los Angeles (ironically this bike was stolen two years later down the street).

Just then, my new roommate Avishay came running down the stairs, with all his buttons undone on his shirt, wearing like four necklaces, and he said to me, "Don't talk to her, she is bitch."

Yes, she is a bitch, I thought. "Well, I don't know what to do, because she locked my bike up, on top of my lock."

He turned to her and said, "Oh my god, you are such bitch."

She started yelling at him. What a cool apartment complex, this is what Craigslist gets you.

Unbothered, Avishay ushered me upstairs and gave me the keys and showed me into the kitchen. My heart was beating and my nipples were hurting. What had I walked into? Nadine looked at me like "You sure you want to live here?" I can't say I blamed her. We started unloading the car into my new room. A warped floor, crappy blinds, small bedroom facing a courtyard with its own bathroom. The bathroom was really old and the side walls had lots of cracks in them, cracks that I later learned housed a lot of insects and small rodents. Those pics didn't make the CL listing. I should have realized when I opened the medicine cabinet and there was roach killer and mouse killer inside, but I wasn't that astute yet. I was still thinking about my bike. I mean, it wasn't *stolen*, I just didn't have access to it. It could have been worse, but I was twenty-seven years old, and besides a few small scuffles on a tennis court, no one had ever been deliberately mean to me in my entire life.

I made maybe fifteen trips from the car and back, and on the tenth trip, I noticed that the bike only had one lock on it, my lock—she had secretly taken her lock off as we had stepped out. I took a deep breath and moved my bike to my bedroom for the time being. As I rolled it into the apartment, Avishay said, "I don't want bikes in here."

I nodded to acknowledge him and also ignored him completely and kept moving the bike to my room. I didn't like doing that but it's what needed to happen at that very moment, and maybe, just maybe, I was beginning to develop the thick skin needed to survive in LA.

• • •

The shower was finicky and shitty and the shower curtain was not fresh. "This is my new shower, this is my new life," I said to myself as I stood there, naked, inspecting my nipples.

My plan was to stop by the Comedy Store on Sunset Boulevard for their Sunday-night open mic. It was a true open mic, meaning anyone could sign up and if you were selected, you would be given three minutes of stage time on this very famous, very important stage. The way I saw it, I would sign up tonight, get selected, perform my three minutes, get discovered, and in about three months I'd be a paid regular at the club, negotiating multiple TV deals with multiple different TV networks. I believed that no one had experienced the true comedic talent that was Michael Kosta and I was here to set the world on fire.

Nadine dropped me off a few blocks away from the Comedy Store (so no one would see me getting dropped off by my girlfriend) around five forty-five p.m. It was a six p.m. sign up, and then they posted the names that made the lineup (fifteen to twenty comics) at seven p.m. Upon being dropped off, I was surprised to see that there was a line that snaked three blocks east down Sunset Boulevard, probably two hundred people. Must be some kind of concert, I thought, maybe Michael Jackson was performing. I walked to the front of the line, and briefly noticed how they *all* were roughly twenty-something years old, mostly white males, mostly not in shape, who looked like they hadn't ironed their shirt, gotten much sleep, and clearly had some kind of chip on their shoulder. As I got to the outside bar of the Comedy Store, it was obvious that the line was the comics, waiting to sign up for the open mic.

"Is this the—" I said to the bouncer who rolled his eyes and said what he had been saying every Sunday at six p.m. for the past fifteen years, to the new kids who had just showed up from Michigan or Ohio or wherever.

"This is the open mic sign up, go back to the end of the line, sign your name at six p.m., we post who makes the show at seven p.m.," he robotically announced.

I walked all the way back past everyone I had just walked past, kind of like when people try to board their airplane early and the flight attendant says "Sorry, you're zone seven, we are boarding zone one now." It was clear I was so in over my head. When you live in Michigan, you think "I'll just move to LA" and you *can* just move to LA. You *can* just drive there—but what you don't realize is that 10,000 other people are also doing that, on that exact same day as you. Physically getting yourself to LA is not the issue, it's emotionally, financially, professionally, spiritually, surviving once you are there.

The Move

At that point, thanks to the help of Mark Ridley and agent Dave I had one TV credit. Living in Michigan, I had flown to New York and performed a short set on Comedy Central's *Live at Gotham*. It wasn't *The Tonight Show*, but it was a real show and considered a legitimate credit. I wasn't shy about my appearance, but I had wondered if I was totally ready for it at the time and I thought my performance on the show was just OK. Whatever the case may be, I figured that TV credit would give me a leg up on the other two hundred comics who were in line. Certainly whoever decided who made the list would recognize my name and move me into the lineup . . . right? Right? I wasn't gonna drive 2,000 miles with a girlfriend I was about to break up with to wait in line at six p.m. on a Sunday for an open mic and then not actually get on it, right? Right? Wrong.

They taped the lineup to the glass door at seven p.m. sharp, and each sack of potato comic, slowly, and pathetically waited in line again to see the list and for the briefest of brief moments each young man had the smallest glint of hope, until they scanned the list and realized they were not on it. I was one of those men. Shit. I ironed my shirt for this? What am I gonna do? Go "home" and hang out with Avishay? He's probably locking my bike up somewhere right now.

I decided I would stick around and watch the show, see how good the talent was, see what I was up against, see how hard this was gonna be exactly. The show started promptly and my first observation was that the MC was making fun of each comic after they performed. Like, really being mean. Not exactly the classiest thing I had seen, and it surprised me. The MC clearly knew each person waited in line for an hour to do these three minutes, the least he could do is support them? Right? Right? Wrong. After one comic, the host grabbed the mic and said, "Jesus Christ someone throw me in the middle of Sunset Boulevard right now, that was the worst thing I have ever seen."

After another, he said, "Well, I won't be surprised if that last comic kills himself tonight." Some people even got it *before* they went on. "This next comic, he, ah, he, let's just hope his jokes are as funny as he is ugly" and then a very strange-looking man (with a facial deformity) entered the stage. The bartenders and other doormen laughed each time, as if they were all in on the joke. This place was *brutal*.[1] If I wanted to make it here, I had to toughen up real quick. It was a big realization for me, as I still had tears in my eyes about my bike being locked up by that Russian twat.

My last memory of that night involved the host calling out the name "Eddie! Eddie? Eddie are you here? Eddie you are up!" Turns out Eddie was a homeless man who lived under a billboard on Sunset Boulevard and each Sunday he would sign up for the open mic. He wasn't a comic, he just wanted to use the bathroom, get some fresh water, sit in the cool air. And there was no rule against that. Well, lo and behold, this night, he actually got on the lineup. This was an odd and confusing pill to swallow. I didn't understand why this happened, or why they would even allow this to happen. A lot of us made a lot of sacrifices and worked really hard to be here, left family and loved ones, quit good jobs just to try and make this our profession. Why would they forgo those people for a man who clearly didn't care about comedy or a career in showbiz at all? Definitely a petty thought, especially considering this man clearly had much bigger problems than I did, but it was my honest reaction at the time. I'd be more kind and understanding now, at this age, with more life experience, but having just driven for four straight days to make it to this open mic, I was frustrated. I went to the bathroom to cool off,

---

1   For those of you unfamiliar with a comedy club and its scene, these jokes are just what they sound like, jokes. The MC didn't actually hate those people and feel that they needed to be brought down, he was trying his best to get *his* laughs that night and he chose to do it at the expense of others. It might not be how I wanted to do comedy, but one should understand this isn't to be taken personally. At any comedy club, in particular the Comedy Store, jokes come first, feelings second.

when I walked in there was a man with his pants rolled up, washing his feet in the bathroom sink. "Hi, Eddie," I said. "You're on." He never even looked up.

• • •

A few days later I had to drop Nadine off at the airport and say goodbye, like for real goodbye. No more tether to Michigan. It was just gonna be me, all alone in this terribly big, terribly different city. It was scary and I was scared. I remember driving with her down La Cienega on my way to the airport going as slowly as I could. I was hoping green lights would turn yellow so I could brake and make the feeling of comfort last a little longer. Nadine and I had only been dating under a year, but she represented Michigan, my home, the comfort of knowing how to get places, knowing who the people were, knowing the rhythm of the region. She was a former collegiate athlete herself, so she understood work ethic, goals, drive. She was extremely supportive of me moving to LA, helping me design business cards, helping me burn DVDs to send to bookers, endlessly chatting with me about comedy. She understood my obligation to write and often encouraged me to write more and explore jokes deeper. It was a really nice partnership, it had probably gotten more romantic than I had wanted, considering my goal was to move out of Michigan, I was trying to *not* settle down.

"I could always move here with you," she said a few times, when she noticed I was feeling weak, like only a woman can recognize. I would ignore that, or say "No, I want to take this on myself." That part was true, I felt that this was an important step in my comedy career and I envisioned heading west on my own. But what no one told me about heading west all on my own was that it was incredibly hard.

After a quick and awkward goodbye at Terminal 3 LAX while a man with a reflective vest yelled at us to hurry up, I raced back up

La Cienega. I was a wreck. I stopped at the Baja Fresh just north of Beverly, parked my car, and wept for twenty minutes. A woman walked passed me and noticed I was crying, she didn't even flinch. "How often does she see people sobbing in their car?" I wondered. I couldn't get out. I cried looking at the water bottle Nadine had left in the cup holder and the note she had left me on the passenger seat. She was *just* here, *just* sitting in this seat, now it's empty. What the hell was I doing? My friends were back home in Michigan, my family was back home in Michigan. I had a house back home in Michigan. I could go there right now, fill it up with people, have a BBQ, and lead a rewarding, happy life. I thought, *you are being tricked by the illusion of fame, of money, of LA and the mountains and the sunshine and beautiful women.*

The good news about crying that hard is that you can't *keep* crying that hard. Eventually your tear RPMs have to slow down, there is nothing left. I took some deep breaths, wiped my face, looked in the mirror. I thought again about the woman who walked by and didn't care that I was crying and I laughed. I started to talk to myself. "This is a lot, yes, but you've wanted to do this your whole life. You used to write jokes in your diary in the first grade, you listened to Bill Cosby's album over and over again. You've been infatuated with jokes and joke structure since you could read. This is where it happens. LA is where all those comics that you loved broke through (Dennis Miller, Steve Martin, Gary Shandling, Joan Rivers, the Smothers Brothers). Get your ass inside, have a bistek burrito, and go to your acting class like the struggling showbiz performer you are, and stop being a little bitch."

I cleaned up my face, put Nadine's note in the glove box, I would read that later, and I headed to my very first acting class at Lesly Kahn's studio in Hollywood.

Midwest comics love to tell you they are moving to LA or New York. Even now, I go home and I see the same comics, hanging around the comedy club, "I'm gonna move to LA next year, just saving a few bucks," or "Yeah, I'll move to New York once my kid graduates," they say. But they don't. Because it's incredibly nerve-racking to leave home. To leave what you know, to then take a hundred steps backwards, for the slight possibility that you might make giant leaps, it's daunting and difficult and isn't for everyone. Maybe I'm delusional, maybe I was young and didn't know better, but at the end of the day, I believed that I would make it, that I would belong, that I would, through hard work and perseverance and talent and toughness, break through. I knew what it was like to be a journeyman tennis player, I saw the traps and failures of being really really good at something (but not great) and I believed that I could take what I learned from that experience, improve on it, and do a better job at comedy. I had confidence going forward in this unknown, intimidating world that was professional comedy because I had struggled to succeed in the unknown, intimidating world that was professional tennis. I knew I could get to #864 in the world in comedy, and most likely, especially if I learned anything, I could get a lot higher. If I had taken an inventory of my comedy career at that point, like I did when quitting tennis—it would be very similar with one exception. I didn't have any money, I didn't have a big comedy "ranking," but I did have self-belief. And that proved to be all the difference.

• • •

Acting class is stereotypically LA and for good reason. It's insane. You take hot young men and women, who all care about their image and want to be stars, and you shove them into a class, in a city that promotes vanity, self-promotion, and networking and what do you get? A bunch of hot young men and women who have sex with each other a lot and sometimes audition for bad TV stuff.

Lesly Kahn's class was no exception. When I walked into my first class, I immediately saw six of the most beautiful women I had ever seen in my life. They were in my class and we'd be spending a lot of time together over the next three to four months. They were my age (or younger), they had just moved here from the Midwest, "loved comedy," and "felt alone sometimes in LA." They had blond hair, dirty blond hair, brown hair, red hair, sometimes a mix of all of it. They were stunning, but it didn't seem like they were trying that hard . . . *Huh, you know, maybe I'll stick it out a little longer and get to know some of these people,* I thought.

The way I saw it, Lesly Kahn's acting studio was nothing but a huge money grab by Lesly Kahn (never saw her once, who even was she?). The real genius behind Lesly was how elaborate her automatic credit card payments worked. She pulled money from you while you slept for classes you hadn't even thought about signing up for yet. I can confidently say one of our acting "coaches" was sleeping with two of the female students, who in return were sleeping with a few of the other male students. The girls in the class were so beautiful and good at making you feel like you were important and special, it took me a good four months to realize they were doing what actors do, they were *acting*. I say "you," but I wasn't on the receiving end of this special attention. It was generally reserved for the people who had the power to cast or recommend them for a project. I was learning quickly that in LA, your network was as important, or more, than your talent. This didn't and still doesn't sit well with me, a work ethic first, Midwest boy. Shouldn't talent overshadow one's ability to shmooze, flirt, and stand next to important people? Man, I had a lot to learn.

One Saturday, my acting class was supposed to "rehearse" a few scenes together. One of the women, whose dad was a studio executive (imagine that), offered to host at her house in Pasadena. I drove up to the address and arrived at a security gate, where a security guard told me, "They are at the pool house, do you need a map?"

The Move

"No, I can figure it out," I said, and I did, but it took longer than you'd expect. This wasn't a house, it was a compound. It reminded me of some of the country clubs I used to play tennis at. Holding my acting sides and notebook, I walked in the pool house to the sound of a blender, beers opening, and giggles from women changing into their bikinis (very openly now that I think about it . . . and I am). The men were putting on board shorts, and these guys had way better bodies than me, even though I was the only pro athlete in the bunch. There was a main tear-shaped pool, a kids' pool, and hot tub. At this point in my life, most of the hotels I stayed at didn't even have a pool. It was clear this wasn't going to be an acting rehearsal, but it also wasn't clear to me how important this acting class was in the first place. Were acting classes supposed to help you "act better"? Or were acting classes where you just met like-minded people and figured out how to have sex with them? Looking back on it now I think the answer falls somewhere in between. Both are important after all—improving your craft and also getting laid—but I didn't move all the way here, forgo a great college coaching job, and leave my friends and family so I could take my small savings and waste it on sex parties disguised as acting classes. The whole experience made me think about acting and actors in a completely different way—basically, that they were a bunch of vain, incredibly good-looking, not that hardworking, fame-obsessed, annoying to be around, children.[2] The ones in this class at least.

When I left that mansion in Pasadena that day, I decided it was time to focus on what I was best at, what I knew I was good at, what the universe was pushing me toward anyway, where I didn't have to rely on the work ethic of actors to succeed. Besides, Richard, the booker for the prestigious Hermosa Beach Comedy and Magic Club, had called while I was at this "rehearsal" and left me a message: "We have a spot for you tonight, if you want it, eight p.m. show."

---

2   Good for you, Lesly Kahn, you figured out how to take their money.

When I called him back and confirmed, he said "You'll get eight minutes and dinner, we have great food."

It was a sign from the comedy gods.

. . .

Slowly, I was settling in, in LA. I started consistently getting booked at the Hermosa Beach Comedy and Magic Club, then I'd get a paid one-nighter an hour out of town, most nights it was just paid-in-drink-tickets bar shows, if I had a show at all. Basically, I was doing my best to get as much stage time as I could (I needed "matches" anywhere I could get them). A few months passed this way. The sun was constantly shining, the trees stayed green, and summer blurred into fall, and then fall into winter. My routine was similarly predictable. I knew no one, so when I wasn't trying to get booked for something or performing, I sat in Avishay's apartment, crushing cockroaches and staring at my stagnant inbox. Then, one day, I received an email from someone named Scott. He wrote:

"You don't know me, but I coach a bunch of really good junior tennis players. Come join us for a practice."

Needless to say, the email was appreciated.

I drove to the West Side and hit balls with some really high-level juniors. Way better than I was at their age. Immediately they wanted to hit again, then I met more coaches and more players. Before I knew it, I had tennis friends and a community. Tennis didn't save me in LA, but it sustained me. It kept me laughing and having fun, totally unrelated to comedy. Previously I used comedy as an escape from the rigors of tennis. But now, as a professional comedian, I needed relief from the challenges of comedy and what felt comfortable and soothing was tennis.[3]

---

3 Scott is still my friend and texts me frequently after listening to my podcast.

The Move

When it came to comedy, I was taking some wins and losses. After *Live at Gotham* (which I shot before I had moved to LA) I had partnered up with a management firm in LA.[4] Two women who came as a recommendation from an entertainment lawyer I met. I had no idea if I needed management or even what they did. Would two managers be better than one? I drove to Sherman Oaks to meet with them and had a list of questions, but they never let me talk. They talked the whole time. I said like one word, seriously. On the way home the lawyer called, "They loved you!" That's how they became my managers. I was a Michigander, if an LA management company loves you, you go for it. It took about a year for me to realize we were not right for each other, at this point I had probably only said ten words to them. They would email me audition sides for really strange projects, real serious acting stuff, I remember thinking "Was this meant for me? Did they accidentally send this to me?" There was a one-hour sci-fi horror drama that they sent once and I kept looking for the jokes in the script but there weren't any. "This sucks," I thought.

Eventually, it was time for me to fire them. I did it at the same time I moved apartments, this timing made sense to me. New apartment, new Michael. I found a highly mirrored, heavily carpeted one bedroom in West Hollywood that looked like the designer did a lot of cocaine in the eighties; I didn't care. It was far away from Avishay's roach den and it was mine. I thought it would be most respectful to fire the managers in person, so I called a meeting with them and went back to Sherman Oaks. I sat in their lobby for an hour. I waited next to a coffee machine and a stressed assistant for an hour, staring at the clock. Every minute that passed, I was more solidified in my decision. When they finally invited me in, I told them I was moving on. "But we love you!" they said.

---

4   The best way I can describe it: managers help build your career; agents sell you to buyers. At this point Dave was still working for me as an agent back in Michigan, but I knew that was nearing the end, as I would need a more tapped-in LA agent eventually.

Relieved that it was over with them, I went home and thought I should let the world know that comedic genius Michael Kosta was now management free—I was available and looking. I had a really janky website at that point, and it took me two hours to figure out how to change my own page, but under "Management" I wrote "Michael is currently looking for management." When I uploaded the changes, I stared at it, a little lost and lonely. I wasn't sure if it was smart or if it looked desperate. I felt like an unanchored buoy in the ocean, I was drifting, I had very little direction and was completely vulnerable to outside forces. I didn't know what I was supposed to do.

Twenty-four hours later my phone rang. It was from a manager named Jordan Tilzer. He worked at a company called Roar and had seen my comedy and liked me. Get this—he asked me questions, and then he shut up: he listened. He said things like "What are five words that you would use to describe your comedy?" "What do you want to do in this industry?" "Who are your favorite comics right now and why?"

It was unreal. He wasn't just a decent guy, he also knew and cared about comedy and wanted to think about my long-term career, not just tomorrow's booking. I was impressed. I made him chase me down for a few more weeks to prove his mettle, but I knew all along I wanted him to be my manager. I've been with him now for sixteen years. He didn't make a dime off me for the first five, but now thanks to you purchasing books like this, he rakes it in.

• • •

If I thought I was aimlessly floating in the vast ocean before, the next two to three years in LA was a lot more of the same—but now thanks to tennis and new tennis friends (plus a new manager that would pick up the phone whenever I called)—I could navigate the trials of show business in an enormous new and different city, a little easier and with a smile on my face. There was something nice about not holding on to comedy success so tightly because I knew I had friends that didn't even know, or care, what a comedy stage was and even if I was on it. I bounced around, doing what I could to pay rent and keep my head above water. I flew to Michigan to host the hockey show for a weekend, then play in a paid exhibition tennis tournament in LA the next weekend, then headline the Juke Box Comedy Club in Peoria the next weekend. I would go on the road as a headliner, get smothered in attention and adoration in some far away real American place, and then come back to LA where my taxi driver from the airport had more TV credits than me.

What really changed things and started to keep me in LA for longer periods of time, because I knew I could get consistent stage time, was the Comedy & Magic Club. It became a really important club for me. While the clubs in Los Angeles proper (the Comedy Store, the Hollywood Improv, the Laugh Factory) were backlogged with comics willing to wait in half mile lines each Sunday just to get three minutes in front of an MC who hated them, Comedy & Magic fostered a much more supportive, familial atmosphere. And thanks to a couple of recommendations from some really funny and really nice comics, plus a booker who took the job seriously (Richard) and had actually watched my *Live at Gotham* set and asked around about me, they were willing to give me a shot and give me a spot on Friday night. I was so incredibly thankful and grateful. Sometimes it was the only thing I had on my calendar (it had been two years and I still hadn't gotten on stage at the Comedy Store). I would think about my spot coming up that Friday at the Comedy & Magic Club all week. Monday to Thursday, as I was eating microwaved rice for dinner, I would think about that free meal they offered comics, "I can't wait to have a nice dinner Friday." Those types of small wins really help when you are grinding out a new profession. Yes, I just called eating a meal a small win.

One thing that I still value about stand-up comedy is that we, as performers, get instant feedback. The audience laughs, that feels good. I did that. A random thought or idea I had in the car three years ago can turn into a bit to use on stage, and it can consistently get laughs. I didn't have to wait for the director to see my audition, or the casting director to call me back and make me do it again for the thirty-fifth time, this time in front of the producers, I just did it, it was funny, people laughed. That was me, all me. I feel good about that, and I feel good about me. No wonder actors are so messed up. Or maybe they are actually quite normal, and they are just waiting for feedback on the audition they spent time and energy preparing. Maybe we all just want feedback in our lives. I think I just figured something out.

Every time I performed at the Comedy & Magic Club, the better and better feedback I got. I was getting more comfortable there, performing more freely and with more confidence. The audience, who was a little more in my demographic, was helping me pick up steam, which was only giving me *more* confidence, which led me to perform even freer and funnier. It was also lucky that this comedy club had a really close relationship with Jay Leno, and he performed there regularly. Thanks to some strong sets, people started to talk about me to the two men who booked his show. For a little guy like me, this was huge. Two thumbs up from these guys and something dramatic could happen. Something that might make moving to LA feel like it was worth it. So, little by little, I started to make some progress. I made sure that every time I was down there for my spot, I did a great job. Because when it came to getting booked on the other late-night programs, I wasn't having much luck, not for lack of trying.

My manager, Jordan, was s-l-o-w-l-y chipping away on the industry, and through both his efforts and mine, we were inching toward progress. My first big shot for a late-night appearance came in the winter of 2009, roughly two and half years after moving to LA. Jordan hadn't just been riding the industry to take a look at me, he had also been riding *his* boss, Will, to start advocating for me to whoever would listen. One uneventful afternoon as I was driving down La Brea, doing nothing, as you do in LA, Will called me and said, "You are auditioning for Conan tonight." This wasn't a question (it reminded me of agent Dave's email years prior "You will be . . ."). But that was OK, because to me, this was a big deal. Late Night was where I wanted to be and this was a shot.

"OK," I said, pleased that I lived in a city where the phone rings and then hours later you have a career opportunity. Jordan and Will had been pushing the Conan booker, J.P. Buck, to audition me for months, apparently. The audition was at the Comedy Union, a club I never heard of before, which turned out to be a black comedy club on Pico and La Brea, where, apparently, black people hung out, news to me. Just my luck, they wanted me to go up first and, not having the experience to know I should push back on that lineup location, mixed in with a very white kid doing very white kid jokes to a very black audience, I ate it. I remember looking at J.P., the Conan booker, sitting in the corner with his notebook not writing anything down. At one point during my set, it was so quiet that I heard a waitress in the back open a bottle of beer. Everyone in the audience heard it, they couldn't miss it, it was the only sound—so I said, "Well, this is a black club, that must have been a Heineken." That was the only laugh I got. I'm glad I had the confidence to try and riff something while the Conan booker was watching me, even if none of my other material worked. Looking back, I don't think I actually had an audition, I think the black comics wanted a white guy to bomb in front of them so they looked better—and I can't blame them. Needless to say, Conan passed on me (that time).

• • •

I tried multiple times to get seen by David Letterman's booker. I persistently annoyed Jordan to send him my tapes, embarrassingly befriended the booker on Facebook, tried like hell to get a showcase spot at some of the clubs I knew. It was all futile and he was very cold. This was a guy who used to advertise an event that he hosted where he would teach comedians about late-night comedy. He would sell tickets to young comics to these events. And like all classic snake-oil late-night salesmen, it seemed you had a better chance of getting a spot on Letterman's show if you bought tickets to the booker's events. Frankly, I thought the way he was taking advantage of people was disgusting, so I decided to stop focusing on Letterman, despite him being one of my late-night role models.

The Hermosa Beach Comedy & Magic Club continued serving many important functions for me: giving me lots of stage time and *good* stage time, with packed audiences, giving me the confidence I needed to succeed in LA (let's just say I wasn't instantly lighting the city on fire as I had expected), feeding me, and introducing me, eventually, to extremely professional (and valuable) people in comedy—two of which were the bookers for *The Tonight Show.*

Around the spring of 2009, they finally expressed interest in booking me, but there was one big problem. *The Tonight Show with Jay Leno* was about to be finito. As has been well-documented and talked about, *The Tonight Show* starring Jay Leno was scheduled to end in May and Conan was going to take over. That wasn't a good sign for me, given the biggest laugh I just got in front of the Conan booker was air releasing from a beer bottle. I tried my hardest to convince NBC not to transition from Jay Leno to Conan O'Brien, because that didn't suit me and my comedy career, but Jeff Zucker never returned my calls.

Poor old me. It felt like a beautiful woman I had tried to court for years had finally told me to come over for drinks and I even drove to her house and parked my car and then when I got to the front door, the house burned down. I got an official "We love Michael but we don't book the show anymore" email and poof—there went my late-night spot. Another way to say it, I was fucked.

Conan took over *The Tonight Show* on June 1, 2009, and I watched the debut on my couch in LA, wondering if I would ever get to see that stage. I remember his opening bit, a clip of him running across the country, finally getting to his dressing room, and right before show-time, he wraps a noose around his neck. A very funny segment and unfortunately even funnier based on what happened to him in the coming year. Conan's run at *The Tonight Show* would only last seven months before NBC famously paid him to leave the show and gave *The Tonight Show* back to Jay Leno. I'm sure the reality of losing that job felt worse than a noose around his neck. Nuts. But for me, and my chances of performing at *The Tonight Show*, it was actually quite advantageous. Possibly I was unfucked?

Chapter 25

Late Night

FITTINGLY, I WAS on the tennis court when I got the call that I was being booked on *The Tonight Show* for my late-night debut. I was at the Cheviot Hills Recreation Center on Motor Avenue, about to play tennis with my friend Julien. My manager, Jordan, called and told me the news. It's hard to describe how I felt in that moment, but I was so happy that I was on the tennis court. I was holding a racket, the sun was out, the smell of a freshly opened can of tennis balls was in the air. It was the perfect mix of me and my life. The tennis court doesn't change, the lines are the same, the net height, the sounds. For a moment, I was taken back to Kosta family tennis at the Racquet Club, sitting next to my brothers, or about to play mixed doubles with my mom. Who would have thought when I was five, learning the basics from my family, as the youngest little guy, that thirty years later I'd be doing the same activity, tennis, but get a call that would ultimately change my life, a call that I would be performing stand-up comedy, of all things, on a TV show—and not just any TV show, *the* TV show. "Life is weird, man," I thought as I tossed the balls over to Julien. I played well and was on a high for the rest of the day. That night, as I tried to go to sleep, the excited energy quickly turned to scared shitless energy. I took a deep breath, thankful that tennis had taught me how to manage (or at least not self-destruct) with those types of thoughts. Before I knew it, I was asleep.

. . .

I received that call on a sunny Tuesday in April and I was scheduled to perform three days later on that Friday. To the annoyance of the bookers, I had asked if I could come see a taping of *The Tonight Show* the day before. I wanted to get acquainted with the space.

"No one has ever asked to do that before," they said to my manager.

Yeah, well, maybe I'm not like everyone else, I thought. Mostly, I was nervous, and I wanted to cover my bases and get a feeling for what it looked like. This is not uncommon in sports. I mean, if anything it shows how incredibly unprofessional comics are that they *aren't* asking to do this. I wanted to see the lighting, the mic stand, the distance to the audience, the entrance gate, the desk, the warm-up comic, I wanted to smell the air and touch the railings and gauge the temperature. In sports this is a called a "walk through" because you walk through the next day's match/game. In comedy this is "no one has ever asked us to do that before."

It's not every day you get asked to perform on *The Tonight Show*, so I wasn't going to pretend like I wasn't excited, and I certainly didn't want to experience this moment alone. I invited a big group. My brother Todd, who was living in LA at the time, came with his then-girlfriend Becca; his former University of Delaware tennis teammate Ken, my friend and former U of Illinois teammate Evan Zeder, who happened to also be staying at my house pushing his now defunct tennis apparel line, Athletic DNA (Evan now represents New Balance and is one of the driving forces behind Coco Gauff's line of clothes and shoes); my childhood friend and former Ann Arbor Closed City Tournament opponent Mark Fisher even drove up from San Diego to be there as support, my manager, Jordan, who had worked very hard for me for three years and, at that point, made a whopping $12 in commissions. I would have invited more family, especially people from Michigan,[1] but you get so little advance notice of your performance that it's hard for any normal person with a normal job to make it. And also, as a comic, who performs last on the show, there is always a decent probability that you get bumped if the show runs late. Needless to say, *The Tonight Show* had to issue more guest passes than they were used to, probably another annoyance, but I didn't care. I figured this was a once in a lifetime opportunity.

I arrived early and alone, the way I wanted it. The air, the vibe, the smell, the entrance gate, it wasn't as daunting because I had seen it all the day before. The only thing that was different was Jay Leno's parking space had a different car in it. Today it looked like some kind of rocket ship. I learned later that he took a different car to work each day. At that point in my life, I probably had seven pairs of underwear, and here Jay Leno has enough cars to take a different one to work each day. I sat alone with my notes and enjoyed the silence. It very much felt like I was getting ready for a big tennis match. It's so quiet and there is such a serene energy and intensity. You know something is going to happen, but you don't know what exactly. Will I rise to the occasion? Will I flub? Will I have a lifelong memory? Will this not live up to the expectations? Will I experience something totally new? So many open possibilities, it's beautiful. Before, is often the best part. After, you know all the answers, it's not as sexy. Remember back when I was waiting with Oli, Smith, Hank, and Paul for our train to come in Tokyo? The night was nothing but possibilities—by far the best part. I still love the brief, quiet moment before performing, it's one of these odd experiences where the world feels like it is stable and

---

1 Like one of my biggest comedy supporters, my sister Kristy. Kristy was and still is a very busy hospice nurse, so most likely she was doing something more important, like helping a family say goodbye to a loved one.

balanced and calm. Calm before the storm I guess—has anyone ever said that phrase before?

Eventually my guests joined me in the greenroom, which was nice also, of course. I needed a little emotional support. It's good to sit quietly, but not for too long, I didn't want to get in my head. I had done the comedy set I planned on performing that night so many times, the jokes were so polished, so practiced, let instinct take over, I thought.

It was the ideal greenroom as far as I was concerned; I had family and I had tennis and I was about to do comedy. That was my life and it was perfect.

At one point a producer popped in and said, "Snoop Dogg was here last week and he didn't even have this many people."

"Well," I said, "Snoop Dogg knows he will definitely be back again. I don't."

There was a tightness in the air; I noticed everyone paying close attention to me, didn't want to say the wrong thing or mess up my head space. I felt like a pitcher in the middle of a no hitter, where the dugout doesn't talk to him, to risk jinxing the moment. This quickly subsided when Todd realized there was a twelve-pack of Heinekens in the fridge. He and Evan and Becca cracked open a few. It was helpful to have real people there, drinking beer, being jovial. Otherwise, ruminating about what I was about to do, perform in front of millions of people, one of whom was a childhood comedic idol of mine, who would be sitting twenty-five feet away behind a desk judging me, the pressure would have imploded me.

About an hour before the show, there was a knock at the door and in walks Jay Leno. "He looks just like he looks," I thought.

"Hi, Michael," he said in his silly voice. "You're gonna be great tonight, we can't wait to have you," and he plopped down on the seat like he owned the place—which he kind of did in a way. He took the time to meet my whole entourage, took pictures, told me to have fun, and told me if I screwed up don't worry about it, they would just redo it. This made me feel better.[2]

Jay was incredibly kind and supportive. I didn't realize it at the time, but a late-night host hanging out with you in the greenroom before your set is not the norm. Compared to his counterparts, Jay was the only host that ever popped in and sat down with me. I will never forget that. Conan, Chelsea Handler, Seth Meyers, love 'em all, laughed at all their jokes, but none of them said hi before I went on their shows. And this wasn't a one-off for Jay—I went on to do his show two more times, and he did the same thing, but each time he would hang out longer. The third time I did his show, he sat down and put his feet on the couch and we told stand-up stories to each other for twenty minutes. At one point I thought, "Doesn't this guy need to get ready for his show?"

Late-night stand-up sets are quite nerve-racking. Even now, after each one I think, I never want to do that again. It's incredible what happens when you think about it—the show, with all its producers, and music, and hype machine, and extremely highly paid host, just give you the show for five to seven minutes. Here, you take the entire show, no one else will talk, we will focus all the lights on you, turn up your microphone, and you do the show and we will all be watching. It's amazing and terrifying and—when it goes well—absolutely awesome.

The set that you do on the show, normally, has been approved by the booker, the host, the legal team, and the network, and the booker often works closely with you on fine-tuning it and tinkering the jokes so none of it comes as a surprise once you start performing on the

---

2   Now, after working ten years in late night, I know this is a lie—the only time they really let you redo something is if there is a grave error, like if a stage light falls down and knocks you out or if a bird flies into the studio and punctures one of your eyes, those are just two examples I came up with but I believe they would warrant a reshoot. If you just flub a little word or mix the words around because you are nervous and millions of people are watching you, they don't do shit, they just air it and you have to live with it.

show. *But*, I have always thought, it's still insane they are just *giving* me the show, I could actually do and say whatever I want. Maybe I'll do that sometime—maybe I'll go through all the steps necessary to get booked on a late-night show and then when the host introduces me I will stand out there and spew conspiracy theories for seven minutes.

After Jay left and about thirty minutes before taping, someone came and grabbed me and said, "They need you in makeup," and walked me over to the makeup room. I sat down and as the makeup artist started working on my face (minimal work needed), I looked over to my right and in the other chair is a wombat, the Australian marsupial, the size of a giant teddy bear, getting his/her makeup done. I nearly jumped out of my chair.

"Ah, what is that?" I asked, baffled.

The makeup artist smiled, unfazed. "Oh, that's Charlie, he's on the show with you tonight."

Turns out one of the other guests that night was Julie Scardina, the wild animal tamer woman. And if humans need makeup, who's to say that animals don't?

"Nice to meet you, Charlie," I said. He just sat there, staring at his reflection in the mirror.

When I got back to my greenroom, which was getting a bit louder, a bit drunker, there was a producer there with an earpiece in his ear.

"Mr. Kosta, we have some bad news," he said.

Shit, I'm gonna get cut, they ran out of time and they have to cut the stand-up act, this happens all the time, this was too good to be true, I knew it. But I have to admit it felt good to be called Mr. Kosta—even in my tennis coaching days the players just called me "Kosta." *Mr. Kosta* had a nice ring to it, it was respectful, even though I instinctively looked behind me for my father.

"Mr. Kosta we have some bad news. It appears that we ran out of Heineken beers. Do you think your guests would be OK with Amstel Light?"

"Ahh, yeah, I think my drunk brother and drunk friends will be just fine switching to a different brand of free beers," I said, remembering my attempt to sneak Heinekens into that Dutch hostel ten years ago.

And just like that, someone lower on the ladder of seniority ran in with a twelve-pack of Amstel Light and put them in the fridge. My brother Todd, never one to miss an opportunity for a joke, said, "Oh, sorry, I don't drink Amstel, do you have any Heinekens?"

Eventually they walked me out of the greenroom to wait backstage. It had a different energy. You could hear the show happening—you could hear Jay's voice and the crowd's laughter. Act 2 was ending.

Someone with a headset on pulled me behind the curtain, "This is where you will walk out, walk straight until you hit your mark. You're gonna be great."

It was so dark backstage. The curtain was huge. I could hear Jay at the desk cracking jokes with the guest, actress Mary McCormack. I couldn't believe I was standing there, about to do stand-up comedy. Or was I? Maybe I was about to trip, maybe I was about to bomb, maybe I was about to puke on my shoes and make TV history for worst debut ever, maybe I was going to die, like actually die of a heart attack. It's probably happened, I bet in the history of TV someone has died before going on stage—especially in the sixties when like 500 million people watched the Ed Sullivan show—I bet someone died. I bet they just plopped down when they realized how many people were going to see—I heard Jay's voice "When we come back we're going to have a performance from a comic who used to be a professional tennis player . . ."

I heard him say that, I heard him say that while I was standing behind the curtain, at Studio 11, moments away from performing stand-up comedy on TV, I heard him say that from about thirty feet away and I actually, I swear to god, thought, "Oh, this will be cool, I wonder who he's talking about." When I remembered, realized, came to, that he was talking about me, fucking me, it took my breath away. One of those take-your-breath-away moments that's good, like when you fall in love or hold your baby or experience all the mystery and magic of the world. Those are special moments, because there are also moments that take your breath away that are bad, sad, hurtful. You never forget when your breath gets taken away.

I closed my eyes. Recovered my breath. I had a million thoughts and I let myself have them.

I probably had two to three minutes before it was go time. There's nothing like the pressure of stand-up. In tennis, you might have a big match coming up, but you know that match, if it's close, will be at least ninety minutes, probably closer to two or three hours. If you don't start great, you can play your way into a match. You can figure it out. Not stand-up. All this energy and judgment and work and humor, all this shit is gonna happen in five minutes. The pressure is higher. Even after a rocket launches it takes the rocket eight minutes to reach orbit, which is why I've always said that stand-up comedy is more dangerous than being an astronaut (and also why I chose to *not* be an astronaut—not dangerous enough). Five minutes of comedy, that's it. Imagine if your entire year's work, the entire analysis of 365 days, came down to five minutes. Would you be nervous before those five minutes? Hell yeah, you would.

My head was racing and I just let it. My first open mic, crotch karate, Kristy being there, and being the only laugh. John, my brother, trying to help me through tears as I lost to Bradley Adams in the Boys' 10 and Under Ann Arbor Junior Open, Todd's Heineken joke from just a few moments ago, I was so happy he was right here with me, I would see him in five minutes—he would still be my brother no matter how this went. I thought about Craig calling me and telling me I had a bad practice because I hadn't shaved. I felt my face, it was smooth, it was going to be smooth on TV tonight. I thought about the match I lost in South Korea being up 5–1, I should have won that match, it's OK, you're doing something different now. I thought about giving Grandpa CPR with my dad. I thought about the bowling alley where I bombed so hard you could hear the pins dropping upstairs. I thought about my dad incessantly telling me to not talk myself out of a dream in Philly. I thought about my mom tucking me into bed as a kid ". . . and what is something that made you laugh today?" I thought about telling Bruce I wanted to leave UofM to pursue my then-fantasy of comedy. I thought about that asshole club owner that put his gun on the table while he under-paid me. I thought about my first ATP point and the car accident and what a strange situation that was. I even thought about that jerk that kicked me out of my hostel in Amsterdam. The thoughts came and the thoughts went. Silence. Silence. I took deep breaths. I was centered. I quickly repeated my set list in my head: "Contacts, parents, penny, not gay. Contacts, parents, penny, not gay." I heard the crowd clap and quiet down. I looked over to my right, the stage manager was staring at me not moving. I heard Jay, Jay Leno, the guy I had watched on TV since the age of twelve, I heard him say my name. The stage manager patted my back, opened the curtain and I walked out. "This is gonna be fun," I thought as I hit my mark, took in the crowd, and launched into my joke about contact lenses.

Epilogue

AS I WALKED out of the NBC Studios after my late-night debut, I thought to myself, "OK, now, at the very least, I have done something."

I stood in the parking lot with my brother Todd, staring at Jay's silly rocket-ship car, the two of us quietly taking it all in. At one point, he turned to me and asked me how I felt and I said, "It feels like when I beat Jack Brasington for my first ATP point."

Todd replied, "Well, I'm sure that prepared you for this."

He was right.

...

The day after *The Tonight Show*, unfortunately it turns out, is just another day. I couldn't believe that there were still cars on the road and people honking their horns. Hadn't they seen my appearance?! I had a college gig at the University of Santa Barbara that night, ninety minutes north. They didn't have a real stage set up, so I was performing in a lecture hall where the math professor had left his notes scrawled on the board behind me. This is why I love stand-up comedy. The work environment is always changing, always challenging you, always making you sharper. Yesterday I was on the NBC lot, Studio 11 in Burbank, drinking beer with Jay Leno, and today I am standing on a lecture floor with math notes behind me trying to make nineteen-year-olds laugh.

The Tonight Show set went well. I had a new confidence. I figured even if I died now, I would have at least *two* things in my obituary.[1] The world was a little lighter. My decision to move to LA felt a little more justified. I, overall, felt more at ease.

On the drive back down from Santa Barbara to LA that night my phone rang. It was Tommy, the legendary booker from the Comedy Store. He saw my *Tonight Show* appearance and wanted me to come by that night and hang out.

"I've been coming there every day for three years," I told him. "I don't want to come by and just hang out, I want to be performing there." Like I said, I had a new confidence. It's like a superpower.

"Jesus Christ, just come by," he said.

When I arrived, Tommy immediately said, "Mitzi saw your *Tonight Show*, you did great, she passed you, you're a paid regular now."

Together, those two magic words—"paid" and "regular"—offered a life changing distinction. Besides the cool fact that they would paint my name in a fancy cursive on the exterior wall, which stays there forever, it also meant no more waiting in the endless line of wanna-bee comics for the Sunday-night open mic. No more slipping and sliding my way through the perceived endless matches of the Dutch red clay "qualifying rounds." I was guaranteed spots on the best stage in LA—I was automatically in the "main draw" of comedy. This is where I wanted to be.

I went to a nearby bar on Sunset and had a Manhattan by myself in a darkly lit booth, reflecting on the steps it took to get to this point. I wrote down in my joke book/journal "Tonight Show and Comedy Store within 24 hours."

It was hard to even reconcile. What a journey it had already been, and the best part, I felt like I was just warming up.

---

1   (1) Being on ATP computer and (2) performing on *The Tonight Show*. Hang with me, we're almost done.

Acknowledgments

THIS BOOK WOULD not have happened without the vision, enthusiasm, and persistence of book agent Andrianna deLone. She spent countless hours reading, editing, and advising on an unfinished manuscript and then reading, re-editing, and advising again. She ultimately made the book better and refused to give up on it, and for this I am eternally grateful. Thank you to Adam Ginivisian and Taryn Ariel for getting this manuscript into Andrianna's hands.

Thank you to Lisa Sharkey for taking a chance on me and this book. It's clear you see the best in people and your support of my vision and ideas was pivotal. Thank you to Maddie Pillari for your diligence, attention to detail, and timeline help. You execute so many of the important unseen details of a book all while keeping it light and friendly, which is not easy! Thank you to Lexie von Zedlitz for all the help along the way (hard drive recovery, photo scanning, so many unseen things I have no idea about). I felt truly supported by the HarperCollins team, which made this book better.

To my former college coaches Craig Tiley and Bruce Berque. Outside of my immediate family, these two men have impacted my life the most positively. Fantastic coaches and leaders who held me and my teammates to extremely high standards and wouldn't accept mediocrity, thank you.

Thank you to every tennis center, club, park, facility, etc. To every underpaid maintenance person fixing a clay court tennis line, squeegeeing wet courts, tightening nets, putting up wind screens, all so we can play this wonderful sport.

Thank you to the countless comedy clubs that have helped propel me along the way. Live comedy is a cherished art form and you give us comics a place to practice and perfect our passion.

To my siblings, John Jr., Kristy, and Todd, nothing make me happier than when we are all together. Thank you for being kind and supportive of your youngest brother my whole life.

Thank you to my wife who elegantly keeps it all together and has supported me and this project since its inception. Thank you for giving me the space to explore ideas, hide away and write, and for understanding that my creative process can sometimes be annoying to others. I love you.

To my daughters, you make me laugh every day. I hope I help you tackle the world with enthusiasm, optimism, wonder, curiosity, and grit. See you soon, I'm writing this five minutes before you wake up.

Lastly, as I was looking through hundreds of pictures of my childhood it dawned on me that my mother was barely in any of them, because she was the one taking the pictures. Mom, your support, kindness, humor, selflessness, and ultimately LOVE made all the difference. Thank you.

Open de Montréal
ITF Men's Futures

CODE VIOLATION RECORD

iTF

Week of	City, Country	Prize Money US$	Tourn. ID	ITF Supervisor/Referee
16/06/03	Montreal, CAN	10000	CAN F2	Tony Cho / William Coffey

PLAYER DATA

Family name	First name	Nationality	
Kosta	Michael	USA	

EVENT AND MATCH DATA

Full tournament title	Type of event	Singles/Doubles	Main/Qual. draw	Round	Date
Canada F2	Men's Futures 10000	Singles	Qualification	2	15/06/03

Match between	Chair Umpire
Michael Kosta vs. Andrei Radulescu	Pierre-Yves Boucher

DESCRIPTION OF OFFENCE

I, the undersigned ITF Supervisor/Referee, certify that I have made a reasonable investigation into the facts and circumstances of the above named player's conduct in the above referenced event/match.
Such player violated the ITF Code of Conduct as described below:

Code section	Offence	Attachments
Q, J	Unsportsmanlike conduct, audible obscenity (2	**Point Penalty Schedule**

Description of offence
*During an argument concerning a not-up call, Mr. Kosta threw a ball at his opponent, deliberately attempting to hit him. Then on two subsequent occasions during the match he shouted "Fuck".

During the match such player/team was assessed (Warning/Point Penalty/Game Penalty/Default) for [offence]
*Warning, Point, Game

FINES

	US Dollars	
In addition, I herewith fine such player for such violation:	50	

This sum is to be deducted from the player's prize money to the maximum possible amount.
Any balance is due and payable by the player.
Any balance not settled will be added to the ITF Outstanding Fines list, for collection at any ITF event.

Organisation receiving the fine
Tennis Canada

PLAYER APPEAL

The player has 10 days from the last day of this event within which to file a written appeal of this fine to the ITF.

Last date for appeals	ITF department to handle the appeal
02/07/03	Professional Circuits

COPIES

SIGNATURE

Copies of this Record and attachments have been given/mailed to:

☑ the above named player

☐ a player representative

☑ the Tournament Organiser

☑ the ITF

Date	Signature
15/06/03	Tony Cho / William Coffey

I won this match, by the way.

About the Author

MICHAEL KOSTA is a stand-up comedian and former professional tennis player. In 2017, he joined *The Daily Show*, and now is one of their esteemed hosts (Emmy award–winning host, he wants you to know). Kosta has performed stand-up comedy on *The Tonight Show*, *Conan*, *Late Night with Seth Meyers*, and has his own one-hour special *Michael Kosta: Detroit. NY. LA.* on Comedy Central. He also hosts the popular podcast *Tennis Anyone with Michael Kosta*. He lives in Brooklyn, New York, in an apartment way too small for his family.